Laughing All the Way
to Freedom

Laughing All the Way to Freedom

The Americanization of a Russian Émigré

EMIL DRAITSER

Foreword by Konstantin V. Kustanovich

McFarland & Company, Inc., Publishers
Jefferson, North Carolina

LIBRARY OF CONGRESS CATALOGUING-IN-PUBLICATION DATA

Names: Draitser, Emil, 1937– author. | Kustanovich, Konstantin, writer of foreword.
Title: Laughing all the way to freedom : the Americanization of a Russian émigré / Emil Draitser.
Description: Jefferson, North Carolina : McFarland & Company, Inc., Publishers, 2024. | Includes bibliographical references and index.
Identifiers: LCCN 2023048907 | ISBN 9781476692982 (paperback : acid free paper) ∞
    ISBN 9781476650654 (ebook)
Subjects: LCSH: Draitser, Emil, 1937– | Immigrants—United States—Biography. | Russians—United States—Biography. | BISAC: BIOGRAPHY & AUTOBIOGRAPHY / Personal Memoirs | SOCIAL SCIENCE / Emigration & Immigration | LCGFT: Autobiographies.
Classification: LCC PG3549.D7 Z46 2023 | DDC 891.78/503 [B]—dc23/eng/20231204
LC record available at https://lccn.loc.gov/2023048907

BRITISH LIBRARY CATALOGUING DATA ARE AVAILABLE

ISBN (print) 978-1-4766-9298-2
ISBN (ebook) 978-1-4766-5065-4

Front cover image: author's family arriving in America (author image); background map and symbols © Shutterstock

Printed in the United States of America

McFarland & Company, Inc., Publishers
  Box 611, Jefferson, North Carolina 28640
    www.mcfarlandpub.com

To my grandchildren, Phoebe, Griffin, Carter, Sergei,
and my great-grandson, Kai

Acknowledgments

This is to express my gratitude to Dr. Jolanta Kunicka and Professor Emeritus Konstantin V. Kustanovich for their time and effort in reading the manuscript of this book and offering valuable feedback. I'm also indebted to my colleagues and friends Anne Gendler, Dr. Gary Kern, Professor Emerita Elizabeth Beaujour, and Professor Benjamin Rifkin for reading selected chapters of the book and bringing to my attention those episodes of my life in America that needed additional elucidation for the reader. As has been the case with my previous book-length publications, my brother Vladimir Draitser rendered invaluable help when it came to computer-related technological problems and hiccups.

Contents

Contents

IV. The Road to Americanization

Notes on Transliteration and Translation

I transliterated Russian words according to the Library of Congress system for the Cyrillic alphabet. However, for some personal names and geographical locations, I retain their traditional rendering in British and American literature. Unless otherwise noted, all translations of excerpts from Russian texts are my own.

The name of the city of Odesa is "Odessa" throughout the book because, at the time of the activities described, the mid–1970s, it was the proper spelling of the city name, which is reflected in the title of one of the author's books published in English about that period of time—*Farewell, Mama Odessa: A Novel.*

"You can take the boy out of the country,
but you can't take the country out of the boy."
American proverb

"Who are you laughing at? You're laughing at yourself!"
Nikolai Gogol, *The Inspector General*

Foreword

Konstantin V. Kustanovich

Despite its title, *Laughing All the Way to Freedom*, the topic of Emil Draitser's book is no laughing matter at all. America is famously known as the land of immigrants, the melting pot of people from different countries and different cultures. From an abstract "bird's-eye view," the process of "melting" seems rather simple: people come in search of freedom or a better life; they interact with locals and mix with them; the mixture then melts, forming one homogeneous whole.

However, when one looks closely at the individual life of an immigrant, the situation is all but simple. Developing the metaphor of the melting pot, one could suggest that different cultures melt at different temperatures, so the resulting substance is never homogeneous. Some ingredients burn out—immigrants who can never adjust and either return home or eke out a substandard existence on government subsidies. Others do not melt fully and remain a hard matter, having never completely fused with the main body of American culture. They keep their old cultural values and do not appreciate their new home, although they can fare quite well here. At the end of his book, Emil asks a crucial question: can people not only cross the borders of the country in which they were born and raised but also leave behind at least some of their old selves? His entire book is an attempt to answer this question.

While my main research interests lay in Russian literature of the twentieth century, from my very first days in the United States, I was struck by how different the social mores and interactions were in my old and new homes. One often comes across a trite notion: oh, we are all humans—we love, we laugh, and we cry, no matter where we are from. It turns out that we do these and many other things differently, sometimes so *much* that we misinterpret our new compatriots' behavior and they do not understand ours. I gradually switched from literature to the exploration of how different cultures work and why they are different.

1

This research, applied to Russian culture, resulted in my book *Russian and American Cultures: Two Worlds a World Apart* published in 2018.[1]

Born and raised in Odessa, Ukraine, the unofficial capital of humor in the former Soviet Union, Emil Draitser developed a career as a freelance satirist. Intrigued by the same observations, he reacted with the entire bag of tricks of his former trade. Several chapters of his previous book, his autobiographical novel *Farewell, Mama Odessa*, are devoted to his first encounter with the Western world en route to America, in Vienna and Rome. In that book, he uses irony, exaggeration, incongruities, oxymorons, and many other comic devices.[2]

As with all new arrivals to this country, the author often experienced a kind of inner resistance and puzzlement as he encountered the views and actions of these "strange" Americans. With self-deprecating humor, the current volume tells the story of a slow metamorphosis in the consciousness of an émigré overcoming his old cultural prejudices and comprehending a new culture. Occasionally, Emil switches from a lighthearted, humorous style to magic realism, which helps him amplify the absurdity of his satirical target as if placing it under the microscope.

Laughing All the Way to Freedom comprises selected essays, his reflections on his earlier writings in America in which he mulls over how stubborn his old views, notions, and values were. Often, he lets his readers come to their conclusions by leaving them to be amazed at and amused by the strange behaviors of strange people in strange circumstances.

When the writer moved to the United States, there was no end to cultural shocks. Everybody has a car! Who could own a car in the Soviet Union? A high-ranking party official; a famous movie star; a hack writer producing socialist realist literature—that's about it. He is awed, yet he never stops laughing at the abundance of foodstuffs in supermarkets ... the abundance of goods in malls and department stores. (Maybe *too* many goods? Who needs thousands of styles and materials of the same thing?) Freedom! (Maybe *too* much freedom? When it is for me or my ilk, it's great, but when it is for others who don't even look or behave to my taste, could it not be curtailed?) Tolerance for everything non-standard, unusual! (Maybe *too* much tolerance? After all, there are ethical and aesthetical standards.) Your old collectivist, authoritarian culture is stuck to you like a piece of chewing gum to the sole of your shoe. And it rules your opinions about your new home. As decades go by, does an émigré from Russia, who possesses the capacity to see and to think, comprehend the deeper reasons that form the cultural phenomena around him? Thus, after so many years in America, Draitser has arrived at the freedom of understanding his new home—free from the baggage of the cultural prejudices he carried across the borders.

American readers of Draitser's book will enjoy observing the "clash of cultures" in one man's consciousness—a consciousness characteristic of practically all who moved to the United States after being socialized in the environment of Russian culture. The book, however, has yet another valuable angle. One could summarize its main idea as "culture matters and culture does not change easily." Russia had an approximately 15-year respite from authoritarianism—from the beginning of the Gorbachev era (1985) to the beginning of the Putin era (2000). What has been happening since then can be illustrated by the famous maxim of the Roman poet Horace, "You can drive out Nature with a pitchfork, but she keeps on coming back." The ancient Russian culture of authoritarianism, collectivism, nationalism, and legal nihilism (disrespect for the law) has come back with a vengeance to climax in Russia's adventurism abroad (Georgia, 2008; Crimea, 2014; and the invasion of Ukraine, 2022) and its cruel suppression of the opposition at home. Reading Emil Draitser's book, one will better understand why the current Russian regime has no problem abusing its population by undoing its economy and sending thousands of young men to unprovoked war, unconcerned about the number of casualties. One can only repeat—*culture matters.*

Konstantin V. Kustanovich, Professor Emeritus of Russian at Vanderbilt University, is a specialist in 20th-century Russian literature and the history of Russian culture. His recent book, Russian and American Cultures: Two Worlds a World Apart, *explores the major factors that influenced the formation of Russian national culture and led it on a path away from Western cultures. He is also the author of* The Artist and the Tyrant: Vasily Aksenov's Works in the Brezhnev Era *and numerous articles on Russian literature and culture.*

Preface

This book is a memoir of immigration, an account of my coming to America almost a half-century ago with certain, mostly mistaken expectations and the process of discovery on my way to becoming an American myself. I arrived in Los Angeles on New Year's Eve of 1975 as one of many thousands of Jews permitted to leave the Soviet Union. This immigration was made possible by the worldwide Soviet Jewry movement, in which Americans took an active part.[1]

My purpose is to reach back over all those years and recall how I thought and acted in the beginning, and how I learned and changed along the way. It is a story of self-discovery of what makes the Soviet mindset and what makes the American.

All immigrants of the world coming to America expect it to be like their home country—only better. What they often fail to consider is that, like any other nation, America was built on its special foundations, that its DNA differs from that of their country, and that it may take a lifetime to adjust to the new country's culture, mentality, and its way of doing everything differently, pretty much, from the way they have known. It means that in coming to America, they are choosing to remake every aspect of their life, yet some ineradicable aspect, their native self, will remain with them always.

In most cases, only the settlers' offspring, their children and grandchildren, will come close to accomplishing this task of remaking themselves in their time. But it is rarely the case for the immigrants themselves. The American proverb "You can take the boy out of the country, but you can't take the country out of that boy" applies to the immigrant experience.

It is even more true when the proverbial "boy" comes to America from a country constructed on different principles, collectivist Russia and individualist America, with opposing political systems—democratic American and totalitarian Soviet.

This memoir consists of a collection of essays built around the author's short pieces written over the first two decades of his American life, both in English and Russian. These essays are self-reflecting; they reveal the author's level of understanding of the unfamiliar country. This explains the fact that often they amount to his misreading of an unfamiliar culture, which sometimes amounts to his bewilderment and inability to grasp it. This took place because of his cultural conditioning being brought up in the Soviet mind-sphere. After all, by the time of the author's emigration in late 1974, the totalitarian system in the country of his origin lasted nearly seven decades and its earth-shaking political, social, and cultural transformation affected the mentality of at least three generations of Soviet people.

However, the satirical nature of most of my American publications doesn't mean I've ever doubted my life-altering decision: to leave the country in which I was born and raised. Some American readers might frown when reading satirical pieces penned by an immigrant, and this is understandable. In his time, the great Russian poet Alexander Pushkin remarked, "Of course, I despise my fatherland from head to toe, but I am annoyed when a foreigner shares this feeling with me."[2] So maybe an American reader may not want to entertain satiric or critical remarks made by a newcomer to the country, even one very grateful to have arrived.

On this point, it's worth noting that satire as a literary genre is as American as apple pie. Indeed, my first acquaintance with the country's literature came from reading Mark Twain's works, such as *Adventures of Huckleberry Finn*, *A Connecticut Yankee in King Arthur's Court*, *The Celebrated Jumping Frog of Calaveras County*, and then *The Devil's Dictionary* by Ambrose Bierce, stories by O. Henry, and later works by Dorothy Parker, James Thurber, and scores of other American satirists.

I also discovered an army of American stand-up comedians, nonexistent in my home country. Many of them were biting social critics, such as Mort Sahl, Dick Gregory, and George Carlin.

In 1987, at the World Symposium of Political Humor in Philadelphia, I had the pleasure of chatting with Art Buchwald, my longtime favorite American satirist whose columns, translated into Russian, had frequented the pages of the Communist Party newspaper, *Pravda*. In his writing, he was never hesitant to ridicule his country's big shots, be they in the White House, the Pentagon, or the FBI. Their counterparts in the Soviet Union were off limits to any critics.

And then let us not forget that every day in America, you can see comedians and even TV commentators poking fun at the current head of the state. When I arrived in America, Merv Griffin was on TV every weekday afternoon and Johnny Carson was on every night. They were very comfortable making jokes about any famous person they pleased. Toward the end of my first year, 1975, *Saturday Night Live* began its long run lasting until today. Very often it begins with a "cold open," a skit ridiculing the sitting president, be it President Ford, President Reagan, or President Clinton. And all the other well-known politicians receive the same irreverent treatment. Seeing this kind of freedom of expression was an uplifting experience; it encouraged me to use my satiric skills developed under very different conditions, over the Soviet part of my life.

It took me some time to realize that satire is not just sharp criticism, not just gross exaggeration, dressed up into something comical, but it also belongs to the lyrical genre; it expresses the emotional life of the satirist. The abundance of satire in America shows the heartfelt attachment of the people to their country, both those who are making jokes about what is going on and those who are laughing. The opposite of love is indifference. As the Russian writer Fazil Iskander once remarked, "Satire is the offended love of your people, of the native land, of humanity as a whole."

Also, especially in my case, writing humor and satire are the author's attempts at adjusting to reality. In his book *The Satirist: His Temperament, Motivation, and Influence*, Leonard Feinberg notes: "If 'adjustment' to life is the basic motivation of all writers, it is also the motivation of satiric writers. [...] The interrelation among the satirist himself, his technique, and the specific problems in his society show that his satire is an aesthetic expression of a fundamental adjustment to life."[3] And later on: "By using his special talent for distorting the familiar in a playful critical manner, the satirist adjusts to the society he lives in."[4]

Here's what Heinrich Heine says about the healing power of poetry and its ability to cure his blues: "From my big sorrows, I make little verses, and, getting wings, they fly away." These words can apply to satire as well.

Satire's mending properties are especially needed when dealing with something an individual feels powerless to change. For example, handling the horrific topic of the risks of total annihilation, Stanley Kubrick's movie *Dr. Strangelove* was one of the best satiric antidotes to the paranoia of the Cold War. During a time of great fear, the film's humorous approach mitigated anxiety caused by the threat of the mutually assured destruction of humanity.

For an immigrant, the need to grasp the nature of life in the new land, to learn its conventions and rules, is often urgent. Examining my early American writings, I have discovered that, contrary to my belief, I hadn't left my satirical cap at Customs in Moscow's Domodedovo Airport on that fateful day of October 8, 1974.

Although for most Americans, the term "Soviet satire" sounds like an oxymoron, the truth of the matter is that several satirists worked in the Soviet media. Their targets were on the okay list of the powers that be. Under the watchful eyes of an army of censors, the regime employed lampooners to fight "individual shortcomings (*otdel'nye nedostatki*) that slowed down our movement toward the shining heights of communism." The phrase "individual shortcomings" was meant to imply the system is wonderful, but some individuals go against it by drinking, being negligent or lazy, messing things up, failing their socialist duty, and they (not the leaders) should be exposed in a satiric light.

For the last ten years of my Soviet life, I contributed satirical pieces to the country's press. Coming of age at the time of a significant relaxation of the orthodox Stalinist ideology, which was known as the "Khrushchev Thaw," I was attracted to satire as an opportunity to launch my writing career. Prompted by a newspaper editor in Moscow, I chose the genre because it allowed me to write and get published without using the dry newspaper format but in a style close to that of *belle lettres*, which I aspired to master. In addition, I was born and raised in Odessa, Ukraine, the unofficial capital of the country's folk humor, the homeland of Ilya Ilf and Evgeny Petrov, the authors of *The Twelve Chairs* and *The Golden Calf*, classic works of Soviet satire. (In 1970, the first novel was made into a hilarious American movie directed by Mel Brooks.)

I was encouraged by my first successful steps in satirical journalism, as it was practiced in the 1960s and 1970s in the Soviet Union. Within a year, my work appeared on the pages of the most powerful satirical magazine in the nation, *Crocodile*, six million copies of which hit the newsstands three times a month.

My rude awakening came in May 1971, when *Crocodile* printed a lampoon by me ridiculing a stupid and vulgar play. The act of panning a poor theatrical piece wouldn't have had such dire consequences if the playwright hadn't turned out to be an untouchable, a man whose official position and high connections protected him from any public criticism. But I didn't know about his presumed invincibility. So I wrote freely, and there was a scandal. *Crocodile* had to spit in its face and call my work, which it had itself published, "unprofessional," and in addition strip me of its correspondent's certification, much coveted by journalists in Russia.

Although, when the scandal calmed down, *Crocodile* invited me back two years later, by that time I realized that I not only couldn't write the way they expected any longer, but I also couldn't even breathe anymore in the country in which I was born.

I belong to the generation of Jewish immigrants who seized the opportunity to leave the Soviet Union at the height of Leonid Brezhnev's rule, a decade and a half before Mikhail Gorbachev's programs of liberalization, known as glasnost (freedom of speech) and perestroika (restructuring). Both Brezhnev and the Bolshevik regime were aging, yet the eventual collapse of the Soviet system seemed unthinkable. What that modern-day exodus had in common with the ancient one chronicled in the Old Testament was that the numbers were comparable. The number of Jews that left the USSR, the country of the Red Pharaohs, between the years 1974–1991, was roughly the same as the Bible accounts of those who had left the country of their bondage, that of the Egyptian Pharaohs, "up to six hundred thousand men, except children" (*Exodus 12:37*).[5]

The question may arise whether it is correct to compare the life of a Soviet citizen to that of a slave in ancient Egypt. Understandably, today the word "slave" evokes an image of a man who labors under the whistle of a whip, who either rows, chained to other unfortunates, or picks cotton on a plantation under the burning sun.

Yet, while the Hebrew slaves and Soviet Jews were not sold off away from their family members, the life of an ordinary Soviet person had some similarities with that of an ancient Egyptian slave.

For example, a Soviet citizen had to work to feed himself and the members of his family, the same as any other head of a household in the world. But the wages were fixed and hardly enough to make ends meet; to survive from payday to payday, many had to borrow one from the other. And since there was no private property, no one owned the roof over their head. Everyone had to live where the authorities allowed them, often in a communal apartment, or only one room, according to the registration stated in their internal passport. No one was free to move from one city to another without permission. Several cities, including Moscow, were closed to nonresidents: a citizen had to deserve somehow the right to live there, for example, by working for the government.

And no one could leave the country as a matter of course, but only with special permission and under supervision. Travel was in a group, on an assignment or foreign tour, and an informant was implanted in the group, and relatives were left at home as hostages, should one think of defecting. Here, the following Soviet underground joke comes to mind:

In the cabin of a plane carrying a bunch of Soviet tourists landing in Paris, a voice is heard:

"Does anyone know how to ask for political asylum in French?"
One tourist rises from his seat:
"Well, well, are you planning to betray our great socialist homeland?"
"Oh no, comrade! I just wanted to know who oversees our group."

And you couldn't even dare to think about emigration! In the late 1920s, emigration from the country ceased. The borders were closed, guarded, and fenced. If any citizen tried to cross the borders in remote areas or refused to return from a foreign assignment, they were called defectors and considered guilty of the act of treason. And not only was the defector guilty but also his relatives who remained in the USSR, regardless of whether they knew of the defector's intentions. They were prosecuted, and their lives were ruined or at least severely impaired.

We had to serve our masters, fight for them, and die for them. And they didn't care if we wanted to do it or not.

In American chattel slavery, it was forbidden to teach an enslaved person to read. In the twentieth century, in one of the world's two superpowers with nearly total literacy, we, its citizens, could only listen to, watch, and read that which was permitted.

We could think only in the approved way and only about what our bigwigs allowed. We had to praise them every day. Any criticism was a serious crime. For telling the truth about them, we could be persecuted.

However, the ancient and the contemporary exodus stories do differ from each other. To begin with, unlike how our biblical ancestors had done it, asking the Egyptians to help them sustain themselves during their flight, to give them "things of silver and things of gold and clothes," it never crossed our minds to ask that from the other Soviets. Very few of them had much for themselves, never mind their reluctance to share anything with us, the outcasts. (Besides, exporting valuables from the country was prohibited; you couldn't pack even a family relic, say, your grandma's wedding ring.) And none of us, the emigres, possessed any "flocks and herds" to take along. All we emigres, could do to provide for ourselves during a long journey into uncertainty was to exchange Soviet rubles for only a hundred dollars per person. That was it. We were on our own, the contemptible traitors to Mother Russia.

Yet no one who fled our native land cried aloud along the way. None of us hungered to return. No one made a peep because it wouldn't do any good. We could buy one-way tickets out of the USSR, and that was it. Stripped of Soviet citizenship, we were forever outward bound. We had to pay a hefty fee to cut off any connection with our socialist Motherland.

While the Almighty, on Moses' request, supplied the ancient

fugitives with water, manna from heaven, and protein as some fowl, two organizations, HIAS (Hebrew Immigrant Aid Society) and "Joint" (American Jewish Joint Distribution Committee), saved us from thirst and hunger and provided us with a temporary shelter. The former paid for our travel expenses, and the latter gave us money for food and lodging for the duration of our journey.

The most crucial difference between the ancient exodus and ours, however, is that none of us spent forty years in the desert (*Numbers 14:34*). It took us only forty days (give or take a few fortnights sometimes) to wait for entry visas. To save its political face—how come some people want to leave the best country in the world?—the Soviet authorities made believe that they allowed the emigration on strictly humanitarian grounds: to reunite families of those minorities, the majority of which lived in the capitalist countries. (To cover up the Jewish character of the movement for the right to emigrate, they included Armenians and Germans in this group. To be sure, there were plenty of these people happy to flee the country...)

So the only way to get out of the Soviet Union was to receive an official invitation from Israel, regardless whether you had any relatives over there. Once you reached Vienna, you were free to choose any country that accepted refugees. Since the only member of my extended family lived in Los Angeles (my cousin; she had left a year before us, joining the American branch of her husband's family), we had to wait for our entry visas in one of the Roman suburbs, Ostia Di Lido. Looking back, we nicknamed that lull in our journey our "Roman Holiday," in honor of the famous Hollywood movie with Gregory Peck and Audrey Hepburn about a love affair set in the Eternal City.

When I first read the part of the *Book of Numbers* (32:11) that "none of the men twenty years or older who came out of Egypt will see the [promised] land," I shrugged. Because of the skepticism of my Soviet atheistic upbringing, and my dismissal of any religion as the proverbial "opium for the people," I couldn't comprehend the profound meaning of this biblical episode. Why should adult former slaves spend forty years in the wilderness before coming to the promised land?

Only after living half of my life in America did I come to appreciate the tale's wisdom. I realized that, like many other things in Judaism, the wilderness, in which God forced the ancient Hebrews to roam for forty years, carries a symbolic import. The opening lines of Joseph Brodsky's poem, inspired by the Exodus story, brought to the fore of my consciousness that the biblical "desert" stands for any terrain where people are not oppressed. In a poetic lullaby, a mother instructs her baby never to forget that he was born free:

> I gave birth to you in a desert
> Not in vain.
> Because no trace of a tsar
> Has ever been here.

And further on:

> Get used to the desert, my little one,
> For wherever you'll be from now,
> It will live in you.[6]

The poem made me ask myself a hypothetical question: what happens to a person born and raised in slavery for more than twenty years, who, instead of spending the proverbial forty years of wandering in the wilderness, entered the "promised land" and lived those years in it? After all, that is the case for me and my generation of emigres who fled the former Soviet Union in the 1970s.

In this book, I have traced my steps in the land "without a tsar," the land of the free, the United States of America. It happened one day when rummaging through my literary archive, I realized I could recreate my spiritual journey if I revisited my writing of the bygone years.

My quest started when, going through the scrapbook I took out of the homeland, I stumbled upon a few old clippings. Rereading them now, so many years down the road, helped me understand I had left the country way before I boarded a plane at Moscow's Sheremetyevo Airport.

PART I

Farewell,
Step-Mother Russia

1

My Inner Emigration

It should hardly come as a surprise to the reader that, way before I even thought of collecting my papers and heading for the Exit Visa Office, like many of my friends and acquaintances, I had emigrated mentally. It came with the territory, so to speak. The former Soviet Union wasn't the first country in which the phenomenon of "inner emigration" took place. The term was used regarding another totalitarian country—Nazi Germany. While several of the country's intellectuals, Thomas Mann being one of the best known, left their homeland in order not to give credence to the regime, more than a few German writers, poets, and artists continued living under the Nazis, often while pretending to conform.

Over the last years of my Soviet life, in the early 1970s, I also belonged to the part of the country's intelligentsia that left the state mentally. While opposing the very tenets of the ruling communist ideology, I stayed employed at the Nedra publishing house as an editor of technological books and, after the *Crocodile* scandal, turned to another kind of writing.

Two years down the road, the scandal had been forgotten. Manuil Semyonov, *Crocodile*'s editor-in-chief, invited me back to his office, mumbled his apology (something like "Who the hell knew the playwright was untouchable!"), and offered to forget the bad blood between us. He returned my correspondent's ID and gave me a new assignment.

They published my satirical note on an approved target of Soviet satire—bureaucracy on the local level, of course, which fitted the mantra of Soviet satirists, "Do not generalize!"

Bureaucracy, as a target of public criticism, was welcomed early in the Soviet state; it was considered a disease inherited from the tsarist time, destined to die out as the new regime would function in full swing. The most publicized example of the intolerance of the powers that be toward this endemic shortcoming of state machinery is the opening line of Vladimir Mayakovsky's poem, which every Soviet schoolchild had to learn by heart. Titled "Verses about a Soviet Passport," the poem describes the moment when he, a Soviet citizen, showed his ID at the border crossing of one of the Western countries:

> I'd tear like a wolf at bureaucracy.
> For mandates my respect's but the slightest.
> To the devil himself I'd chuck without mercy
> every red-taped paper.
> But this...[1]

Then the poet describes how proud he is of owning his Soviet passport.

In my time, a lot of ironies were attached to the ownership of a Soviet passport. To begin with, there were two kinds of it. One, for domestic use, every Soviet citizen had to carry on him or her. It was the instrument of the police state to learn everything about you on the spot. Not only did the internal passport have your name, home address, and date of birth, as any American driver's license does, but it also denoted your father's name (your patronymic), your place of birth, your ethnicity, your marital status, and your record of military service. It had a police seal certifying its permission to live at your place of dwelling (the notorious *propiska*).

However, in his poem, Mayakovsky refers to a passport of a different kind, a special one issued to those few whom the state considered loyal beyond any doubt, therefore permitting you to travel abroad (*zagranpasport*). Regular Soviet citizens only hoped to be allowed to have one.

Because of this situation, the very notion of "inner emigration" for Soviet people was different. Unlike citizens of Nazi Germany, who, at least in the first several years of the Nazi regime, had a choice of whether to stay in the country or leave, we Soviets were spared the agony of making such a fateful decision. For decades on end, the exit gates of the country were shut down and locked with a huge warehouse padlock.

However, the case of bureaucracy I was offered to make fun of in the pages of the country's leading satirical magazine was on a much smaller scale. A document the editor handed me, based on which I wrote my satirical note, certified that a regular person, a train conductor, fell victim to clerical negligence.

In the September 1973 issue of *Crocodile*, the piece was published. To be truthful, I wasn't aware that, for the last two years since I fell victim to a scandal, my writing took on a much more pessimistic tone. My close friend, screenwriter Boris Lobkov, brought this to my attention.

"Look at that!" he said upon reading my note. "You imbued this short piece with such spirit of the hopelessness of our whole Soviet way of life. People live by inertia.... They accept the humdrum of life as a norm."

I reread my note. He was right. It looked like, unbeknownst to my consciousness, my pessimistic view of Soviet life informed my writing. Not only does bureaucracy wield full power over the life of a little person, but regular people are also indifferent to the fate of one of their own. Both his neighbors and co-workers show no empathy for the man in trouble. They show no solidarity, always taking the side of the authorities:

"The Dark Copy"

It was the month of May. And the train conductor Ivan Gavrilovich Sviridov felt very good. First, because of the blossoming of nature. In addition, it was payday.

Not only that, but the amount he received was also more than expected—more than usual. Substantially.

"What's this for?" inquired Sviridov.

"What for, what for?" muttered the bookkeeper, not raising her head. "They give it, you take it; they hit you, you run!"

"But still!" insisted Ivan Gavrilovich.

The bookkeeper sighed, ran her finger along a column, and pointed to the figures opposite Sviridov's name:

"This code means a bonus."

"What for?" the train conductor broke into a smile. "What for, exactly?"

At this, the bookkeeper tore herself away from the register, to have a look at this pest:

"What's the difference? Didn't I say they give it—you take it?"

When Ivan Gavrilovich encountered his colleagues, the other conductors, in the corridors, they asked why he looked so radiant.

"A bonus," he answered. "Only exactly what it's for, I don't know...."

"They gave it to you. It must mean something," his colleagues said and clapped him on the shoulder. "Why should you be surprised, Gavrilovich, when you've got twenty years of flawless service? Sure, they're entrusting you with more responsible work. This calls for a celebration. You owe us a drink!"

And his wife noticed his enthusiasm at the doorway.

"Look here," he said to his wife, "a bonus. For.... Well, in general," he said, "for everything good."

And his wife said to the neighbors:

"They honored my husband at work. And with nothing less than a bonus!"

And every time they saw him, all the neighbors congratulated him:

"To your bonus, Ivan Gavrilovich!"

"Thanks for your kind words," he answered and departed on his next assigned run.

And having returned in a no less pleasant month of June, he went as usual to the cashier's office. To pick up his next pay packet.

Again, the sum didn't agree with the usual amount he expected.

Only in the opposite direction: it was less. Substantially.

"What's this for?" asked Sviridov.

"What for, what for!" muttered the bookkeeper, not raising her head. "They hit you—you run; they give it—you take it!"

"But still!" insisted Ivan Gavrilovich.

"This code means a deduction."

"For what?"

"For the bonus. We gave it to you by mistake. They sent us a dark carbon copy, a very poor specimen, from the head office. And we confused you with another comrade who had earned it."

"But that means I didn't...."

"That's what it means."

The conductors met again in the corridors:

"Ah, Gavrilovich! What's with your bonus? Did you forget about us?"

"I don't have a bonus," Sviridov said. "They took it back."

"What happened?"

"It happened," Ivan Gavrilovich said, poking the air. "A poor specimen, they say...."

"They took it back. It must mean something," said his colleagues to each other, following Sviridov with their stares. "There he is with twenty years of flawless service. And look, in the twenty-first, he screws up. Who'd have thought it of Gavrilovich!"

And his wife noticed his dark mood in the doorway. She asked about the missing sum.

"They received a dark copy...." Ivan Gavrilovich squeezed out of himself.

"You're keeping something in the dark yourself," said his wife. "How could they have taken it away if you paid taxes and union dues with the bonus?"

And it was the same with the neighbors. Sviridov couldn't make them understand anything at all.

"A poor specimen..." he said, but not a further sensible word would come to him. Something interfered.

He tried to figure out who was to blame here.

It turned out to be nobody.

The Head of the Directorate of International and Tourist

Transportation of the Moscow Railway, Comrade Tsaplin was not to blame. He had signed a clear copy.

The Head of the Wagon Section of the Eastern Direction, Comrade Stratiychuk was also not to blame. He approved the same clear copy.

And the accounts department was less to blame than anyone since it had received a dark copy.

In short, the man was hurt, but there's no one to blame....[2]

I shouldn't have been surprised by my friend's assessment of this piece. After all, two years earlier, soon after my debacle at *Crocodile*, I had joined several other satirical writers who engaged in the age-old Russian literary game of writing between the lines. Well, in my first case, the offense wasn't even saying something subversive between the lines; it was ignoring the long-standing literary demands imposed by the Soviet regime. At first glance, there is nothing anti–Soviet in that story, which appeared in the famous "12 Chairs Club," which occupied the sixteenth page of the *Literary Gazette*. However, the literary work is centered on the life not of an advanced shock worker or a collective farmer fighting bureaucrats and trying to introduce a new way of growing crops, as the reigning communist ideology requires, but on that of ordinary Soviet white-collar employees. There is not a single line in the story about what they do in that state institution, for they hardly care about it. All their creativity is concentrated not on how to increase their productivity, but on how they could make their daily life convenient and pleasurable. No hint of any "sacrifice for the glory of the ideals of socialism" is expected of them.

"Like at Home"

We used to bring sandwiches to work. At lunchtime, we lined up at our office's boiler and gulped them down with hot water. For tea brewing, we collected ten kopecks per person and bought a large can of Indian tea leaves.

"Why are we eating sandwiches all the time?" said one of my co-workers. "Let's buy a hot plate and cook some dumplings. It's fast and tasty."

Everyone agreed. We collected ten kopecks per person and bought a hot plate. And pots too: you need to cook the frozen dumplings in something! Then, again, we collected ten kopecks each and bought forks.

And plates. First, the flat ones. Some people wanted to taste the dumpling broth, so we bought soup plates as well. And spoons.

Before the holiday break, we had a little party. We wanted to have some wine. So we pitched in ten kopecks each and bought wine glasses.

From the office bookcase, I removed two catalogs, a reference book, and a three-volume encyclopedic dictionary. So, now we have a home bar.

Now we felt much more comfortable. An hour before lunch, the women took turns shopping and cooking. We could also use our lunchtime to take a walk, get some fresh air, and meet our loved ones, those who worked nearby.

Now the women felt very much at home. They brought home slippers and knitting with them. I brought an electric shaver from home. Then I realized I could wash a nylon shirt in the office washbasin and hang it on a hook of the clothes stand; it would dry quickly. This freed up my evening even more.

I cleared the desk drawer of papers and put some underwear in there. Then I decided, why waste two hours every day commuting? And so, I spent the night on the sofa in the director's office.

Irina from our department also lived far away....

Soon we got married. Colleagues presented us with a refrigerator, and our parents gave us a chest of drawers. We didn't have to buy a TV set: Ivan Ivanovich, our director, allowed us to use the one in his office.

A year later, our son, Misha, was born. They put his crib in the library. Irina's mother moved here from the archive department to look after her grandson. My father-in-law had just retired and got a job at our place as a night guard. So, in the evenings, the whole family was together.

On Saturdays, guests would come, and we'd receive them in the clerical office. Irina, my wife, hung little pictures there made of printed chintz with flowers. On the door of the head of the supply department, we put up a watercolor, "The Early Birdie," done by our nephew Tolya. We decorated the corridor with petunias and cacti in ceramic pots.

Gradually, the countless telephone calls, the shuffling of messengers, and the crowds of out-of-town businesspeople annoyed us. I sued for the right to living space. On moral grounds, they agreed in my favor to leave me the fireproof cabinet from the research department and a tea set in the visitor's room.

I won the suit. Our institution has moved out.

Now we take sandwiches to work again....[3]

For a while, writing and publishing in the *Literary Gazette, Literary Russia*, and *The Week* several stories of the same ilk, I felt disappointed. After all, the very fact of publishing stories of that kind amounted to only giggling in satisfaction among my fellow writers that we've fooled our literary censors. I realized that, although we, the Soviet satirists, don't want to admit it to ourselves, we are only the livery servants making jokes behind the doors of our masters' chambers. The true masters of the country don't give a damn about our writing. Although we are not the watchdogs of the Soviet regime—we don't pen the editorials in *Pravda* and *Izvestia*— they, the powers that be, treat us like harmless little poodles, entertaining our owners with our cute yapping. Quite in the spirit of the Russian proverb "Whatever a dog barks about, the wind carries away" (*Sobaka laet, veter nosit*).

Therefore, it is only natural that the next stage of inner emigration was writing for that proverbial "desk drawer," that is, composing stories that couldn't be camouflaged as an innocent humoresque in which a satirical sting is hidden, no matter how skillfully.

I devoted one such story to a taboo topic—that of the utter concentration of power over a vast country in its capital.

Arriving in America and settling in Los Angeles, I was struck by how decentralized life in my new country was. The capital is not the country's largest city (New York), but a much smaller Washington, D.C. The capital of the state of California is not millions-strong Los Angeles, San Francisco, or San Diego, but provincial Sacramento. I'm not even talking about a situation unimaginable in my home country where the laws of some parts of it could differ from the all-union ones, as in America, where some state laws could differ from federal ones.

In the USSR, the total concentration of power in the country's capital, Moscow, was indisputable. (The capital of France is Paris, not some Marseille, although Marseille isn't some backwater.) It was also accepted given that the country's capital regulated every aspect of everyday life in an enormous geographical space, up to deciding how many stockings the knitting factories had to produce year in and year out.

It is believed that total subordination to the Center had been instilled in Russian life since the time of the Moscow princedom. The very word "state" (*gosudarstvo*) in contemporary Russian comes from the Old Russian word "sovereign" (*gosudar'*), as the prince-ruler was called in old Russia, which is associated with the word "master" (*gospodar'*) from the Old Russian "Lord" (*Gospod'*). That is, linguistically speaking, the centrality of power in the state is assumed ordained by the Almighty, no subject for dispute…. Therefore, the capital, the sitting place of the country's ruler, is where everyone gets orders to be carried out locally.

This principle of execution of the old Russian sovereign power was preserved in Soviet times. Soon after the Bolsheviks' takeover in October 1917, the seating of the supreme power in the country became

Moscow. And it became a stand-in for the entire country. The refrain of the song "Moscow in May" (*Moskva majskaia*) written in 1937 for the 20th anniversary of the establishment of Soviet power identifies the capital with the entire country:

> Ebullient,
> Mighty,
> Invincible,
> My country,
> My Moscow,
> You are the most beloved.[4]

Ideologically speaking, it was assumed it was just a matter of time before Moscow would rule not only over the land of the old Russian empire but over the entire world. During my time growing up in the USSR, that wishful thinking of the powers that be was expressed in a form that even the first-graders could comprehend by reading in the children's primer, "Everyone knows the Kremlin is the center of the World" (*Vsem izvestno, chto Zemlia nachinaetsia s Kremlia*).

During my travels around the country, more than once, I was struck by the fact that the local authorities all over the vast territory sought Moscow's approval for everything they were about to undertake. It felt as though they looked up to the capital not only for advice but for permission to breathe.

The following story is a *reductio ad absurdum* of that phenomenon. Of course, I didn't even think of sending the story to any Soviet publishing outlet.

"Soccer Game at 5:30 PM"

I finished my business in the small town with plenty of time to spare. The train back to Moscow ran at night. At the bank, someone mentioned, "There's a soccer game today."

Walking through a little square with stunted little bushes, I approached a man sitting on a bench and reading a newspaper. His face showed intense interest in every line. He even moved his lips, whispering to himself as he read.

"Excuse me," I said, "when does the soccer game start tonight?"

He folded down the paper and looked over the top at me.

"How would I know?"

"Well, the paper...."

"What about the paper?"

"The paper would list it, wouldn't it? Isn't it local?"

"Yes, it's local. But that doesn't mean a thing. What a place to find out the starting time for a game of soccer! In the local paper! Ha-ha!"

I was surprised:

"Where else?"

"A letter should come. From Moscow," he said.

"For the start of a soccer game? From Moscow?"

"Of course!"

"Why?"

"To know for sure when it'll start."

"What, there were cases when they didn't start on time?"

"God forbid! They start right on the minute."

"Then why the letter?"

"What else would you recommend? A letterhead, two or three signatures, a round seal, a case number, and a date. Everything as it should be."

"Isn't it enough to inform people through the paper?"

"No."

"Why not?"

"It's not valid. Where, tell me, where is the letterhead?"

He thrust the paper at me, crumpling it in his agitation.

"Why do you need stationery? If you're such a stickler for formalities, then here's the date of the paper, and here's the number from the first publication. And the signature has been also set up—'Editorial Board.'"

"Aha!" the man ripped the paper back to him and pressed it to his chest. "Right! That's just it, the Board. Where are the names of the Editorial Board members? Any signatures?"

"Who needs it? It's printed right here—"Editorial Board.'"

"Some aunt Masha can type too," he remarked.

"Don't you believe our press?"

"I believe it," he said. "More than I believe myself. But where is a signature?! At least one facsimile!"

And again, with a sweeping gesture, he threw the newspaper to me.

I smoothed it out and read, "Soccer today, starting 5:30 p.m."

"Here it is," I say. "And you didn't believe it. It's here in black and white."

"That's right," the local man quipped. "But maybe today is the birthday of the typesetter's son-in-law! They are to gather at 7:00 p.m. in the banquet hall of the café 'Forget-Me-Not.' And here's a soccer game. How to make it work for everyone? To schedule the game at half-past five."

"Well, God bless it," I gave up. "What's the difference after all!"

"I agree, none," said the man. "If the weather won't interfere."

"The match takes place in any weather," I said.

"And are they also flying in any weather?" the stranger asked, narrowing his eyes. "Sorry, even there," he nodded his head towards the setting sun, "they also nod off for a day or two at the airports. Waiting for it to clear up."

"What does a plane have to do with it?" I said.

"Hello?" he said. "Would the circular come on its own? On its little legs?"

"But why do they need it? That circular? What nonsense?"

The man stood up in indignation.

"Well, you know, I'll tell you, something is suspicious about you. You don't understand the simple essence of things! How would we know the final score of a match without a circular?"

"Well, you," I said, feeling that the veins on my neck were about to burst, "you'll be sitting in the stands, and when they score, you'll see it."

"We'll see. Yes. And how could anyone know whether it is a valid score without a circular? I see you're still wet behind the ears."

"If!" my eyes almost popped out from the strain on my forehead, "the referee! ... Points! ... To the center field! It means—it is a score!!! ... Isn't that clear enough?!"

"I feel you got it finally," he calmed down and sat back down on the bench. "Only the opposite takes place. The Center will inform the judge. In short, let me explain the whole procedure to you. They kick the ball from morning to evening. At a time unknown to anyone in advance, a plane arrives from Moscow. In a special booth, they open a secret package right on the field. It gives the result of the match. They acquaint the head referee with the circular. He shows it to the players. And everyone sighs with relief because now they know how to play and who will score and how. They send the circular to the newspaper for the sports commentators, and the spectators go home."

Feeling that I was going out of my mind, I backed away from the stranger, nodding my head in agreement.

I didn't go to the soccer game. I hastened to the railroad station. My faith in the train schedule was shaky.[5]

Over time, I became increasingly aware that I was living in a country with cultural and moral premises different from those in Western countries, the so-called "capitalist world." There was a vast abyss between the Western ways of life and those I knew at home, an abyss that couldn't be bridged.

Of course, I could judge life in the West only from reports written by Soviet foreign correspondents, and these were filtered by political censors. Everything that worked in a democratic society built on the principle of individual freedom was incomprehensible to the culture of the country in which I lived.

This realization came to me gradually. Once I was certain of it, I wanted to express it in writing but felt I had to disguise it as a humorous short story about a simple-minded fellow who took it in his head to copycat a social service he read about in a Soviet paper. A provincial humor magazine called *Chayan* (Kazan) accepted it and published it just at the time I was summoning up my courage and gathering my documents to apply for emigration. Here it is.

"The Special Occasion Service"

Recently, while perusing a fresh issue of *Pravda*—as usual, from the front page to last, from headlines to TV programming—I noticed a tiny article under an intriguing caption: "Their Way of Life" (*"Ikh nravy"*). It talks about a sad innovation in one of the Western countries. Because of an increase in depression among the general population abroad, they came up with a special service to save those who, in their dark despair, think of cutting short their life path. They announced a phone number people could call when life was unbearable to them, and a whole staff of psychologists on the other end of the line would try to talk them out of doing something stupid because the sun was still shining, though maybe not for them at present, and maybe not in the future either. The article also reported that the service had had little success because of the inhuman capitalist system.

And the next day I come to my factory committee with an idea. "Of course," I say, "we don't need such a social service in our country; we have no grounds for it. But since it's possible to extract a grain of wisdom from any foreign experience, I propose to organize the S.O.S.—the Special Occasion Service. What should we count as a special occasion? A sudden drop in mood, which, we must admit, anyone can experience from time to time. Sporadically, in different seasons of the year, at different hours of the day, it happens. Like before payday, or right after it. Or even from something insignificant...."

"Well, therefore," I say, "for such rare cases, I offer my apartment and, of course, my telephone for the service."

They heard me out at the factory committee and said:

"Why don't you, Comrade Portnov, go to ... get back to your workplace! Together with your ideas. You're always coming up with crazy ideas!"

All right, I thought. I had to take the initiative into my own hands.

I hung a note on the bulletin board in our workshop. With the message that if anyone ever feels not happy, they're welcome to call my home number. After I'm back from my shift, of course....

That's how, in my single life, an incentive appeared. As soon as my shift is over, I rush home. To monitor my telephone. I've read some related literature. On all sorts of hypnosis and methods of persuasion. I got a grounding in these techniques as best I could.

I spent the first three weeks in vain. Nobody called. I thought my idea had failed miserably when I got the ring. Semakin was on the phone, a toolmaker from our workshop and a fellow resident who lived on the eighth floor of our building.

"Well, well!" I said excitedly, sat down at the table, and moved the manuals toward me. "What's gone wrong with you? Tell me!"

"Yes, there isn't much to tell ..." he said, as if against his will. "What're you doing?"

"What-what!" I said. "I'm the one who should ask you questions. And you should answer, hold nothing back, you'll surely feel better, I promise."

"Why are you so antsy?" he asked. "What's gone wrong?"

"There you go again, meathead! It's with you that something went wrong. I'm fine...."

"And what then went wrong with me?" he quizzed anxiously.

"Aha," I say, "I see! A special case: you can't sort your things out by yourself.... Well, this is not a problem for us.... So," I glanced at the manual, "stretch out your right hand in front of you!"

"What's that for?" he asked even more anxiously.

"Stretch it out," I said, "it's none of your business. It's necessary!"

"But where do I stretch it out?" he got angry. "My phone is in my hallway. There's no room for my elbow to go."

"Don't interrupt!" I shouted, "Do as I say! Repeat after me, 'My hand is warm, heavy.... I'm calm.' Three times.... Then, 'My head's warm, heavy. I'm calm ...'"

"That's right," Semakin interrupted me, "my head *is* heavy. You guessed it right. I'm at a loss where this gravity comes from."

"Shut up!" I shouted at him even louder to get his will under control, "repeat after me, 'My hand is warm and heavy.'"

"Why do you keep poking your hand at me?" Semakin foamed.

Annoyed that the man spoiled my entire session of helping him, I almost smashed my phone to pieces.

"All right, Semakin, that does it!" I screamed. "You're such a pain in the neck! I'm trying to save you, and you've driven me to madness yourself. That's it! Go to hell! I don't feel sorry for you, you fool!"

And I hung up.

And Semakin called me back right away.

"I'm sorry, Portnov," he said. "I didn't quite get it. Now I'm seeing what's going on. Ah, that's why, over the last few days, you've been walking around the workshop as if something was bugging you.... Well, tell me what it is, unburden yourself.... After all, you and I are neighbors, and what's more—we work in the same shop."

"Well, for goodness' sake!" I felt my face turning pale from pent-up emotions. "I'm coming to you with a humane remedy, and you're making a mockery of me."

And would you believe it, I even burst into tears from my inability to explain to Semakin his disappointing behavior.

And Semakin tragically said into the phone:

"Oh, what a blockhead I am, Portnov! How could I not have guessed it at once? Now I understand where your sadness comes from. Wait, I'm coming over."

And a minute later he showed up at the door.

"Well?" he said and pointed at the clock. "It's twenty to seven. The liquor stores will be closing. Will we make it?"

I saw the man is in decent shape. Although he gave me a tough time, it worked. My S.O.S. worked.

"It shouldn't be too hard to make it," I said and took out an empty vodka bottle to return. "It shouldn't be over ten minutes even without hurrying."[6]

2

"Lessons of Montreal"

As soon as I settled in America and found a means of sustenance for my family and me, I wanted to check out whether everything was yet in place, whether anything was lost in the perturbation of emigration. My writer's eyes were still turned backward, to the country I left forever.

The year was 1976, and the international behavior of my former homeland revived my satirical spirit. Perhaps I also felt the need to reassure myself that I did the right thing—that is, escaped from a system in which lies and forgery were its way to project its superiority, to claim and uphold its prestige.

That's why, upon reading the reports about the Olympic Games held that year in Canada, I turned to my Russian typewriter, which I had brought with me, and typed out a satirical piece titled "Lessons of Montreal."

The article reflects such realities of that time as the shortage of grain in the USSR. For years on end, the Soviet Union had to buy it from Western countries, the United States and Canada. Despite their inevitable doom, as the communist ideology had it, the capitalists still produced so much grain that there was enough for the Soviets, short of it, year in and year out.

Also, several political embarrassments occurred during the Olympic Games, highly publicized. Thus, Soviet diver Sergei Nemtsanov and four members of the sports team of the brotherly Romanian Socialist Republic asked for asylum.

Soviet modern pentathlete Boris Onischenko and the whole Soviet pentathlon team were disqualified because of his cheating. He embedded a pushbutton into his sword that registered a false hit.... A Soviet diving arbiter offered a bribe to his American partner.... And, to avoid embarrassing defeat, the Soviet water polo team feigned illness....

"Lessons of Montreal"

The Olympic Games have ended. The emblem of the next meeting place of world athletes—the USSR, Moscow—appeared on the huge tableaux of the Montreal stadium. A Russian girl, touched up with rouge by the makeup artists of Moscow television, appeared on the screen with traditional Russian bread and salt. It is easy to see the symbolism of the Olympic relay here: without a doubt, the bread has been baked from Canadian wheat....

Thus, 1980! What awaits the athletic world and its countless fans over there, in that faraway Moscow? Considering the goings-on in Montreal, it's not too hard to predict what it would be like, the Soviet jousting field, long-awaited, hard-won in the battles at the Olympic Committee meetings.

The scandal around the fencer Onishchenko will not be repeated in Moscow. As is known, in Montreal, he installed a device in his sword, showing a false hit. Onishchenko will be called on the carpet to face the high Soviet sports authorities.

"Shame on you, Onishchenko!" they will say. "They dishonored you before the entire world for good reason. What a shameful thing you did! Coming up with such a wonderful invention—and not a peep about it to anyone! Ugh, how ugly of you! ... You're a miserable individualist, Onishchenko, that's who you are! Where is your team spirit? If you'd share it with your teammates, there would be no scandal. Together, we would have brought your invention to perfection, so that not a single dog would have dug it up. How despicable!"

Most likely, they would correct the situation when preparing for the next Olympiad....

It's safe to assume that, back in Moscow, the Soviet diving judge got bawled out for offering a secret deal to the American arbiter.

"What a nincompoop!" they will tear him to pieces. "How come you forgot who you were dealing with? How could you expect that he, an American, would know the ways we do things here, in Moscow? You know.... You scratch my back and I'll scratch yours.... One hand washes the other, etcetera.... After all, he is a gentleman, pardon my French! If you just give him Stolichnaya vodka with medals, even then you might have had a better chance.... Maybe he'd have tossed a prize or two our way."

And the Soviet water polo players have fallen flat on their faces in Montreal altogether. Seeing that the Olympic medals weren't in the cards for them, they pretended to be sick. Didn't show up at the next game.... And they were caught in a lie.

Oh no! Such a disgrace won't happen in Moscow. If they lose again, the KGB will step in and help the Soviet sports federation. They will throw some stuff their way from their reserves. You don't have to worry then. No medical commission will smell the sham there....

To think of it, of all people, you won't envy the KGB workers at the time of the Moscow Olympics. Judge for yourself. Millions of foreign tourists will come to Moscow, all at once, and each of them is a potential spy, or saboteur, or even a Zionist.

Only one thing would be good not to worry about: no Soviet athlete will attempt to defect, as occurred in Montreal to the diver Sergei Nemtsanov. There would be no need to ask the grandmothers for help to get the prodigal grandchildren back…. And for the Romanians, brotherly socialist campers, there would be no need to worry. Unlike what happened in Montreal, you can hardly expect any of them to seek political asylum in Moscow.

Truly happy about the future Olympics will be ordinary Soviet people. Hundreds of thousands—what am I saying?—millions of them from all over the country will head for Moscow, and their eyes will blaze with real hunters' passion.

However, they would hunt not for the autographs of world-famous athletes, but for souvenirs. Souvenirs of a special kind, unknown in the West. For smoked sausage…. Oranges…. Lightly salted herring, which is produced for export only…. The Moscow visitors will take these souvenirs to all parts of the country in quantities limited only by the physical stamina of the individuals. All over the great nation, people know how much Soviet authorities are keen on fooling visiting foreigners by creating a semblance of abundance. And, when it is feasible, Soviet people take advantage of this knowledge….

When, in the summer of 1957, for the first time in Soviet history, the World Festival of Youth and Students took place in Moscow, my parents egged me on to go on a long journey from my hometown Odessa, a thousand-mile trip.

"Go," my parents told me. "You're on your college break, anyway…. We must not miss the opportunity to buy you a decent suit."

I went to Moscow with a lengthy list of goods compiled from the requests of my many relatives. To their immense joy, I got a lot. In lines, with blood, but I got it. Toward the opening of the World Festival, the shelves of Moscow stores were filled with goods unseen for many years. Then I bought a suit for myself that would serve me until my next trip to Moscow. When the World Trade Fair which took place several years down the road….[1]

Finding in my papers the clipping of this satirical piece published in the New York newspaper *Novoye Russkoye Slovo* reminded me not only of my literary activities of the time but also about my state of mind, that of a recent immigrant coming from a totalitarian country.

I discovered I signed the article with my initials only. It looks like this was my first, timid attempt to get my real name back. As I describe in *In the Jaws of the Crocodile*, back in my Soviet life, when I first tried to get published in a Moscow paper, I was told that my surname was "not for newspapers," which was a paraphrase of the fact that it was Jewish. I had to come up with a Russian-sounding pen name instead.

In the haven of emigration, thousands of miles away from the Soviet Union, on the other side of the globe, I could stop playing Soviet games and sign my work with my real name.

In time, I did it. Meanwhile, still mindful of the ways Soviet, I used my initials only. I wanted to protect those members of my extended family who still lived in Soviet territory. I knew too well the Soviet system's practice of persecuting relatives for the political sins of their kin. Especially those who left the best country in the world....

3

"Dust"

Now, at a distance of three decades, rereading this satirical piece, I recall writing it, feeling the hopelessness regarding the future of the country in which I was born and raised. The immediate impetus for taking to my typewriter was my trip to Moscow in January 1991.

Until recently, there were grounds for optimism. The trip was my second return to Russia since my emigration. The first one had taken place just half a year before, in the summer of 1990. When I emigrated in late 1974, none of us, emigres, thought that the USSR would ever collapse. After all, the lack of hope that things would ever get better in the country was the major impetus for taking the risk of applying for exit visas. We all felt compelled to get out of the country at the first opportunity.

But then, ten years down the road, the political climate relaxed to a degree unheard of in Soviet times. Incredible news came from my homeland: over there, they allowed you to speak about things you could only whisper previously. It was a time of political liberties, known as Gorbachev's glasnost and perestroika.

Among other frivolities that the regime felt it could afford was loosening restrictions on travel that had been severely restricted for almost all Soviet citizens and the lifting of the curse on those who left the country in the 1970s and 1980s. Suddenly, we émigrés could go back and visit the land where we were born and raised.

I have to admit that, on the eve of my visit to the old country, I was anxious. Accustomed to not trusting the Soviet government on any issue, I had bad dreams.

According to one of those dreams, a dream that recurred in the first years of my life in America, I am back in my hometown, Odessa, Ukraine. I walk the streets and visit with my old friends, but it's time to leave. I hurry to the railroad station. The customs officer is at the booth. I hold out my passport and notice—there is no exit visa. The high-cheeked border guard is very young, of high school age (they seem to hire such young people because they are not corrupt yet; you can't bribe them). He looks at me and says, "Step aside, citizen." I rummage in my pockets, turn them inside out, and dig through my carry-on. But there is no piece of that pinkish checkered paper—the exit visa with which I had left the country many years ago. What will happen now?! Fear grips me. The situation is not resolved. The border guard, playing with the nodules of his cheekbones, looks at me disapprovingly. On the edge of despair, I wake up in a cold sweat.

Then I learned I wasn't the only one having this kind of dream; many other emigres who had left Russia had it, too. Those who emigrated after the revolution, during the civil war, and those who were taken out of the country by the Germans during World War II to be part of the Nazi regime's workforce. I kept asking myself what kind of power a country has that both beckons you and scares you to death?

It was a bittersweet reunion.... I visited the editorial offices of newspapers and magazines I'd frequented back in my Soviet past as a freelance journalist. They greeted me as if I were a ghost. At the time, Russians had fallen into a habit of wringing their hands in remorse for how they had treated those who had left the country. The editors of widely read publications, such as *The Week*, *The Literary Gazette*, and *Evening Moscow*, asked me for articles about America and published them on their pages. They supplemented these publications with their write-ups, reminding readers about my previous work and giving a résumé of my American life. In his preamble to two of my short pieces, the editor of the popular magazine *Ogonek* wrote, "Now we repay our debts and give those whom we compelled to leave Russia the opportunity to speak—it is time to gather scattered stones."

However, while it seemed to be that glasnost politics gave some hope for the country's future, the state of the country's economy gave no cause for optimism. Perestroika stumbled in a big way.

Wandering the Moscow streets, I thought of the Soviet underground joke of the time, which summed up the situation in the country:

They ask a doggie, "How are you doing now, Polkan, under glasnost and perestroika?"
"What can I tell you! It's still a dog's life.... True they lengthened my chain, but they moved my bowl farther away. And I can bark about it as much as I like."

In short, everything was more or less all right with glasnost. With perestroika, things stood not so great, to put it mildly. The standard of living of the population declined in the country. The production of food plummeted. They introduced ration cards for many food products and goods for everyday use. Inflation soared. There was unemployment in the country, and crime increased sharply.

I strolled along the streets of Moscow, perplexed by the in-your-face evidence of the country's stark poverty. The Soviet economic system had broken down. Rows of poorly dressed men and women with emaciated faces stretched around the entrances of the city's subway stations. They held up domestic relics, which they hoped to sell—amber earrings, medallions, silverware, antique books.... This brought back my childhood memories of the wartime years, which my mother and I spent being evacuated to a remote part of the country, in Central Asia. As a young boy, I used to wander around the makeshift black markets where people offered whatever they had of any value for food, just as they were doing now in Moscow. Hunger left them little choice.

Pale, sleep-deprived people with eyes narrowed by exhaustion walked around the city, frail, skinny, and degenerate. They walked through the streets hoping to make some money. They stopped at the small street stalls and inquisitively examined whether there was any product that could be worn or eaten without a threat to life.

I met old friends. One of them, Rita, a journalist, a dark-haired beauty, shared with me her sadness arising from the circumstances of everyday life.

"My husband is a good and kind person. I'm ashamed he works for what is a handout. He is a translator from English to Russian, and his employers don't pay him a salary. Instead, sometimes they give him a carton of American cigarettes, sometimes a pack of laundry detergent...."

"I can't live like this," she continued. "Yes, now I can sign up to get a coupon entitling me to buy a new sofa through the trade union committee. But I'd rather have two beds so that there would be more space for me. I enjoy sleeping in a position with my body sprawling. But I cannot buy two beds, only one. I'm ashamed to tell our trade union committee what I want. I know that the very next day, a rumor would spread in our editorial office that there is marital discord in my family.... That I sleep with my husband in different beds.... It's awful! I feel I have nothing personal."

"Or here's another thing," she hesitated for a minute. "I'm sorry to talk about it but, since the store shelves are empty, I can order a pair of panties for myself through our trade union committee. And there they ask me, 'Rita, what panties do you like to have? There are two types of them available: striped and solid.' And now I am dying of shame when I walk down our corridors. Now everyone knows my panties are striped. It is a disgrace!"

However, there was one aspect of the country's life that remained unchanged. It was the ever-present fear of the country's secret police—the notorious KGB.

"I'm afraid," Rita said. "I'm still afraid of them. No matter what you tell me, I'm dying of fear."

"Well, they don't take people away now," her girlfriends said with some pride for the new times and their country, the Soviet Union. The revolutions of 1917 led to the establishment of the USSR five years later, and now that country, before it even reached the seventeenth anniversary of its founding, is shaking itself up a little. It's dusting itself off. It casts away its past like a lizard does its tail when pursued by a predator.

"They aren't arresting people and taking them away now," Rita said, all with the same passion. "But they took away my grandfather and grandmother. And they would do it to my dad, too, if he wouldn't keep his mouth shut. And since they are still *there*," she raised her eyes, "how can I not be afraid that they might think it over and resume arresting people?"

Here she reminded me she was by far not alone in fearing the unchallenged power of the country's secret police; its hands were bloodied for all of Soviet history.

"Have you heard already what people joke about these days?" she said. "'What will happen after perestroika? Shooting everyone [involved in it] [in Russian, it's a pun—*perestroika ... perestrelka*]. Here is another joke, if you feel it's funny for you."

And she cited the following lines:

> Comrade, believe it'll pass,
> The so-called glasnost,
> And then, the state security
> Will remember our names.

It was the satirical switching of the concluding stanza of Pushkin's poem "To Chaadaev," which every Soviet schoolchild had to learn by heart:

> Comrade, believe it'll rise,
> The star of captivating happiness.
> Russia will wake up from her sleep
> And, on the wreckage of autocracy,
> They'll write our names.[1]

I said goodbye to my old friends, not without regret. Same old fidgety glances around.... Haunted gazes.... Fear of an uncertain future.... Could it be that everything that has happened in the country has changed nothing?

I left Moscow feeling much more skeptical about the future of the country compared to the one I came with. I wanted to believe in a miracle.

However, on my next visit in January 1991, there was again hope that the country would change. In the middle of the month, a protest rally was held on Manezhnaya Square in Moscow under the slogan "Down with the Occupation of Lithuania!" As soon as an opportunity appeared, in March of the previous year, Lithuania became the first of the Soviet republics to declare independence.

And then they tried to suppress this movement by military force. Blood was shed when Soviet paratroopers stormed the television tower in the Lithuanian capital, Vilnius. According to various sources, the public demonstration in Moscow gathered from 100,000 to 500,000 people.

However, just ten days after this uplifting event, I witnessed something that plunged me into confusion and instilled pessimism about the future of the country. It was about how Muscovites behaved when it came to, it would seem, their very ability to survive under the conditions of the economy collapsing before their eyes.

It was announced that new 50- and 100-ruble banknotes were introduced. Old bills of the same denomination could be exchanged for new ones in the shortest possible time—within just three days, from January 23 to January 25. In addition, people could exchange no more than a thousand rubles.

People's savings accounts were frozen. You had to prove the legitimacy of your savings. This meant that people who had been saving for their old age for years on end could not access their savings.

Huge lines for many hours stretched out at the entrances to savings banks and post offices, where the exchange of currency was conducted.

I couldn't believe my eyes. I was flabbergasted, thinking, Look at that! They stand meekly in lines as if it's the natural order of things? ... If something like this were to be tried in America, mass protests would break out all over the country.

The pessimism generated by these impressions remained with me when I returned to New York, and you'll see the reflection of that pessimism in "Dust." Composed in the spring of 1991, it sums up my reaction toward the entire period of glasnost and perestroika in Soviet history. From a distance, the goings-on in the country over the five years since Gorbachev came to power seemed to be no more than a time of endless public discussions on a variety of social topics with no action taken, an illustration of the Russian proverb "like pounding water in a mortar" (equivalent to the American one "like pouring water through a sieve.")

Such a vision of that period of Soviet history resulted from my Americanization. Over the past fifteen years of my life, I embraced the American way of valuing deeds over words.

One target of ridicule in "Dust" is the excuse for inaction in the form of the Russian addiction to reading, which has deep historical roots. Since at least the first quarter of the eighteenth century, from the time Peter the First "hacked through the window to Europe," Russian culture developed a profound reverence toward literature. While, in the West, it is customary to think literature exists to reflect life, Russians often seem to assume that literature comes first. While in English we talk about a writer's "work," Russians use a word of higher style, having Church-Slavonic roots—*"proizvedenie,"* which is more like the English "creation." In Russian culture, a writer is treated as a holder of higher truth, a visionary, a prophet, and, if not a celestial being, then a being of higher order. As Russian poet Eugene Evtushenko summed it up, "a poet in Russia is more than a poet."

This attitude toward literature and reading in the period of glasnost was enhanced by the sudden lifting of state censorship imposed on publication from the early days of the Bolsheviks' takeover of power. Announced as a "temporary measure to safeguard the gains of revolution," state censorship lasted decades on end.

Thus, as soon as taboos were removed one by one from the censors' lists, an avalanche of books appeared in the stores. For the first time, Soviet citizens, young and old alike, could read works of émigré Russian writers that had long ago established themselves in world literature, such as Vladimir Nabokov and Joseph Brodsky. The same goes for many volumes of *tamizdat*, that is, works by Soviet authors smuggled out and published abroad because their writing couldn't see the light of day in the USSR for political reasons. This was the case with works of Soviet literature cursed in their own time, such as Boris Pasternak's novel, *Doctor Zhivago*, and Alexander Solzhenitsyn's *The Gulag Archipelago*.

In the glasnost-era, a lot of books were published in the Soviet Union that previously had appeared only in *samizdat*, that is, were self-published by retyping the forbidden text by hand using carbon paper. Such was the fate of memoirs of former camp inmates.

Also, because of the stringent and puritanical standards upheld by Soviet publishing houses, during this time, readers could get hold of many works of pre-revolutionary Russian and contemporary foreign literature.

Besides that, popular outlets, such as the magazine *A Little Light* (*Ogonek*), the journal *The New World*, and newspapers such as *Moscow*

News and *Arguments and Facts* as well as *Izvestia*, began publishing many materials that exposed the bloody events of the Stalin era.

Now it was possible to read Russian publications about the abuses of the Communist Party and Soviet government officials, economic difficulties and commodity shortages, negative social phenomena (for example, drug addiction and prostitution), and musical and other subcultures, especially among Soviet youth.

However, the outburst of reading activity in the Gorbachev era was hardly more than the phenomenon of forbidden fruit made available. The press censorship established after the Bolsheviks' grab for power, called "temporary, to protect the gains of the revolution," wasn't lifted until the beginning of glasnost in 1986. (It should be noted that, as soon as communist ideology ceased to be official and was replaced with a capitalist one, Russians' high spirituality disappeared into thin air. The country with the highest reading rates in the world correlated with works of great literature rushed to get hold of cheap mysteries and watch mindless TV series.)

My lampoon, titled "Dust," proved to be an ominous, but accurate, premonition. About ten years passed after I wrote it, and it turned out that my intuition did not let me down. Even though at the end of August of the year, the lampoon appeared in the Russian-language New York newspaper *The New Russian Word*, mass protests were held in Moscow against the coup. The Communist Party retrogrades attempted to seize power in the country. The coup failed, causing the collapse of the communist totalitarian regime, which led to the fall of the entire USSR.

However, while the Communist Party lost its monopoly, on the eve of the year 2000, about a decade later, the power in the Russian Federation returned to the hands of those to whom it had always belonged— the KGB. Ailing Russian president Boris Yeltsin resigned, making Vladimir Putin, former KGB officer and one-time director of the Federal Security Service (FSB), the successor of the KGB, acting president of the Russian Federation. Since then, that very man has been holding all the power in the country. And he may well keep it in his hands for the foreseeable future.

"Dust" is written in the literary style known in Russian literature since the end of the eighteenth century. This style is called Aesopian, which, in tsarist and Soviet times, served to circumvent the ubiquitous censorship. The style involved the use of allegories, hints, and images that an initiated reader could decipher, but which the censor couldn't find fault with. Although there was no need to fear it in an émigré publication, as a writer, I was attracted by the pleasure of the literary game inherent in the Aesopian language which the immigrant Soviet reader could easily decrypt.

The key to understanding who the author means by "electricians" of various levels of command and "electricity" itself is the propagandistic phrase repeated *ad nauseam* that explained the principal task of Soviet society as building communism, "the bright future of whole humanity." Hence, the "inventors of the foundations of electricity" are none other than Karl Marx and Friedrich Engels. Since the slogan widely known in Soviet times "Communism is Soviet power plus the electrification of the whole country" belongs to Vladimir Lenin, he is, of course, the "Chief Electrician," and Joseph Stalin, the excesses of whose leadership a lot was said during the Glasnost period, is the "designer" of an "electric generator."

It's easy to guess that the "SST" (State Sanitation Team) is none other than the KGB, the secret police. For those who followed the events at home, it was also clear that "Small-POX" is a highly vocal nationalistic and anti–Semitic society which called itself "Memory."

The lampoon also makes fun of other Soviet propaganda clichés. Regarding the undesirable statements of certain public figures, it was customary to blame foreign interference, commenting that such statements have been "sung from someone else's voice" (*propety s chuzhogo golosa*). They parrot foreign (meaning, the capitalists') ideas.

It's quite transparent that the "countries of the setting sun" are none other than the Western countries.

"Dust"

Few people now remember how it started, but the first to sound the alarm were individuals obsessed with cleanliness and those with conjunctivitis. At the same time, they drew the attention of the healthier part of the population to the fact that dust, coming from out of nowhere, covered mirrors and lids of desks at a rate exceeding the usual one.

After some time, an indiscernible substance, more and more distinguishable to the naked eye, appeared in the air. Soon all the roads, bridges, and monuments to both the Chief Electrician of the country and the inventors of electricity—the foundations of the bright future of humanity—were covered with a layer of dust. Life, however, went on as usual. In the subway, before sitting down on benches, the population swept them clean with their handkerchiefs.

The amount of dust in the air increased. Practical young women adapted by carrying small sponges in their purses with which they removed the settling dust from the lips of their beloved before kissing them.

Newspapers wrote little about dust since they were busy with much more important things: the main generator of the country was rusted and was threatened with collapse. It was necessary to rewind the anchors, re-seal the ends, and polish the brushes—in short, a major overhaul; and this threatened a temporary blackout with no idea of when the light would return, even if at reduced strength, but at least enough for reading—the country's major hobby, without which the population could not imagine itself as a population.

Since it became customary to respond to even minor inconveniences of readers, newspapers interrupted for a while debates on electrical topics and refuted rumors that both the capital and the provinces were covered with a powder of unknown origin. The rumors were called absurd, a song sung by outsider voices, but they continued to circulate, somewhat even more energetically than before. Then the Chief Laboratory Assistant of the country was interviewed, and he calmed the population, saying that, based on an analysis of the substance falling from above, there was no radiation in the dust. Dust emanating from an unknown source, he said, contained common silicon compounds, spores of ripe plants, and dried dinosaur semen. The dust was regular and vulgar; it didn't represent any special intrigue of non-friendly powers, such as claimed by the representatives of a small, but highly vocal Society for Preservation of Old Xeroxes (nicknamed "Small-POX").

This society called a press conference and announced that, first, it demanded the people not confuse the dust on the streets with the dust that it had vowed to preserve for future generations, and second, that it was all the fault of the dust storms produced with the help of superpowerful ventilators belonging to the countries of the setting sun, who are known for their ill will. Another, a more aggressive faction of the "Small-POX" declared that what the cities of the country were covered with is not dust at all, but nothing more than heavenly manna of Jewish-Masonic origin. This dust was being poured upon us with the sole purpose of instilling unjustified hopes into the gullible indigenous population of the country and, in doing so, first morally corrupting the population, and then undermining its physical health.

In the meantime, the State Sanitation Team (SST) was deployed against the dust, whose top priority task was to fight evil spirits of all kinds. It was a terrifying organization equipped with water cannons and pumps of monstrous power. In the not-too-distant past, SST's water cannons were developed to have a such powerful force that they washed away everything that came under its stream from the face of the earth. After some time, it turned out the washed away was not at all some kind of evil spirit, but gold dust. Upon clarification, a commemoration of that gold was arranged. But no one thought to abolish the SST. It has been stated that the SST recently completed the rewinding of its local transformer, and the current SST, thus updated, had nothing to do with the infamous SST, except for its name.

Meanwhile, dust covered the sidewalks of the cities, ankle-deep. Some hotheads called on the population to take a whisk in their hands and sweep the dust. But they were stopped by those who had wised up the hard way.

"We know this business back and forth," they assured. "Well, let's say we sweep off this dust, which is unlikely, given the lack of experience and our loss of the habit of coordinating our body movements. But even if we succeed, what's the point? More dust will come soon. Here you have to look at the root of the problem. It is necessary to develop such a system that would ensure a decisive and final sweeping. The current approach is not adapted to such cases. The whole damned system is to blame."

Those who had used the dust as a pretext for a redesign of the entire system were stopped. It was pointed out to them the unreasonableness of wasting efforts on a systemic redesign, since the system has already begun to change itself, and there was no need to interfere with that process. As a sign of impending changes, it was noted that recently the system, like a lizard being pursued, had dropped its tail. And now we just have to be patient for a bit, since other limbs may fall off too, following the tail.

Reptile experts issued a cautionary note: you shouldn't rely too much on comparing the system to a lizard. Observations have shown that lizards discard their tails for the sole purpose of deceiving their predators. Diving under a rock, lizards quickly grow back new tails, no worse than the previous ones.

Zoologists have been dismissed as too narrow-minded. Everybody agreed it was necessary to place all our hopes on time. In time, everything will resolve itself and everything will be put in its place. Well, let's make it to September, the population said with a sigh.... Well, at least until March.... And would you look there? It's already been announced, that a law should be approved regarding state measures to combat dust and the tasks of local vacuum cleaning authorities. Then we'll breathe more freely and, having prayed for a new law, we will begin the sweeping.

Meanwhile, the dust in the streets reached people's knees. The population, accustomed to natural disasters of all kinds, did not lose heart, and once again showed an outstanding ability to survive. Say what you like, people told each other, but there are no people as long-suffering and patient as we are. Others would crack, but we're okay, we're holding out. We only have to wait for a decree permitting dusting off things when we're not at work. Then, when we get down to business—just watch us! The world will only gasp and shudder, astonished....

There was, however, a certain curator of antiquity, a small-bore, no matter how you look at him, who remarked that they say things hadn't taken such a turn for the first time. The world, they say, has been doing nothing but gasp and shudder for decades on end, given what has been done on this earth.

But they shushed the curator, calling him a reactionary, a man who looked backward, not forward....

In the meantime, while waiting for the resolution, some bright minds came up with a way to deal with dust. Caring for the next generation, they invented gauze bandages for children's mouths and noses. True, there arose a shortage of gauze, but it was also overcome by limiting the amount to be sold per person so that there would be enough to cover the children's noses. To keep the gauze patches in place, they put two and two together and adapted rubber bands from pharmacy vials. It was suggested to the population that they wrap those rubber bands around the ears in a special way. To give a visual representation of the process, Central Television performed an act of hitherto unheard-of civic bravery. It interrupted for three and a half minutes the broadcast of the speech of the country's Chief Power Engineer at a permanent meeting of representatives of the lighting community.

This speech comprised three phases. The first phase, which lasted three years, nine months, and seventeen days, was devoted to criticizing the design of the existing generator. In the second phase (two years and three months), the Chief Power Engineer focused on the personality of the designer himself, who, however, had long been dead, but whose disgusting personal qualities the speaker considered it necessary to dwell on for the future generation's edification. The third phase of the speech, the most businesslike and energetic, by the time of the historic break in its broadcast, lasted about seven months and addressed the pressing issues of rewinding the generator anchors. The need for such an operation was not objectionable. Deep disagreements of the electricians were revealed around the question of how the winding should be laid—in an old-fashioned way, crosswise, as some called for, or in the new-fangled, close-fitting way, as others no less zealously insisted....

The dust, meanwhile, was waist-deep. The population, after thinking about it, found a way out and got used to moving on skis, the runners of which were lubricated with Vaseline.

When the dust reached people's necks, some of the least hardy parts of the population became despondent. But the majority still found reasons for joy and hope. First, the majority reasoned, that in the past, things were much worse than this had happened. For years on end, we've been stuck up to our necks in something worse than dust. Second, although being up to your neck in the dust is an unpleasant thing, it still does not yet interfere with reading. We don't care about our ears. If they were to be buried under the dust, it would be no big deal. Some people have already had cause to put plugs in their ears. But the eyes, the eyes! It is rare luck, if you think about it, that the eyes are up there, almost at the forehead! For the dust to reach the eyes, given the size of the country, you'd still have to have much more of it. So, you can still read stuff. Oh, you can read swell! And everyone read and read everything—translated philosophical treatises and manuals on karate techniques during acts of marital intimacy, historical novels of pre-electric times, and instructions for opening water taps.... The contents of the books were not so important, but there always needed to be a fresh supply of them. The quality of life wasn't much to write home about, but it was a first-rate reading experience.

The most stubborn ones still pursued the answer to the question of where did the dust come from, in such an enormous amount. But no one listened to them, just as no one listened to the mutterings of the curator of antiquities, a well-known bore, who swayed from side to side and whispered under his breath:

"...And then one day some gray-haired old man looked down, shook his head, and said in a low voice, with obvious indignation at his pride: 'It is an unheard-of impertinence on my part to believe that all ideas and sketches must be realized into something meaningful, into something that must make sense. Creativity, who invented you! Who came up with this sophisticated torture, the act of creation? Where is the poet who never crossed out a line that goes nowhere? Where is the artist who has not made a single sketch, in which, upon further reflection, he found no use? A stray thought flashed and disappeared.... But this is the power of the creator to find the strength to stop the flight of a crazy fantasy if there is no fruitful continuation of it.'

"And with that, with a gentle movement of his hand, the old man pressed the handle of the lever that tipped the enormous receptacle upside down."

"And a substance especially prepared for such cases—silicon compounds, spores of ripe plants, and dried sperm of dinosaurs—rushed down to the ground, a substance that is very easy to confuse with ordinary dust."[2]

PART II

Discovering America

4

"Increditability"

Perhaps none of my first writings in America reflects best my state of mind, my confusion, and even bewilderment regarding various aspects of the American way of life than the story "Who Is Who."[1] Rereading it now, many years later, I conclude it is not by chance the book titled *Future Shock* is mentioned in it. This work by futurist Alvin Toffler, published a few years before I arrived in the country, deals with America undergoing an enormous structural refashioning, a revolution from an industrial society to a super-industrial society. The author treats the term, which gives the volume its title, as a personal perception of "too much change in too short a time," which overwhelms people, producing "shattering stress and disorientation." They become "future-shocked."

In my case, that of an immigrant growing up behind the Iron Curtain, it was a present shock. While being a formidable military threat to the free world, aiming at it with its ballistic missiles furnished with nuclear warheads, the Soviet Union in the early 1970s was inferior in many other, non-military aspects. Margaret Thatcher wasn't too much off the mark calling it "a third-world country with missiles." Coming to America, I entered a land where, daily, I encountered a multitude of things and had to absorb various notions that the inhabitants of the land took for granted.

The story "Who Is Who" reflects my world perception over my first years on American soil, my lack of confidence in, even bewilderment over, the reality of the surroundings. It seems that the author of the story does not believe that he is still on earth, not on another planet. Like an astronaut on the moon, he bounces a bit at every step. Indeed, I found myself in a land in which not only humans but the local animals need an interpreter as well. Here, instead of *guv-guv*, as Russian dogs go, an American one produces *woof-woof*. The local frogs utter croak or *ribit-ribit*, not the way they are supposed to express themselves—*kva-kva*. An American pig utters a mysterious *oink-oink*, while its Russian cousin says *khriu-khriu*. Couldn't they come up with some lingua franca among themselves?

No wonder the action in my story takes place in a supermarket, the central nerve knot of adaptation to a new land. Stepping into it, we, ex–Soviets, found ourselves transported from a life of perennial shortages of basic necessities into a life of oversupply. Here you have to strain your brain not over where and how to get a scarce product, but what choice to make from a seemingly endless variety of it.

Besides overflowing with lots of recognizable products, the supermarket had many items we, the newcomers, had never seen in our Soviet past. We never tasted mango, kiwi, or grapefruit. Of the tropical fruits, we apprehended lemons, but not their undersized and green (with envy?) cousins called "limes." Growing up in Odessa, Ukraine, I knew oranges and bananas only as rare, much-welcomed guests. From time to time, because of sea storms, rain, or other excuses for mismanagement, they were slow in reloading these gifts of nature from the holds of the steamships, bringing them to our Odessa harbor from overseas onto the cargo trains heading for Moscow. (It was important for the powers that be to show the tourists from the capitalist countries that we are not worse than others.) So, if oranges and bananas were deemed not to make it to the country's capital intact, they were delivered to the local Odessa stores and sold out in a flash.

My generation of people born twenty years after the Bolsheviks' takeover of power in the country knew another tropical fruit called "pineapple" (*ananas*, in Russian) only from the lines composed by the poet of the revolution, Vladimir Mayakovsky. We had to learn them by heart in our secondary schools. We didn't know either how it tasted or even looked, only that it was expensive, judging by who had consumed it in pre-revolutionary Russia:

> Eat your pineapples and chew your grouses.
> Your last day is coming, [you despicable] bourgeois.[2]

There were many other never-seen items in the supermarket. We looked over containers with deodorant spray, trying to guess what they were for.

Back in our Soviet life, in our hometown Odessa, my younger brother used to mystify our family members visiting us from other cities by pronouncing: "If you want to know how capitalism smells, pass by the hotel London."

Erected in the style of the early Italian Renaissance with luxurious accommodations, in the Soviet time, this best hotel in town was used to house visitors from capitalist countries only. The fragrance of the air around the entrance to the hotel resulted from the hotel guests' use of deodorants, a product unheard of in the USSR.

Now we could get hold of these products and smell like those foreign tourists. We discovered spray cans with air fresheners for bathrooms and fridge odor absorbers.

However, we, Soviet immigrants, were by far not the only ones in this situation. As I learned later, a curious episode took place with Viktor Belenko, a Russian pilot who, in 1976, defected to Japan on his secret MIG-25 (Foxbat) warplane. After one of his first debriefings, as he took him back to his hotel, the CIA curator asked him whether he wouldn't mind dropping by a supermarket along the way—he forgot to buy a pack of coffee for his home.

They spent only a few minutes in the store. When they got back into the car, Belenko frowned. His face took on the hostile expression of a deeply offended man.

"I don't deserve to be treated in such a manner," he said, his teeth clenched. "Why such distrust? Why overdo it? I'd chosen to come over of my free will. Damn, I'd risked my life.... I delivered a top-secret plane to you Americans. Why this show? I'm already here.... Why this circus?"

It never occurred to the CIA employee that, coming from the land of perennial food shortages, seeing an American supermarket packed with goodies, Belenko would not trust his eyes. It never crossed the CIA man's mind that Belenko would think the supermarket was a "Potemkin village," hastily erected to seduce him with the Western way of life, that he wouldn't believe it was an ordinary American commercial establishment.

Many other realities of American life gave us, the newcomers, pause. Back in our home country, we only knew cash. Here, we could pay with a snippet of printed paper named a "check." You just signed it (no seal of any kind to confirm its validity?), and your bank would honor it, no questions asked?

I am not talking about such a bizarre thing as paying for your purchases with a piece of plastic. This is the height of gullibility. You are in the land of the naïve and dewy-eyed.

However, outside the material world as well, there was a reason to scratch the back of our heads. In the highly-controlled Soviet press, you had never found even a mention of school-age girls' pregnancies, as you could find in American papers. And mind-boggling were the publicized cases when some individuals corrected nature by subjecting themselves to a sex change operation. What, did they have too much free time on their hands?

For us, coming from a country with the unlimited power of those in whose hands it was for three generations, it was hard to get used to the fact that even the highest authorities in America could be subjected to the court of public opinion, at the very least. Thus, the American media reported that Thomas Bertram "Bert" Lance, Director of the Office of Management and Budget under President Jimmy Carter, resigned because of a scandal during his first year in office. Although he was later cleared of all charges, for six months, the press and Congress discussed his alleged mismanagement and corruption when Lance was chair of the board of some local bank. The man became a butt of jokes on the *Saturday Night Live* TV show, and a Washington-based journalist earned a Pulitzer Prize for covering the opprobrium.

In my story, I make use of second-hand knowledge as well. My American friends told me about another high-level government scandal, which took place a couple of years before I came to the country. In 1973, Vice President of the United States Spiro Agnew was investigated on suspicion of criminal conspiracy, bribery, extortion, and tax fraud. The man accepted kickbacks from contractors during his time as Baltimore county executive and governor of Maryland. I'm not even talking here about the overwhelming Richard Nixon Watergate scandal.

So, it's no wonder that, upon reading my story originally titled "Who is Who," Martin Tucker, editor-in-chief of *Confrontation* magazine, published it, noting in his introduction that the author's "journeys spring [...] from the politics of conformity," and the story's author's view "can be credited to his relative lack of American experience."[3]

Perhaps the best instance of that lack is that, in the story, I (the narrator) project all my (the newcomer's) insecurities and a sense of bewilderment about the American way of life onto an unlikely character—the supermarket manager. Here, another cultural misapprehension takes place. The fact is that, soon after I settled in America, I learned that only a small percentage of American writers made their living by ... writing. They have to support themselves by doing other things, like teaching or using whatever other skills they possess. At the time, it was a far cry from the notion of a writer in Russian culture. Traditionally, literature represented the nation's consciousness. Belonging to the small elite enclave of writers was equal to that of the high priesthood, full of reverence. Very few of us knew that, in Soviet times, a handful of writers made a good living and enjoyed such privileges as special resorts and accommodation for creative work. Not the readers' market, but the government decided how to compensate for a writer's labor. So, in my story, portraying an American who tried to become a writer and eventually settled for being a supermarket manager was an attempt at ridiculing things I had no first-hand knowledge about. No wonder the American editor changed my story title to a made-up one.

"Increditibility"

I ran into the supermarket to pick up a trifle and was soon at the checkout stand, offering my dollar bill to the checker. He stretched out his hand, took it, and said:

"Do you have an ID?"

"What for?" I asked, surprised.

"...And two credit cards," the checker added.

"What??"

I looked at him with sympathy: Poor guy! The day has just begun, and he's already worn out. What will he be doing later? He'll end up weighing the customers instead of the produce!

"I am paying cash," I said, pointing to my dollar in his hand.

"Sorry, sir, but it's store policy."

I looked around me, bent toward the checker, and asked out of curiosity:

"Have you been getting counterfeit money? Boy, the counterfeiters these days are scrapin' the bottom of the barrel. It's not as if they needed to print one-dollar bills! They are taking a big enough risk anyway—they might as well go for the hundred ones. Maybe that's clever. Who'd pay any attention to a dollar bill these days?"

"Naw," said the checker. "It's got nothing to do with counterfeiters. It's just the manager's new policy."

"Has he gone nuts? Whoever heard of verifying cash with ID and credit cards? Did he fall into some kind of marasmus in his old age?!"

The checker thought for a minute:

"Excuse me, he fell into what? How is it spelled? M-a-r-a-s-m-u-s? What's that, some kind of plastic? You'll have to excuse me, I quit school in the eighth grade ... and he's not that old, anyway."

"He's gotta be out of his mind! Didn't you learn how to spell this word in high school?" I fumed.

"Okay, okay," the checker said. "He's in his office, to the right, at the end of the corridor."

"Sir!" I began before I entered.

The manager, quite young-looking, jumped up from his desk and offered me a seat.

"I know what you want to say," he said. He did not show any signs of madness. He was an ordinary-looking bureaucrat with a steady voice and a smile on his face. "Just one dollar, and what a hassle. Well, sir, are you sure that your dollar is a real dollar?"

"What kind of joke is this!" I exclaimed. "I know, I know, inflation, higher prices, the price index.... I agree that a dollar is worth now, let's say, thirty cents."

"Twenty-seven," corrected the manager. "But that's not the point. Just look," he took my dollar, "everything seems in order. The seals, the signatures of the treasurer of the United States and the Secretary of the Treasury.... It's like they're trying to tell us, 'Trust us, people.' Tell me honestly, keeping in mind the events of the last decade, do you have any trust in these people?"

Running over in my mind the headlines of governmental scandals, I examined the signatures on the bill.

"Heck.... I can't even make out their names," I mumbled. "What difference does it make, anyway?"

"Where do you live?" the manager asked.

I was about to answer, but he went on:

"I'll tell you where—in a vacuum! Don't you realize that nowadays you can't believe in anyone or anything a hundred percent?"

He started pacing around his office.

"Just think of the events of the last decade. The Budget Director couldn't keep his hands out of somebody's pocket. The Vice President was on the take.... The President of the United States himself...."

"I don't get mixed up in politics," I hastened to say, trying to get a hold of my dollar that he was waving around.

"Okay," he said. "Let's leave politics alone. What do you think this is?" he said, flourishing a bright pink object like a magician.

"An apple," I stared at it.

"It only looks like one," he said. "It has neither smell nor taste. The apple has more wax than a candle. They want it to look better!" he said. "They want it to catch your eye! They don't want people to notice other apples that aren't so nice."

"I know, today's produce ... leaves a lot to be desired," I nodded in agreement.

"You think it's only the produce? What about people? Let's take you, for example."

"Why me?" I asked.

"As an illustration.... Let's take your whole family."

"Oh, no, no," I said. "You can have me if you wish so but leave my family out of it."

"Fine, you don't want your family, let's take mine."

"Okay," I agreed.

"My wife!" said the manager with pathos. "My children! Let's not worry about whether or not they're my kids. Let's just say that if they live with me—then they're mine. It'll be easier that way.... But are children really children nowadays? If thousands of kids in the country have babies? Just read the papers—how many high schoolers have already become parents and still don't know the subject of a sentence from a direct object? A pregnant teenager doesn't surprise anyone nowadays. You agree that kids somehow aren't kids anymore.... And your wife!"

"What about my wife?" I shrugged. "What's so mysterious about that?"

"Aha, and what mysteries! You just wait! These days you must peek over your shoulder first thing in the morning to make sure that she's still a female. Here, get a load of this." He pointed at the paper on his desk. "A marine sergeant, a real jock, a family man—a couple of operations— bang! He's a woman and transferring to the nursing staff. It's enough to drive you out of your mind! Not to mention women—with their natural curiosity and their newly developed taste for liberation! She goes on vacation and when she returns, she's a 'he'! And the mail carrier hurries to give you the good news—'You're invited to a gay convention.' For crying out loud! Before you know it, everything's all turned around. You've only begun to figure out what's going on when you catch yourself taking a little longer than usual in front of the mirror. *My God!* a crazy thought creeps into your head, *just think of it: a few strokes of the scalpel, and you don't feel the pressure anymore, the pressure to succeed as the head of the family.* It's a blessing that your wife soon got fed up with being a male and switched back again. A certain man, not stupid by any means, authored a book recently: *Future Shock.* What 'future' when we all have present shock? Well, anyway, tell me: you are you?"

"Well," I said, "who else?"

"Lucky guy." The manager's eyes showed real envy. "One in a million! I, for example, am not myself. I'm not what you take me for."

I looked around his office and didn't understand.

"No, no," he caught my eye. "Everything's okay here. I'm the manager here. An orange vest, like the road crew wears. The salary is nothing to sneeze at. A house ... but all the same, it's not me."

"And who is it?"

"I don't know.... Some stranger.... In my youth, I dreamed of being a writer. In the meantime, I earned a few bucks at the store bagging groceries. I didn't even notice how I got to be a manager. Well, what more can I say?" He waved his hand. "Give me your dollar."

He pressed the note on the table and wrote, "Accept for payment."

I left the store. I found my car. Or, to be more exact, a car of the same make and color. With my license plate.

I kicked the tire before I opened the door. My foot bounced back. The tire pressure was fine.

Or so it seemed....

5

Buying a Used Soul

Although on the surface of it, the following archeological finding, a piece I published in America, in both Russian and English, is also about white-collar crime, it mostly makes fun of another phenomenon of American life, totally new to the immigrant from the Soviet Union—the come-ons and other trade gimmicks widespread in America.

"Would You Buy a Used Soul from This Man?"

I was struggling through my income tax forms late one night when somebody knocked politely on the door. I looked through the peephole before opening the door. There stood a gentleman dressed like a door-to-door salesman—beige shoes, a three-piece suit, and an orange tie. He looked like a typical Southern Californian with a maybe a bit darker suntan.

"May I?" he asked pleasantly, offering me his business card. I read, "D.V. Lucifer, trade representative, Lucifer & Sons, Inc."

I smiled, "Did you come to buy my soul?"

"I can see right away that you're a recent immigrant," Lucifer grinned. "It's not so much your accent as your inability to understand our main economic principle. Remember. In this country, buying is no problem. The problem is selling."

"Do you sell people's souls, then?"

"Precisely. And we don't make a bad living at it, either."

"But, what the hell—oh pardon me!—What do I need somebody else's soul for? I don't know how to get rid of my own soul sometimes—that's how rotten I feel."

"Sorry, right now we're a little overstocked. The supply has been exceeding demand lately…. But please keep us in mind—the best prices in town. What do you need somebody's soul for? For the same reason we do—to sell it."

"Well, if things were hopeless, I'd probably sell my own."

"You're a pretty self-confident man," the visitor remarked softly.

"Do you think you'll feel hopeless only once in your life? And what will you sell the next time? And the third time.... No, believe me, it wouldn't hurt to have a spare soul for a rainy day."

"Hmm...." I cheered up. "It used to be that once you sold your soul to the devil, you'd solved your problems for good."

"That's right," Lucifer sighed. "But life was simpler then. Nowadays, you can't get along with just one soul. If you could, we'd have gone out of business long ago. But we're still around."

I thought it over for a while and agreed. Really, what guarantee do you have that you'll get that desperate only once?

"How much is a human soul worth these days?" I asked, out of curiosity.

"Oh, not at all expensive. Three thousand dollars."

"Quite a respectable sum," I said, not without pride for humanity. "At one time, thirty was a reasonable price."

"My dear sir!" Lucifer threw up his hands in despair. "Thirty in biblical times was the same as $3,000 now. You've forgotten about inflation."

He shook his finger at me jokingly.

"Three thousand is too much for me," I said.

"We give credit. Of course, only if someone takes responsibility for you: a bank, let's say."

"Are you kidding? Would a bank give a loan if they found out I was selling my soul to the devil?"

"You're not selling, you're buying," Lucifer reminded me. "But even if you're selling, they might not lend you the money at the usual interest. Offer them a higher rate and maybe they'll take the risk."

"Well," the conversation was becoming fun, "how much could I get for my soul later on if I had to sell it?"

"It depends on the goods," Lucifer said.

I opened up my soul to him.

"Well," said Lucifer after a few moments, "it's as good as any other. Enough sin, enough virtue. I can give you a rough estimate."

He told me the amount.

"That's all?" I was a little insulted. "But look how much you sell them for!"

"My dear man, what about our production costs? Remember, our company supplies souls of the best quality only. To clean up an average soul, we have to use a lot of high-quality, expensive bleach. Then there's packing, invoice typing.... All manual labor. Not to mention our advertising costs. Do you know how much those bastards on TV charge for a minute of prime time?"

"It doesn't matter. I can't afford $3,000," I said.

"Buy two, get one free. You'll save money that way. Incidentally, you can do some moonlighting on the side. Sell a couple to your friends. We pay a pretty good commission. And now it's the height of the season, they'll snap 'em up."

"The height of the season?" I was surprised. "Can souls be in or out of season?"

"You're talking like a foreigner again!" Mr. Lucifer laughed and patted me on the shoulder. "Half the country flirts with the devil around income-tax time. What am I saying—half the country? Almost everyone cheats on taxes. Maybe just a little, but they do cheat. Besides, your purchase is tax-deductible."

"You don't say!" I was shocked.

"You'd be surprised at what people deduct."

That did it! I bought a soul from him. A used one, of course, but giving the devil his due, it was in pretty good shape. Maybe it'll come in handy someday....[1]

Rereading the story now, many years later, I recall being irritated by the barrage of advertisements in America. The sheer novelty of the experience, its oddity, made me feel like mocking the popular sales tricks. Coming from a country of perennial shortages of the most essential goods, I was unaccustomed to being persuaded to buy anything. In my former homeland, you didn't purchase the desired product, in the direct meaning of the word; you "got it" (*dostat'*). That is, you got hold of it by any means possible, which involved, besides money, standing in long lines, or using whatever pull (called *blat*) you had at your disposal. The American elaborate and pervasive trade calls revived in my subconsciousness the Soviet newspapers' ever-present scorn of Western commercialism, of the "capitalist sharks" that pounce on you, trying to deceive, smelling their victims' blood.

In the ideological realm I grew up in, salesmanship of any kind was considered lacking in social prestige. I remember my old friend, scientist Alexander M., speaking with disdain about the occupation of his relative, whose job was to supervise a huge vegetable warehouse in Odessa. Alexander slighted him as if the man did not have his hands full, making sure tons of potatoes and cabbage under his charge did not rot before being transported to our hometown stores. In Alexander's eyes, the man was little better than a parasite.

The term for a tradesman in Russian (*torgovets*) produced a derogatory spinoff—*torgash*, a huckster. Of similar design was the pejorative word *kommersant* ("merchant"). When applied to the West, to America, the papers used the denigrating expression "wheeler-dealers" (*del'tsy*), as in the "Wall Street wheeler-dealers." The English word "deal" (*sdelka*), in Russian translation, meant not a business agreement, but a "shameless arrangement," as in "to make a deal [compromise] with one's conscience." Selling your soul to the devil, that is.

Another commerce-related epithet, "traveling salesman" (kommivoyazher), was especially poisonous. Used for satirical purposes in the press, it meant a "shady character," a "snake oil salesman," a "con artist." The bite of such a nickname came from both the in-your-face foreignness of the word to the Russian ear and its estrangement from Soviet reality: widespread shortages of goods made it superfluous for the salespeople to travel all over the vast country.

No less derogatory than the word *kommivoyazher* in the Russian language were the words *biznes* ("business") and *biznesmen* ("businessman"). Transliterated from English, they were stock pejoratives from the vocabulary of the state's anti-capitalist propaganda.

It also took me and other ex–Soviet newcomers a long time to get used to another feature of Western life—the concept of private property. Already on the way to America, in Vienna, over our first stop, we stared at the store signs carrying the names of their owners. Instead of generic Soviet signs like "Grocery" (*Produkty*) or "Fruits and Vegetables" (*Frukty i ovoshchi*) or "Haberdashery Store" (*Galantereia*), the shops in the Viennese malls carried the names of their owners or the designers of their wares—"*Swarovski*," "*Tiffany*," "*Viktor-Adler-Markt*," and others. The very sight of those signboards felt unusual, as if, trailblazers in the unknown world, we time-traveled backward, into the pre-revolutionary Russia of our school textbooks. Starting with our primers, those shopkeepers were invariably portrayed as bloodsuckers, thick-faced, their cheeks shining from fat. The very word "private owner," *chastnik*, was tinged with contempt.

From our Soviet history textbooks came another emotionally charged word—"a fist," *kulak*. It was terror inflicted on a child's imagination. The term applied to a person not only implied that he is stingy, keeping it tightly in his hands and unwilling to share any of it with anyone, but, if challenged, ready to hit you in the face. In Soviet propaganda, the word connoted a merciless user, exploiter, and bloodsucker.

Therefore, it is easy to guess where the outrage came from when, in our first year in the new land, settling in the Greater Los Angeles area, on a hot day, my wife and I arrived at the beach in Malibu where Hollywood stars' bungalows lined up along the coast. The Pacific Ocean's silver scales glittered in the sun. We spread our beach towels on the sand and unpacked our swimsuits, foretasting the pleasure of splashing in the ocean and sunbathing, as we spotted the "Private Beach" sign. We looked at each other in dismay. Wow, what rich bastards! They own this beach, ha!

This was not our first encounter with private ownership, however. In Vienna, we were taken from the airport to a small boarding house that agreed to shelter several dozen emigrants from the USSR while we waited for travel visas.

The boarding house was located in a narrow lane lined with cars. I, who never owned one, could only make a wry face in squeamish jealousy. I felt morally superior to those filthy rich. They were obsessed with their cars. They don't have a space to park them!

I'm not even talking about the owner of the boarding house bearing her name—"Bettina." Throughout our Soviet life, we were taught to hate shopkeepers, tavern owners, and owners of any property in general. And here—look at that, some kind of Bettina![2]

However, on her face, there was not a shadow of what was expected—hubris, haughtiness, all those attributes of private ownership, of possessiveness, which we were taught to hate from an early age. On the contrary, she had an almost ingratiating, confusing look. Only now I understand. Russian emigrants, often with small children, fell on her head (it seems she ran the place alone) like nuts from a tree after a strong gust of wind. How can you manage to feed them all in time and place them in your tiny boarding house?

Now, many years down the road, I understand how shortsighted it was to see *any* private enterprise as necessarily predatory, as a source of lucre filth, not of mere existence, as it is in many small companies in America, the so-called "mom and pop" stores.

When I recently shared my sad memory of staying in Bettina's boarding house with one of my fellow emigre acquaintances, his face darkened.

"Yes, all of us, ex–Soviets, were poisoned since our childhood," he said, shaking his head. "In our minds, incapable yet of processing information critically, Soviet school textbooks have successfully hammered in the idea of the justice of Lenin's slogan 'Rob the loot!' [*Grab' nagrablennoe!*]. In that very boarding house, which was run by a middle-aged woman, bewildered by the flow of Soviet emigrants, I stole several tubes of apple jam, which she served for breakfast. I was traveling with a child; my daughter was a three year old. I noticed where Bettina put away whatever was left after breakfast: onto a high shelf, covered with a dark green curtain. I picked a moment and climbed there. Now, whenever, with incredible shame, I recall my action of that time trying to remember why I went to such petty baseness, I conclude that then, still to the roots of my hair, a Soviet person, I considered myself entitled to do it. 'Rob the loot!'"

He shook his head again. "I wish it were only that!" he said with a bitter laugh. "On the eve of my first New Year in America, I shouted at a woman for the fact that the price for the Christmas tree she was selling was as much as twenty dollars, which then, I, the newcomer, couldn't afford.... Now I remember this episode with burning shame.... The woman was even confused.... As I later realized, she had nothing to do with the price setting. She was hired to stand outside of the shop, in the street, and help the prospective buyers choose a Christmas tree. But I, who came from a country in which everything belonged to the state, including the trees, thought she owned the shop; in reality, she was paid as a seasonal worker, most likely a minimum wage."

And he waved his hand in desperation. He couldn't go back in time and make amends to the woman.

Another aspect of our new life was a different, if not opposite, work ethic. Of course, back in our homeland, none of us ex–Soviets took to our hearts the ubiquitous Soviet slogan "Labor in the USSR is a Matter of Honor, a Matter of Valor and Heroism." Rather, a cynical underground joke was more to the point: "They pretend they pay us, and we pretend we work." At the first steps of our lives in the new land, we found that, for many Americans, like for us back in the Soviet Union, labor was hardly more than a matter of making a living. However, they didn't even feel like keeping appearances that it is anything more than that. That's why we were flabbergasted that a fast-food restaurant chain was called "TGI Friday," which stands for "Thank God/goodness it's Friday," that is, let's celebrate that the week of damn work is finally over.

By the same token, it's embarrassing to recall how, in response to my new American acquaintance's question about whether I liked my new job as a technical writer at Hughes Aircraft Corporation, I answered in the Soviet way. That is, I was glad that, in the interim period between big projects I had to handle, there was an opportunity to take a short nap right there, in my cubicle, guarded against my supervisors' eyes.

The American, who happened to be an owner of a small business, wasn't amused, however. In a disapproving tone, he commented that what I described was nothing to be proud of. Moreover, my napping during working hours was outright shameful, nothing but an act of stealing. I should have found some use of my free working time for the pleasure of my employer. After all, I received my salary for working, not for napping.[3]

The term "business" remained abstract for me for the first decade or so of my American life, until one day when I learned what it could mean in reality. It happened in the summer of 1991, fifteen years after my family and I arrived in the country.

Our émigré acquaintances, the Greenbergs, a couple whom we had known from the days of our stay on the outskirts of Rome waiting for our entry visas to America, suddenly became the owners of a business. Their distant American relative died, bequeathing them his small stationery store on West Pico Boulevard in West Los Angeles. Since neither the husband nor the wife had skills in high demand in America, such as that of an engineer or at least a technician (in their homeland, they were warehouse stock clerks), they seized on the sudden opportunity to make a decent living.

Over a year of their life as business owners passed, and, in the summer of 1990, one of the Greenbergs, the husband, called me and asked whether my son Max, who had just graduated from high school, could help them out. To find out what exactly he needed to assist them with, I dropped by the shop.

My visit produced a life-changing revelation. The discovery that beyond this imposing term—a "businessman"!—lies so much daily painstaking work stunned me. Myriads of tiny merchandise, which you couldn't easily tell apart. That alone, what does it take just to remember the countless names and shelf locations of all office supplies! Notebooks of all sizes and shapes, a multitude of ballpoint and fountain pens, a wide variety of calculators, rulers, paperclips, and other clerical sundries! It turned out that, for the newly minted business owners to make even a modest living, was hardly a piece of cake at all. The Greenbergs' anxious and stressed facial expressions signaled that their life was a daily struggle, and they still tried to comprehend their situation. How the hell did it happen that, in the country of the free, they found themselves chained, like slaves in the galleys, to the counter of their stationery store? Fearing that, if they close their shop for a week, they could lose their customers, they asked me to let my son, together with their teenager, replace them, so that they could finally, after a year of work, have a breather. To go on a short vacation, at least to Palm Springs, a hundred miles away. They could be on hand on the off-chance the teenagers could not handle some emergency.

That visit once and for all dispelled the notion etched in my brain over my Soviet school years that any business is a genetically vile occupation, and that all "*biznesmeny*" were unscrupulous human beings.

Come to think of it, it was even more astonishing that I never questioned that notion, even though, back then, in my raw youth, I saw with my own eyes what was involved in running a private business. As I described it in my memoir, *Shush! Growing Up Jewish Under Stalin*, my father ran a small, private (unlawful in the USSR) house-painting business in my hometown Odessa, Ukraine. I saw how hard he worked. In the summers, the time when his services were in the highest demand, he even skipped resting on the weekends. After long hours of work, he would come home at dinnertime, sometimes even later, exhausted and sweaty. He worked hard, yet he was conscientious when it came to charging for his services. When some poorly paid school teacher came to him asking for his services, he would say: "Okay, lady, I know how miserly they pay you for your hard work. I wouldn't want your job for any money, anyway. Children…. They are handfuls, even just two of them," he said, smiling shyly and looking at me and my brother, a teenager. "Let's do it this way: I'll freshen up your apartment, and you pay me as much as you can afford."

Now, I am scratching the back of my head in astonishment: how could I forget it when I wrote the following piece many years later in America? While there was no shortage of white-collar crime in America, how could I portray any business as an inherently dishonest occupation?

I also ponder why the publisher of the New York–based *The New Russian Word* printed the story on his paper's pages. After all, he ran a small business and knew firsthand what was what. Or did he think most of the paper's subscribers, being fresh-off-"the-Soviet"-boat immigrants, would appreciate the story because their brains were conditioned along the same lines as the story's author?

"A Difficult Case"[4]

As I stepped into the examination room, the new patient, a middle-aged man in a dark-blue business suit, sat there looking very pale. His eyes wandered vacantly. He seemed distracted and in pain. I introduced myself, washed my hands, and asked him to take off his shirt.

He thought a moment and did as told but paused another moment to look at his reflection in the mirror.

"What seems to be the problem?" I asked, taking the stethoscope in my hand.

"Save me, Doctor!" he said with a heavy accent.

"Save you?" I repeated, listening to his heart. The beat was fast but steady. I shined a light in his eyes and turned up his eyelids. "What do you mean, save you?"

The reflex was good; there was no inflammation.

"For years, she drives me crazy. Already she ruined my career!" he said. "Like cruel fate, she opposes my every step. I hate her!"

"Why don't you divorce her?" I asked, checking his chest and arms. He had a moderate layer of fat, but no lumps.

He burst out laughing:

"Oh man! ... If only I could divorce her! I would give anything to do it!"

"Well, if that's how you feel," I said, pressing his elbow and joints. "Get a good lawyer—you can do it. If you go on like this, you'll drive yourself into the grave!"

"Don't talk to me about lawyers!" The patient dismissed my suggestion with a wave of his hand. "No lawyer can touch her. I consult with everybody.... Disgrace, shame. Because of her, I become the laughingstock of the entire town."

"Yes, it's hard to live in a small town," I said. "People start talking, and you can't run away...."

"No, that's not it!" he said. "It's all the same to me what people are saying."

I didn't see anything physically wrong with him and stepped back. He glanced at the chair behind him and sat down as if he were doomed. "If only I could get control of her," he said, "then there would be no more problem."

"How long have you had this problem?"

"As long as I can remember."

"I understand," I said. "It must seem like a very long time. It's like a job you can't quit. Was it an early marriage? Are you fed up now, after so many years?"

"*Fed up*—that's a good expression, but it hardly describes how I feel!"

I noticed that his Adam's apple was slightly enlarged, but not overly much. He was in fairly good physical shape. There wasn't much I could do but continue to talk about his emotional problem:

"Are you still in the same house? Have you considered moving out? Can you afford it?"

"What good would it do?" he said in desperation. "You don't know her. You can't hide from her. She'll find you no matter where you go. I even tried to change my appearance. To pretend that I was not myself, and she was not mine. No, Doctor, here decisive measures are needed. Your scalpel, that's my only hope!"

"What, are you serious?" I asked, peering again into his eyes, which had rolled up and become half-crazed. "I'm a doctor, not a hitman!"

"Right, you're a doctor. You know how to do it. If I could murder her, I would have done it long ago. I tried everything—but nothing works. Please!" he said, seizing my hands. "Take any amount of money—and finish her off once and for all."

I understood—he'd gone crazy. I had to humor him.

"You know I can't do that," I said in a soothing tone. "Man to man, I sympathize with you. Sometimes my wife complains a lot. For example, about being squeezed for money. Can you believe it? Her husband is a doctor, a specialist with a private practice, and yet she complains! So we all have to put up with such things. But I would never ask you to murder my wife," I said in a humorous tone, trying to turn the whole thing into a joke.

He sat there immersed in his suffering, then suddenly picked up on my last remark.

"Why not?" he said. "Why not ask me? You save me from my problem, I save you from yours. Believe me, I have nothing to lose. I'm at the end of my rope."

I couldn't believe my ears. Were we talking about the same thing? I needed to spell it out. This visit was getting far too serious.

"You mean," I began, "you will kill my wife, and I will kill yours? Do you realize you're talking about homicide, and that means going to prison? You might have extenuating circumstances, but still, it's premeditated murder. They'll put you away for a long time. And what will you achieve? After you serve your term, you might get married again, and then your second wife might become like your first, and you'll start all over again...."

As I was taking this line, I began to notice that my patient was looking at me quizzically. He interrupted me.

"Wife?" he said. "What does my wife have to do with it? It was she who thought I should come to see you. She says you're a luminary of neurosurgery. She said you could help."

He stood up with an air of disappointment and started to put on his shirt. Now I was confused.

"So, who was it you wanted me to murder?" I said. "Were you talking about your mistress?"

He stopped at the door, still buttoning himself up.

"I've been trying to tell you for a long time already. I'm a businessman for many years. My friends and I run businesses of similar kinds. They get rich, I stay poor. They laugh at me. I do business as well as they do. But there's one problem—my conscience. I can't cheat. She won't let me."

"She?" I asked.

"She is my conscience. She talks to me. I tell her: to make money you have to cook the books, squeeze your employees, bribe your suppliers, write everything off on your income tax, including gifts for your wife, and describe them as promotions for the firm. They can do it, but I can't. When I was a schoolboy, my face would turn red, but now.... I saw five doctors before you. They all make the same diagnosis—a congenital defect! But modern medicine can cut out congenital defects, can't it?"

"Why do you call your conscience 'she' and refer to it as 'her'?"

"I think about things close to my heart in Russian. My parents brought me to this country as a youngster, but I retained the language.... Conscience is *sovest'* in Russian. A feminine noun. She speaks to me."

"You want me to cut out your conscience?"

"Yes, Doctor, can you be the one to do it?"

"All right," I said, happy that murder was off the table. "Well, as I understand it, you have nothing to lose. Perhaps we can try something.... You'll have to sign a consent form, and we could do it later this week."

The patient was delighted. We drilled into his skull with a special machine in the office and relieved a bit of pressure.

He recovered soon, but I never heard from him again.... To be honest, for the first time in my life, I was happy that my bill remained unpaid. After all, a professional triumph is worth any money.

6

"He Won't Make It"

One day, a few years after arriving in America, passing by a big dumpster near my home in Santa Monica, California, I spotted a few ditched copies of a book, its covers torn. The very sight of a book in a dumpster stopped me in my tracks. I picked up a copy and could not believe my eyes. It was not some cheap paperback for "beach reading." This American term sounded bizarre to my ear, as did another one related to it—"summer reading." Are there books designated as "winter reading" as well? Back in my old Soviet life, reading wasn't conditioned by the degree to which Earth was tilted on its axis. Another term nonexistent in my past life was "pulp fiction."

The book I picked up was a short story collection by Isaac Bashevis Singer. The pages were smeared with red dye, but most of the book was still readable. What the hell? Bashevis Singer! I first discovered this writer in America and admired his work. I could not comprehend why copies of his book had wound up in the trash. He wasn't some dime-a-dozen scribbler. I read his stories in *The New Yorker.* Last month, they interviewed him on Channel 13, the PBS station in L.A.

I shared my bewilderment with one of my UCLA grad school classmates. A tall, lean, youthful man, he heard me out, gave it a thought, and, pinching his short blond beard, replied: "Well, Emil, welcome to capitalism, my friend."

After a pause, he continued with a note of guilt in his voice: "For you, a book is an almost sacred object, but for the bookseller, it's just merchandise. It may well be they needed more shelf space for a new blockbuster in that bookstore, and this Singer title didn't move fast enough. After an agreed time, the publisher accepts the returns of the unsold copies."

"Okay, I understand that," I said. Having lived in America for a few years, I was already familiar with the profit principle. "But why disfigure the book? Why tear off the cover?"

"Well, to cut down on the postage cost." My classmate produced an orange-wedge smile. "If the publishers feel a particular title won't sell quickly enough, they might suggest that instead of sending back the unsold copies to get the refund, the bookstore just sends proof of these copies being destroyed—their torn covers."

At the first stage of their life in an unknown land, after they have found a job or other source of livelihood, immigrants experience acute spiritual hunger. "There isn't much of culture over here," my compatriot friend, an educated man, said with a grin, producing a nostalgic sigh. By the will of fate, he's found himself in a vacuum. Having left Russia, he broke away from its culture at the level at which he could consume it, whether it was books, movies, or theater. And now he can't partake in the host country's culture because of the language barrier. But not only because of it. American culture, in its consumer-friendly form, bewilders an immigrant from the Soviet Union. The abundance of popular literature, including detective yarns and romance novels, is difficult for him to accept. I'm not even talking about books dealing with same-sex love, which, in the Soviet Union of the time, was punishable by law.

The cultural vacuum takes place because, conditioned by their past, Soviet immigrants consider all printed matter in America to be official. For them, this means that it is approved and encouraged at the state level, i.e., almost mandatory, for the public to consume. The very idea of choice is alien to them. No amount of reasonable advice—"If you don't like this book or movie, don't read it or watch it"—will help. The reflexes instilled over many years of Soviet training, especially concerning literature, are not easily shed. After all, these immigrants come from a country in which literature occupied a special place in the firmament of culture.

Though back in my Soviet writing career, I always had to be sure not to overstep ideological moats, I was conditioned to regard literature with the highest respect.

Traditionally, a writer had a special place in Russian society. A person of letters was perceived as belonging to the world of the celestials. In America, the terms "writer" and "author" are used almost interchangeably. Even experienced writers and published authors may not know the difference between the two. In Russia, the word "writer" was never used lightly, and it didn't apply to anyone who writes. Though over my ten-year career in the Soviet Union I published more than a hundred satirical pieces, feuilletons, and short stories, I never dared to call myself a "writer." At best, I could be considered a "litterateur"—that is, someone who has something to do with literature. In America, even a newsletter scribbler is called a "writer."

In the Gorbachev era, a delegation of Soviet writers arrived at my college. Having learned that our English department had a creative writing section, the head of the delegation asked how fierce the competition was, that semester, for each opening in the class. When they told him that there was no competition, he looked up in surprise.

"Not at all? Ahem ... and who told those who signed up that they have any talent?"

"No one," the professor replied with a shrug. "You know, we don't have any problems with that. After the first semester, people drop out on their own. They try their hand and decide for themselves whether it's worth going on."

The Soviet writer just shook his head. Americans ... you sure are something....

In its glorious past, in the nineteenth century, with the absence of free speech, Russian literature addressed the deepest of social problems in belletristic form. The very sense of what the Russian nation was all about, its national self-consciousness, was expressed by its greatest poets and prose writers.

Soviet authorities succeeded in the cultural appropriation of classical Russian literature, making it seem a natural part of the new regime's heritage. They republished the works of the Russian greats many times over. They wanted readers to feel that these giants had waited for the October Revolution with bated breath. It was as if Pushkin, Gogol, Turgenev, Dostoevsky, Tolstoy, and Chekhov had approved of the Bolsheviks beforehand, and had expected that, one day, Russia would turn things upside down and become paradise on earth.

For one to sense how the Bolsheviks had achieved such a sleight of hand, it is enough to cite the title of one of Lenin's works: "Leo Tolstoy as a Mirror of the Russian Revolution."

If one or another work by a classic Russian author was deemed inappropriate from an ideological point of view, it was suppressed for a long time. Throughout Soviet history, while Dostoyevsky's *Poor Folk*, *The Insulted and the Injured*, *Crime and Punishment*, *Brothers Karamazov*, and other works were frequently reprinted, his novel *The Possessed* was only sporadically included in academic editions of his works. It was available to a small circle of academicians. As a standalone edition, it appeared only with the advance of Gorbachev's *glasnost*. Thus, the underground Soviet joke from the 1920s regarding Dostoyevsky's *The Possessed* was revived in the 1970s. In this novel, which was first published in 1871–72, Dostoyevsky forewarned Russian society about the disasters that would unfold if the radicals of his time gained the upper hand. In the post–WWII time, the following underground joke circulated in the country:

The Bolsheviks erected a monument to Dostoevsky in the center of Moscow. The pedestal bore the inscription: *To Fyodor Dostoyevsky, from the grateful possessed.*

By the same token, Soviet literary publications were never meant to serve as entertainment. Stalin considered writers to be the "engineers of the human soul." Under his watch, many were not so much "engineers" as "supervisors" of the souls. If any literary work were to be deemed dangerous to the regime, it would be arrested together with its author, who, without much ado, would be sent to a labor camp. That was the fate of one of the greatest Russian poets of the twentieth century, Osip Mandelstam. His fate serves as proof of his appraisal of the value placed on literature in the USSR: "Only in our country is poetry treated with respect. They murder you for creating it."

In the post–Stalin era, during the years of Khrushchev's and Brezhnev's rule, contemporary literature was still the source from which members of the Russian intelligentsia sought to draw droplets of hope. Thus, after walking through the desert for days, dehydrated, these lonely travelers sucked on little twigs moist with morning dew. Yes, there were plenty of novels about the struggle of milkmaids to produce high yields on collective farms. No one read them, but the state publisher ticked them off the list of requisite propaganda activities. Yet now and then, highly regarded "thick" journals—*The New World* (*Novyj mir*), *The Friendship of Peoples* (*Druzhba narodov*), and *Youth* (*Yunost'*)— published bold (considering the fierce censorship) works. We pored over these works, hunting between the lines for any minor truthful reflection of our lives. Because not everyone could afford a subscription to these journals, we borrowed them from each other to read overnight.

There was also *samizdat*, retyped copies of literary works prohibited from being published in the USSR. When I mentioned the word *samizdat* to my American classmates who knew Russian, they shrugged. The word meant self-publication. What's the big deal? Take whatever you wrote to the print shop on your block, make them print it, and do with it whatever you feel like doing.

When I came to America, I knew the country was not devoid of serious literature. It was enough to recall the names of Edgar Allan Poe, Walt Whitman, Jack London, Mark Twain, and William Faulkner, to name a few. Soviet authorities made sure we read Theodore Dreiser's *An American Tragedy*, which dramatized the human cost of advancing in a capitalist society, and Upton Sinclair's *The Jungle*, which depicted the harsh conditions in which immigrants were forced to work in the United States.

When, in 1955, after Stalin's death, the journal *Foreign Literature*

(*Inostrannaia literatura*) appeared in the Soviet Union, all the country's intellectuals became engrossed in new American writing. We would get Ernest Hemingway's *The Old Man and the Sea,* John Steinbeck's *Travels with Charlie,* F. Scott Fitzgerald's *Tender Is the Night,* J.D. Salinger's *The Catcher in the Rye,* John Updike's *The Centaur,* and Kurt Vonnegut's *Slaughterhouse-Five.*

However, the very fact of literature's availability in America—its democratic nature, its attempt to cater to all human interests—was hard to swallow for us immigrants. It seemed superfluous and inappropriate. I still remember feeling quite confused in the early years of my American life. Although new works by John Updike, Philip Roth, and other highly regarded contemporary American writers were published, bookstore windows were filled with volumes featuring scantily dressed beauties and square-chinned gentlemen with languid smiles. How come? Literature as pure commerce?

To my surprise, my unpleasant discovery found a sympathetic ear in an American editor. A skit of mine was accepted by *Studies in Contemporary Satire,* a scholarly journal that also published original works.

"He Won't Make It"

Doubledom Publishing House.

SECRETARY (*entering the Editor-in-Chief's, Bob Plainchild's, office*): There's a man at my desk who wants to see you, Bob. Says he's a writer.

PLAINCHILD: Oh no! I've had enough of their tribe this week! Jeez, don't they know by now we don't talk to writers directly? If he's good, an established agent will represent him. If he's bad, well, we don't have time for graphomaniacs. As if we have nothing better to do than to just sit and chat with them! That guy at your desk suffers from delusions of grandeur. Thinks he's Stephen King!

SECRETARY: Says he's Russian. That might explain it.

PLAINCHILD: A Russian? Unless he's Solzhenitsyn, tell him to hit the road. That's just what we need right now—an obscure Russian writer! What does he look like?

SECRETARY: Kind of middle-aged.... With a big beard.

PLAINCHILD: Then it must be Solzhenitsyn. (Tightens his tie.) Let 'im come in. How do you do, Mr. Solzhenitsyn! We haven't heard from you in quite a while....

VISITOR: I'm not Solzhenitsyn.

PLAINCHILD: Who are you then? I must admit, to my American eye, it's hard to tell Russians apart. Easier than Chinese, but still hard.

Visitor: Count Leo Tolstoy.

Plainchild: Tol-stoy.... Mary, do we have an account under this name?

Tolstoy: I'm a Count! Not an account....

Plainchild: Pity.... Well, don't tell me, count, what you're holding under your arm's a pile of short pieces. You can't make it with shorts nowadays. Unless you're Andy Rooney or Fruit of the Loom, ha-ha!

Tolstoy: It's a novel. I named it *War and Peace*.

Plainchild: A novel is better. Not as good as a memoir, though, but you have a chance here. Have you published any novels before?

Tolstoy: No, this is my first one.

Plainchild: The first novel by a nonentity.... It won't sell.

Tolstoy: You mean you won't even read it?

Plainchild: You must be kidding. Look how thick it is! We're in business, sir. We don't have your long Russian winter nights with nothing to do but drink vodka from a samovar, dance squatting, and sing lingering Gypsy songs. You should send me an outline first. A synopsis of four ... maximum five pages.... Well, since you're here already, I'll give you two minutes to give me your elevator pitch. What's your novel all about?

Tolstoy: Well.... It's rather difficult to summarize the entire novel in just a few phrases....

Plainchild: That's it! I'm convinced—if you can't sum up your novel in two sentences, the public won't understand it. It means you don't understand what you've written either....

Tolstoy: Well, sir....

Plainchild: Never mind. I don't have time for arguments. I'll give you a second chance, however. Imagine your novel's been sold to television—you never know, anything might happen! You're asked to summarize the plot for the *TV Guide*. How would it sound?

Tolstoy: Well.... This is a story about ... two friends.... Both are in love with the same girl.... Mmm.... She's about to marry one of them.... But, when he dies from battle wounds, she marries the other....

Plainchild: Not too bad. Might do for a daytime soap.... I have a couple of questions. These two friends of yours, is anything going on between them?

Tolstoy: What do you mean? They're close friends....

Plainchild: How close are they?

Tolstoy: In what sense?

Plainchild: C'mon, Leo. Don't be so old-fashioned. If you want your book to succeed, you'd better get your two friends involved as well.

TOLSTOY: Involved in what?

PLAINCHILD: Involved with each other. It would add tension to your—admit it—traditional triangle.

TOLSTOY: But excuse me, sir....

PLAINCHILD: Listen, Leo, get it straight from the horse's mouth— there are only three salable topics. Health, wealth, and sex—not necessarily in that order. The formula is simpler. You can hardly have sex without health. And without wealth, sex isn't worth writing about. So, it's sex, sex, and sex. Triple sex, for short.... Here's an example from our front-list titles. Please note, that it's in its eighteenth printing.... Whenever the male protagonist feels like making love, he takes his girlfriend, a world champion in acrobatics, aboard his private jet. When the lovers' imaginations run dry, they ask the pilot to jazz up their sexual routine. A dive here and there, a sharp climb, you know, depending on who's in the mood for what at the moment. Terrific yarn, I tell you. They grab it like ice cream on a sultry day.... Where were we? Oh yes, your novel.... What did you say the title was?

TOLSTOY: *War and Peace.*

PLAINCHILD: No good. Keep the "War"; scrap the "Peace."

TOLSTOY: Scrap the "Peace"?!

PLAINCHILD: Don't even hesitate for a moment! A title must disturb or at least intrigue. Remember—disaster sells, tranquility doesn't. Call it *The War.* Which war did you write about?

TOLSTOY: It's a nineteenth-century war.

PLAINCHILD: Oh, it's a historical novel. Why didn't you tell me in the first place? That's not bad either. High-society intrigues, romances.... Am I correct?

TOLSTOY: To some extent....

PLAINCHILD: Then the title isn't good. Change it to *From Russia with Love.* I know, it's already been used once, but if a title suits your needs, it's okay to recycle it. Thank God there's no copyright for titles. Go ahead, change it. You have my blessing. Besides, the housewife will love it.

TOLSTOY: What housewife?

PLAINCHILD: Don't you know? You Russians are living on the moon. We exist thanks to our huge female audience. Statistics don't lie, Leo. Our average reader is a bored housewife. She dictates everything, including the size of the book.... How long's your manuscript?

TOLSTOY: Around a thousand pages.

PLAINCHILD: You must be crazy! You've got to cut it at least in half. Otherwise, nobody here will touch it with a ten-foot pole.

TOLSTOY: Cut? Did you say "cut"?

PLAINCHILD: With an iron hand, Leo. The housewife is a weak creature, my dear man. She isn't Arnold Schwarzenegger. She can't hold all your thousand pages in one hand and stir her garden vegetable soup with another....

TOLSTOY: Can't she put the book aside and stir her soup?

PLAINCHILD: Not on your life! If she can, then we're in trouble. That means the book's no good. Not involving enough.... Is there any movie potential in your novel?

TOLSTOY: Well, there are some philosophical ideas in it. I don't see how they could be adapted to the screen.

PLAINCHILD: What? Philosophy? That better be a joke. We'll both laugh and forget about it right away. The housewife doesn't care about philosophy. Neither about your philosophy nor about anybody else's. Since you must cut it anyway, philosophy's an excellent place to start.

TOLSTOY: I won't cut it.

PLAINCHILD (looking at his watch): Oops, time's up. Listen, Leo, I understand perfectly well. I know how hard it is to cut your novel. It's like cutting your own throat. But hey, you're in a free country! Thank God America isn't Russia. Nobody will punish you for self-publishing. People have been doing it for ages. Take Moses, for example. He had a title on the rather thinnish side called *The Ten Commandments*. I believe it's some inspirational stuff. I know what did it. He cut his production expenses. Produced a camera-ready copy in stone and dragged it to a publishing house. But it was worth doing. Now it's a super-bestseller! People say he had a ghostwriter. But you know how that is—everyone envies success.... I could recommend some shops to you. They'll print your novel.

TOLSTOY (leaves in dismay mumbling on the way out): Two men ... involved with each other ... stir their garden vegetable soup ... with a ten-foot pole.... Cut! Cut!

SECRETARY (enters the office): Bob, I'm curious.... How did it go with the Russian?

PLAINCHILD: To tell you the truth, Mary, I knew his book wouldn't make it from the moment he walked in. The fact is he won't do well on talk shows. Too overweight, and the public won't like him. Unless he cuts his beard and starts doing aerobics, he won't make it in the American market. He might have a lot to say, but it's a weird world out there, Mary. If a writer doesn't make Oprah, he's zero, nil. Nobody will ever know his book even exists. Except for perhaps two dozen skinny New York intellectuals who take pride in being unemployed. And I'm sure no writer in his right mind wants that.[1]

As my Americanization progressed, some twenty years down the road, my attitude toward democratic literature soften up, which a lighter tone of the following piece signals.

"Gone into Literature"

"Give me back my husband!"

With these words, a tall, strong-boned, middle-aged woman entered my office one rainy morning and hit my desk with her umbrella.

"Excuse me, who are you?" I said. "And what would I need your husband for?"

"It doesn't matter who I am. As for my husband…. What you need him for is no mystery to me. It's for your vocation."

"What are you talking about?"

"Isn't that obvious? You're a writer. You need characters."

"So, what has this to do with your husband?"

"Every-thing!" the woman said and dropped an opened envelope on my desk, out of which fell a piece of paper; the following note was written on it with a felt-tip pen:

Irina, sorry, but I can't go on like this anymore. Don't judge me too harshly. And don't look for me. I'm gone into literature.

"Well, why me?" I said. "Why do you think I have anything to do with this?"

"It wasn't easy," my visitor sighed. "It took some effort, but I figured you out…. Do you recall the artist's retreat at Banff? That's right, the one in Canada, in Alberta province. At the foot of the Rocky Mountains…. Yes, Banff…. With two 'f's…. August 1999?"

"Well, yes, I do recall that. I was there."

"I bet you were. My husband and I lived nearby then. He's always been obsessed with literature, maniacally in love with it, and he's never missed a public reading in Banff. For some time now—why, it'll soon become clear to you—I never let him go to those readings alone. I always went along. That evening, you read some of your stuff there, at Banff. As soon as the reading was over, he rushed up to you. Devil only knows how I got distracted for a sec. I waved to my girlfriend whom I had spotted in the crowd, and he seized the moment. 'May I ask you for a favor,' he whispered so that no one would hear, 'please don't make me a character in any of your stories.'"

I recalled something....

"Well," I said, "how do you know what he whispered to me? You've said that he whispered. So how could you hear him?"

"I didn't need to hear it. I know that from experience. Over the years of our marriage, quite stormy, I know my scoundrel in and out. Know all his moves. Even to the point of the tone that he invoked when talking to you. He said it ingratiatingly, but without much hope. As if it was his destiny.... As if he's been doomed.... He's quite thorough when it comes to details."

I shrugged.

"Well, most likely you were surprised to hear such a strange request," the woman continued, paying no attention to my reaction. "But he knows how to press his point. I bet he said something like 'I know, I know, it's not a conscious process. You'll put me in one of your tales, not right away, but after a while. After I get nestled into your subconscious.' What can I say? He's good at drawing a writer's attention," the woman sighed. "Yes, yes, don't think you were his first. In the same year, also in Banff, there was a writer's workshop for beginners. They gave them an exercise: choose someone they encounter in the nearby village and write a short piece about him or her. And what do you think? Seven thousand people lived there, but, out of a dozen of new writers, three of them picked him. Well, of course! His nose is bluish. Means he drinks.... Half-bald.... Half gray-haired.... Has a Canadian accent. Plenty of room for imagination. Those beginners were from the U.S. and the UK. It's a known fact: the farther you are from your native land, the more your imagination grows."

"Even so, how do you know that he's run off into some book...." I said.

"Oh, stop it, please. As if that trick is new to him! I've seen him do it more than once. Once he even left the same note," the visitor pointed her umbrella at the envelope on my desk, "and he sneaked into some beach novel. You know, the light read people take along when heading for a summer vacation. And what else would you expect? He got involved with some bleached blonde there. You know yourself the kind of goods one gets mixed up with. I barely pulled him out of there.... Then he got into some thriller and came back missing two front teeth, his rib broken. Can imagine the medical bills I got stuck with!"

I rushed to my old manuscripts and began flipping through everything I had written from the time spent in Banff.

Soon, I came across a character that was reminiscent of the man who, back in my Banff days, had approached me with a strange request. He stuck in my memory, and, a few years later, he wound up in my novel. I thought about him when I needed a prototype of one of the minor characters in my novel. Then he grew into an almost major protagonist.

It's true that literary characters often go rogue and begin carrying on as they please. Sometimes, they are capable of such pranks that the author can only scratch his head in bewilderment. However, with great difficulty, I persuaded the man with the bluish nose to return to his wife.

At first, he resisted rather rudely.

"Get lost," he said. "You want me to do it, but you don't know my wife. If you knew her, you would not be pushing me. If not out of male solidarity, at least, out of sheer charity.... If you think she's so sweet, *you* marry her."

In the end, I prevailed and sighed in relief.

A few days later, I got a phone call from the man's wife. She thanked me for the favor and said that her newly restored husband was taking her to Maui in the Hawaiian Islands. "He says it'll be like a second honeymoon."

I congratulated her on the fortunate turn of events and was about to hang up when she said:

"By the way, do you happen to know? I checked it out on the net, but sometimes they organize these things at the last minute.... One can't be too careful.... Do you happen to know, if, in the next few weeks, there, on Maui, there's going to be any writers' conference?"[2]

7

Forbidden Laughter

October 26, 1978. A phone call comes to my home.

"Is this Emil?"

"Yeah...." I say guardedly.

It has been just three years and ten months since, as a Soviet immigrant, I arrived in America. In the old country, the only call from a stranger you could have received on your home phone (if you were lucky enough to have one, that is) was from some KGB officer inviting you to a "friendly chat" in his office. Here, in the States, I have already gotten used to receiving all kinds of over-the-phone solicitations: car insurance, sales discount offers, bank credit promises, you name it. My newly gained American friends advised me not to engage in conversations with strangers and not to accept any proposals, no matter how tempting they may seem.

"Emil ... Draitser?"

"Yes...."

"Hi there, Mr. Draitser. How are you today?"

I know by now that this question is merely a salutation in America, that the caller doesn't expect me to give him a detailed report on my well-being.

"Fine," I say, thinking of an excuse to hang up.

"We'd like to invite you to take part in our show. I mean, *The Merv Griffin Show.*"

The man pauses, letting the information sink in, then continues cheerfully: "Merv likes your book.... You know, the one you put together. *Forbidden Laughter: Soviet Underground Jokes.* He wants you to come over and talk about it a bit."

I mumble something to the effect that I am honored. The caller asks me a few more questions, as I realized later, to test out whether my English is good enough, and not too thickly accented.

It so happened that, as soon as we, a group of Soviet immigrants who settled in Los Angeles in the mid–1970s, regained our footing in the unknown land, we decided we should—no, we must!—show our gratitude to the hospitable Americans by sharing with them the greatest cultural treasure that supported our spirit through many years of our former life. These were the only valuables we could export, ones that could survive the body search at customs. We sneaked those underground jokes out of the country in our double-bottom boxes (called "skulls"). No KGB officers could seize them as they did dissident literature committed to paper (*samizdat*) and accuse us of "attempting to defame the honor and dignity of the USSR."

Before long, in the small immigrant publishing house called Almanac-Panorama in Los Angeles, which produced a newspaper supported by doctors, dentists, and lawyers whose services catered to the local Russian-speaking community, an idea arose to compile a sampling of the best underground jokes—about Stalin, Khrushchev, and Brezhnev, about the Communist Party and the KGB....

We created *Forbidden Laughter* as not a Cold War, anti–Soviet enterprise. We included jests about everyday life—marriage troubles, unhappy love, intrusive mothers-in-law, and other private calamities. The publisher entrusted me, a former servant of the Soviet satirical muse, to compile the gems. I asked my American classmate, Jon Pariser, a grad student at the Department of Slavic Literatures at UCLA, to translate the entries.

The day after my conversation with the TV producer, during a break between lectures, I tell my classmates Deb McLean, a vivacious brunette with a charming smile and terrific sense of humor, and Selim Karady, an Iraqi refugee with soft manners, about the strange phone call. I am still trying to figure out what happened.

"Do I hear you right?" Debbie says, looking at me with a dose of polite mistrust. Being fresh-off-the-boat, and from a far-away enigmatic place to boot, I could have mixed things up. "*The Merv ... Griffin ... Show*? ... Are you certain? Do you watch it? ... It's the most popular talk show after Johnny Carson! Merv Griffin, ha! ... Did you know that he also created *Jeopardy*? And *Wheel of Fortune*? Merv Griffin.... Are you sure?"

"Yeah," I reply, now doubting my memory. "I think so.... That's what the man said."

"Well, well, Emil," she is still not convinced, "who else will be there? ... You won't be there alone, just you and Merv, right?"

The caller had told me the names of other people who would appear on the show. I had only half-listened. None of them rang any bell in my immigrant's ear.

"Mike Connors, I think.... Dody Goodman.... Bob McGilpin...."

After each name, Debbie produces that characteristically American exclamation—"Wow!"

Only later am I to learn the reason for my classmate's excitement. I, an outlander, would be in the company of American celebrities. For almost a decade, actor Mike Connors has been playing private detective Joe Mannix in the eponymous TV series, for which he got a Golden Globe Award. Comedian Dody Goodman played the mother of the title character in the series *Mary Hartman, Mary Hartman*. Widely popular. Bob McGilpin was a disco artist best known for his recent hit, "Superstar."

Upon hearing the name of yet another of Merv's guests, instead of uttering "Wow!" Debbie paused, then asked: "Ralph ... Nader?! Are you sure?"

Though today some may remember him as a man who ran for the presidency, back in 1978, Ralph Nader was a vocal consumer advocate and the author of a bestselling book about car safety, *Unsafe at Any Speed*.

The phone call inviting me to appear on one of the most-watched American TV shows at the time is a total surprise. Being ex–Soviets, neither the publisher, Alexander Polovets, nor I knew how to advertise and distribute books in Western society. In the USSR, the state took that headache upon itself, deciding how many copies to print and how to get them into stores and libraries. We didn't know what a "press release" was, or that, in writing it, you should somehow tie the content of the publication to current events, or that we should contact the editorial offices of newspapers and magazines, radio and television stations. The Almanac publishers printed a few copies of the book, but we had no inkling of what we should do with them.

As the Russian proverb goes, "You're better off having a hundred friends than a hundred rubles." Here, one American friend was worth more than a hundred Russian ones.

His name was Simon Frumkin, a tall, intensely attentive fellow. He was the first American who visited me and my family upon our arrival in Los Angeles, in our small two-room apartment on North Genesee Street.

A survivor of Dachau and an active participant in the Soviet Jewry liberation movement, he made his actions on our behalf the center of his life. Driven by the cause, he not only fought for our freedom to emigrate but also helped new arrivals in any way he could. (The time would come when I would dedicate my autobiographical novel, *Farewell, Mama Odessa*, to him, his assistant Zev Yaroslavsky, and, through them, to all the people of goodwill who took part in the Soviet Jewry movement.)

When I presented him with a copy of our publication, he leafed through it, read a few entries, smiled into his wheat-blond mustache, and said that we would hear from him soon.

We were stunned when, the coming Sunday, June 4, 1978, Si's review of *Forbidden Laughter* appeared not in some neighborhood paper but in the pages of the *Los Angeles Times*, which was, as we had already learned, one of the biggest papers in the country. He titled his review "Understanding Russia through its Humor." After reminding readers of Winston Churchill's definition of Russia as "a riddle wrapped in an enigma," Si suggested unwrapping it by reading our book. He corroborated the authenticity of our collection; just a few years before its publication, during his trip to the Soviet Union as the chair of the Southern California Council for Soviet Jews, he had heard underground jokes of the kind we included from "taxi drivers in Moscow, Jewish refuseniks in Leningrad, and servers in Kyiv."[1]

We did not know that the content of our small publication was to be such a surprise for many Americans. And that's how I found myself on the set of one of the country's most-watched talk shows. When Merv introduces our book to his audience, he hits the nail right on the head: "We are busy watching the Russians, their defense system…. Their missiles…. Competing with them…. We're not thinking of the possibility they have humor and wit over there…. Besides their May Day parades and an occasional invasion, we see very little of a Russian sense of humor…."

Unbeknownst to us, *Forbidden Laughter* had undermined the decades-long stereotype of the Russians as people incapable of smiling, never mind laughing out loud. In movies and TV shows, the faces of Russian characters were bleak and overcast, like the skies over their vast country.

Perhaps part of the blame lay with classical Russian literature. In Dostoevsky's *Crime and Punishment*, a man probes his philosophical outlook by axing a woman he dislikes. Tolstoy's Anna Karenina finds no better way to solve her problem than throwing herself under a train. Before the curtain descends at the end of Chekhov's masterpiece, *Uncle Vanya,* the title character's niece, Sonya, reassures him with the following words, "We'll patiently endure the trials that fate will send us…. We'll die obediently and there, behind the grave, we'll say that we suffered, that we cried, that we were bitter, and God will take pity on us."

No wonder English humorist P.G. Wodehouse describes the state of mind of one of his characters by saying that he "experienced the sort of abysmal soul-sadness which afflicts one of Tolstoy's Russian peasants when, after putting in a heavy day's work strangling his father, beating his wife, and dropping the baby into the city's reservoir, he turns to the cupboards, only to find the vodka bottle empty."[2]

It was hardly surprising that a poll taken at the time of our book's publication revealed that only three percent of Americans thought Russians were cheerful and fun-loving and had a sense of humor. In American popular culture, the Russian name Igor (sometimes Ygor) was given to such unsavory characters as Dr. Frankenstein's henchman. To underscore their unpleasantness, they made them hunchbacks, or, at the very least, deaf and mute. And if physically deformed and evildoing humans named Igor were not enough, in the 1946 Three Stooges short feature, *A Bird in the Head*, they called Igor the mad scientist's *gorilla*.

As irony would have it, besides the editor and compiler, our book's title page credits the illustrator, whose real given name was ... Igor. Together with his witty illustrations, we used a few of his original cartoons. One of them, for example, depicts a beggar asking for alms beside a bunch of ready-to-be-launched Soviet missiles. To protect his relatives still in the USSR from being harassed by the authorities for his taking part in what they would consider anti–Soviet activities, the illustrator asked us to omit his surname. And so here was Igor: not a sullen hunchback, as he appeared on American TV and movie screens, but a clever, funny artist. Igor wasn't the only Russian villain in American popular culture.

There were also Boris Badenov and Natasha Fatale, spies on *The Rocky and Bullwinkle Show*, which ran from 1959 to 1964. It presented the male spy as the "world's greatest *no-goodnik*"; his surname was a pun on that of the sixteenth-century Russian Tsar Boris Godunov. Although Badenov works for the fictional nation of Pottsylvania—which mashes up the Yiddish word *putz* with Dracula's home homeland of Transylvania—his heavy mock-Russian accent makes it clear what evildoing country he's meant to evoke. If any doubt remained, when frustrated, Boris hisses the surname of the murderous protagonist of *Crime and Punishment*—"Raskolnikov!" No wonder that, as we learned much later, they banned the show in our old country as anti–Soviet propaganda. And it is hardly surprising that Badenov's equally pernicious assistant, with the Russian given name "Natasha," is the only child of Count Dracula. Boris is also the one-eyed, grim hunchback executioner in Mel Brooks' *Blazing Saddles*.

The Russians weren't depicted as *entirely* gruff, though. In *Ninotchka* (1939), one of the first American movies that portrayed the Stalinist Soviet Union as a gloomy and gray place populated with frigid and humorless commissars, the filmmakers made the greatest film star of the time, Greta Garbo, squeeze out a grin.

Thus, they proved that when stimulated—especially with amorous feelings—the Russians can produce at least a faint smile. But there were no smiles on the face of the mirthless villain Colonel Rosa Klebb, the chief antagonist of the 1963 James Bond flick *From Russia with Love*. (Her name is a pun on the international labor unions' slogan for the women's rights movement, "Bread and Roses" [*Khleb i rozy*].)[3]

So, how were Americans to square all these images with an insider's compilation of Russian underground jokes, whose authenticity was reaffirmed by being rendered both in the original Russian and in English translation? The publication humanized the Russians. It proved beyond any reasonable doubt that not only do they have a sense of humor but they also share the same anxieties as many Americans. For example, they joke about the ongoing brinkmanship between the superpowers:

> "Will there be a Third World War?"
> "No, there will not be a Third World War. But there will be such a fight for peace that not a single stone will be left unturned."[4]

Despite much apprehension, my appearance on an American TV show goes well overall. However, at one point, as I'm to find it out, later on, I put my foot in my mouth. During the interview, the host asks: "Do Russian people know anything about us? About our lifestyle? What do they envy most about American citizens? What about McDonald's?"

In a high-pitched voice, I reply: "Place any Russian in a McDonald's, and he would feel himself in paradise."

I should have stopped right there. But being a greenhorn and wanting to prove that I was as funny in life as our book was, I blurt out: "I know, in America, there are jokes about McDonald's serving junk food...."

The customary smile on the host's face disappears at once. Merv hurries to interject.

"No, no, not all!" he says, startled. "I often stop there after work. It's fast food...."

Here I have another opportunity to keep my mouth shut, but I don't: "Yeah, it's fast, but it's still junk."

A thunder of laughter rolls over the set.... Post factum, I feel embarrassed. I said it out of sheer desire to be funny, not from experience. Coming from a socialist country with pervasive shortages, I was not acquainted with the notion of "junk food." Back in the USSR, food was food—you either had it or you didn't. Period.

To soften the blow of my blooper, Merv and some of his guests on the show talk about how much they enjoy eating at McDonald's. The next day, my newly gained American friend, Dr. Anthony Saidy, calls me laughing and explains that McDonald's is one of the show's sponsors. They expect their product to be promoted, not badmouthed.

Alas, that wasn't the only time I put one of my extremities in a place where it did not belong. These awkward acrobatics of mine relate to the book's contents as well.

We had assumed that, by sheer fact that one quality all humans share is the ability to laugh or, at least, to smile, all Americans would understand our jokes. Well, minus those that are based on linguistic play, on puns. That assumption proved inaccurate. It turned out that cultural sensibilities could interfere with the perception of humor.

The collection betrayed our recent Soviet immigrants' utter ignorance of the American culture. For all our lives, the Soviet state had shut us off from the outside world with the Iron Curtain. Unable to travel to any Western country, we had no proper sense of what went on over there. All that we could do was try to catch short-wave radio broadcasts of the Voice of America, the BBC, the German Wave, and other Western stations, all of them jammed. They forced us to rely on Soviet journalists' reports, which were always laced with distortions and exaggerations.

Such negligence on our part betrayed our provincial haughtiness. And here's another consequence of our isolation. The avalanche of Soviet journalists' reports from the capitalist abroad made us feel that the entire world thirsted for learning more about Russia too. How else could it be? Just think of the sheer vastness of the country, with nearly a dozen time zones, one-sixth of the globe's landmass, and its overwhelming geopolitical importance.

The pitfalls of our knowledge of things American become clear when we receive detailed feedback from readers. It comes to us as an article in *The New Leader*, a bi-weekly political and cultural magazine. Noted Sovietologist Abraham Brumberg bases his write-up on a talk he delivered to the Kennan Institute of Advanced Russian Studies. The reviewer breaks down our collection into items readily understood by American laypeople and those that require more substantive knowledge of things Soviet. Without it, certain entries seem to him "somewhat bizarre and incomprehensible."[5]

As we expected, Russian jokes at the expense of the Party, its self-righteousness, its burdensome intrusion into the private life of Soviet people, or about endemic product shortages were appreciated. However, we could not have predicted that Americans may not care to know about Vasily Chapayev, a military leader in the Russian civil war and a lasting hero of Soviet propaganda. So, the following entry proves to be a waste of space:

A tour guide in Moscow's Museum of the October revolution is explaining:

"In front of you, comrades, is the skeleton of the immortal hero of the Civil War Vasily Ivanovich Chapayev. And this smaller skeleton next to it is the legendary Vasily Ivanovich Chapayev as an eight-year-old child."[6]

We also could not imagine that any anti–Stalinist sentiment could be frowned upon because of American cultural sensibilities:

A man is standing in Stalin's museum in front of a portrait of Joseph Stalin's mother. He shakes his head in grief and sorrow and heaves a sigh:

"Ay, ay, ay! Such a lovely lady. It's a pity that she didn't get that abortion in time."[7]

The reviewer finds it cruel. Only later would we learn that the punchline of this joke touched upon an issue too sensitive for Americans. Back in our homeland, because of the scarcity of contraceptives and general disregard for females' health, abortions were part of many Russian women's life.

The best compliment paid to the book, however, is the fact that its satirical spirit inspired the reviewer to call on American Sovietologists to change their approach. In his view, it would be much more productive if, instead of tediously studying the boring speeches of Soviet political leaders, they would laugh them off.

As I try to forget about the country I left behind, it finds an opportunity to remind me. Merv Griffin's mention of the Soviet Union's penchant for "occasional invasions" when he introduced Forbidden Laughter to his TV audience back in October 1978 proved to be prophetic. In just over a year, on December 24, 1979, detachments of Soviet tanks crossed the border into Afghanistan.

This significant loss for world peace turns out to be a small gain for Forbidden Laughter. As soon as the alarming news spreads, our compilation of Soviet underground drolleries receives its second wind. It looks as though, for the sake of comfort, Americans place their last bit of hope in the possibility that the Russians might have a sense of humor after all. Maybe their invasion of a neighboring country was just a practical joke that went awry? A reviewer for the Texas magazine *Vision* writes, "Maybe Americans and Russians have something in common after all."[8] "You know what the Russians are like—humorless, dour, sulking hulks of unhappiness, right?" *Los Angeles Magazine* teases its readers. "Not according to the new book, Forbidden Laugh-ter."[9]

Atlantic Monthly compliments it by saying that "these anti-government jokes are presumably told in whispers in native Russia, but it is hard to see how secrecy can be maintained, for most of them produce a noticeable yelp of mirth."[10]

After a *New York Times* reporter attends this editor and compiler's public talk at Long Island University, titled "Soviet Satire, Condoned and Condemned," his write-up, together with the speaker's picture and a cartoon from *Crocodile Magazine*, appears on the pages of the paper. Then comes an interview with United Press International, which the *Washington Post* and other papers print. The Voice of America broadcasts the piece translated into Russian.

The Soviets are not amused. Shortly after the broadcast, in its May 18, 1980, issue, *Crocodile* publishes an editorial retort. When I read it in the quiet of my home in Los Angeles, two contradicting feelings spar for dominance. On one hand, denouncing me as a miserable and worthless traitor to his glorious and benevolent Motherland hurts me. On the other hand, it reaffirms my belief that parting with it was, though life-altering, the best personal decision I had ever made:

"Such a Joke..."

As the Voice of America radio station recently reported, citing an article in The Washington Post, a famous Soviet satirist, forty-two years old, who emigrated from the Soviet Union, where he enjoyed great popularity among readers, appeared in the United States. This outstanding columnist and writer, who compares himself to Art Buchwald, whose fate became a guiding light for him, travels all over the United States with lectures on Russian satire and has just published a collection of "jokes prohibited in the USSR."

Today, this prominent litterateur is a professor of Russian literature at the University of California at Los Angeles and is preparing soon to defend his doctoral dissertation on Russian satire.

So that no one would suspect us of a hoax, we will reveal the name of this celebrity: Samuil Draitser. We strained our memory and recalled not without difficulty—yes, there was such an engineer who worked at one of Moscow's technical publishing houses. He visited other editorial offices and offered his opuses, but more often than not he heard the answer, "Alas, no...." There was only one reason—an unfortunate lack of literary talent. Resentfully pouting, S. Draitser went overseas in search of laurels and honorariums.

However, the letters of this future "classic" to his Moscow acquaintances did not sparkle with humor. Rather, they could be classified as tearful confessional prose: with difficulty, he got a job as a simple blue-collar worker. Monotonous labor and complete alienation—white-collar factory workers contemptuously turned away from the little blue-collar immigrant, no matter how much he fell over himself to make their acquaintance. And then, desperate S. Draitser realized he possessed goods that are now valued in the United States much more than a blue-collar worker's hands—vicious and stupid anti–Soviet jokes. He sold them wholesale and retail. And right then the head honchos of propaganda in Washington, D.C., noticed S. Draitser, fished him out from under a heap of immigrant garbage, and showered him with benefactions.

S. Draitser is as much a "professor of satire" as a goat is an archbishop. But if a goat is ready to switch to an anti–Soviet pasture, Washington is ready to proclaim him a professor, a classic, Sabaoth....

Such a joke....[11]

In the grand Soviet tradition, they consider anyone who escaped the country an ungrateful and despicable traitor. First, to denounce the editor and compiler of *Forbidden Laughter* as a graphomaniac who, no matter how hard he tried, never made it into the pages of the famous Soviet satirical outlet *Crocodile*, they do not use my pen name, "E. Abramov," under which the magazine published over twenty pieces of my work, from paragraphs to full-size feuilletons. They had entrusted me with the magazine's correspondent ID #267, valid until December 31, 1974, the day I came to America. Second, by calling me by my first name and surname registered in my Soviet passport, both unmistakably Jewish to a Russian ear, they let their readers know that the traitor of the Motherland is not an ethnic Russian, but a Jew. What else to expect of such a person!

The editorial also invents my American life along the lines of the script Soviet propaganda used to describe the fate of anyone who left "the best country in the world." Per this scenario, the misfits regret their defection for the rest of their miserable lives abroad. They wind up at the bottom of the society they chose instead. Homeless, they ask for handouts in the streets and die in the gutter.

The reality didn't fit that scenario. Shortly after arriving in Los Angeles, falling back on my engineering training (in 1960, I graduated from the Odessa Polytechnic Institute), I landed a job as a draftsman at A-OK Electronic Company. A year later, they invited me to teach beginning Russian as a lecturer at UCLA. Then they accepted me as a grad student in the Department of Slavic Languages and Literatures, where I worked first as a teaching assistant, then as a research assistant. So much for being a destitute blue-collar worker...

But worse than this falsification of my American life was the editorial's hypocrisy. Ironically, describing a "pitiful lot of an immigrant," the *Crocodile*'s editorial projects onto America the dismissive attitude toward blue-collar workers prevalent in Soviet society. Yes, the Soviet Union was supposed to be such a workers' paradise, but it still treated them as members of a lower social stratum—even though a highly qualified lathe operator earned more than a starting-level engineer.[12]

In portraying me as a mental case, suffering from delusions of grandeur, they cite the name of Art Buchwald as being my "shining star." Bizarre. *The Washington Post* article quoted me saying:

> Buchwald is widely known in Russia because they print all his columns that make fun of the White House and the CIA. Things like that.... I thought, "Oh God, they have such freedom there. In Russia, you would be in jail for even thinking such things as Buchwald does, much less writing about them.... What amazes me about America is the level of what they permit. My totalitarian mind still is not used to such frontal attacks on governmental personalities."[13]

So much for my "shining star."

At the time of this *Crocodile* betrayal, I never thought they might, one day, seek my forgiveness. Well, not straightforwardly, but in a roundabout way. Fast forward ten years.... In the summer of 1990, at the height of Gorbachev's campaign of *glasnost* and *perestroika*, the political climate relaxed to a degree unheard of in Soviet times. Among other frivolities that the regime felt it could afford was the lifting of the curse on those who left the country in the 1970s and '80s. We émigrés could go back and visit the land where we were born and raised.

So here I am. It is a bittersweet reunion. I stroll along the streets of Moscow, perplexed by the in-the-face evidence of the country's rampant poverty. The Soviet economic system has broken down. Rows of poorly dressed men and women with emaciated faces stretch around the entrances of the city's subway stations. In their hands, they hold domestic relics, which they hope to sell—amber earrings, medallions, silverware, and antique books. This brings back memories of the wartime years, which, fleeing from rapidly advancing Nazis, my mother and I spent in the hinterland. As a young boy, I used to wander around makeshift black markets where people offered whatever they could in exchange for food, just as they do now. Hunger leaves you little choice.

I also visit the editorial offices of newspapers and magazines I'd frequented back in my Soviet past. They greet me as if I were a ghost. The Russians have fallen into a temporary habit of wringing their hands in remorse before those who had left the country rather than suffocate. The editors of widely read papers like *The Week*, *The Literary Gazette*, and *Evening Moscow* ask me for my American stories and promptly publish them on their pages. They supplement these publications with their write-ups, reminding readers about my previous work and giving a résumé of my American life. In his preamble to two of my short pieces, the editor of the popular magazine *Ogonek* writes, "Now we repay our debts and give those whom we had made to leave Russia the opportunity to speak—it is time to gather scattered stones." I likewise pay a visit to the editorial offices of *Crocodile*, on the twelfth floor of the Pravda high-rise building. My visit starts weirdly. The first person who lunges happily toward me, his golden tooth glittering, is a broad-shouldered man my age, whom I recognize as the head of the *Crocodile*'s Culture Department, Alexei Khodanov. It was through him that my last contributions to the magazine had passed to the editor-in-chief's desk, including the ill-fated feuilleton "Shut up, You Scatterbrain," which gave me the first real push toward emigration.

The man grabs my neck and hugs me. Tears flash in his eyes.

"Oh, how glad I am to see you again!" he says. "What people we've lost!"

Having an adult man hugging me and crying into my chest takes me by surprise. I can't remember anything like this ever happening to me—maybe one case. About a year before leaving the country, they diagnosed me with some kidney malfunction and sent me to get special tests at one of the Moscow hospitals. My parents lived in Odessa, a thousand kilometers away. When my father learned I had serious health problems, he flew to the capital, fearing the worst. When they released me from the hospital, weakened by long confinement to bed and the exhausting medical procedures, I found him waiting for me. Pale with fear, but rejoicing at the sight of me standing upright, this unsentimental man gave me a big hug, holding back his tears. The last time he had felt that way was when he returned from the war and found out that I, his only child at that time, had survived.

And here Khodanov, not a close relative, is weeping on my chest out of the happiness of seeing me again after over fifteen years.

Then Sasha Moralevich, *Crocodile*'s Special Correspondent, with whom I had a warm relationship, comes out of his office. Tall and broad-shouldered, with a big smile on his lips, he cups my hand in his big palms and shakes it.

"You can't even imagine how happy I am to see you, buddy," he smiles. "You did the right thing, leaving.... A country of mice and frogs.... Come over to my place—we'll have a drink."

The next day, during a reception at the House of Journalists, Mark Vilensky, the head of the *Crocodile*'s foreign department, approaches me. I do not remember whether, back in my journalistic years, we had ever talked. And I have every reason to assume that it was he who had authored that despicable editorial smearing my name a decade earlier. His department published pamphlets exposing the American, British, and West German imperialists under such titles as "The Wall Street Exchange is Feverish," "The Anti-People Course of Tory's Ruling Cabinet," and "The Muddy Waters of the Rhine are Flowing."

"I know, Emil," he says, his face wearing the expression of an undeservedly offended teenager. "They probably told you that it was *I* wrote that libel. I give you my word of honor that it wasn't me. It was Khodanov."

He walks away. Thinking back on my visit to the *Crocodile* editorial offices and Khodanov's reaction to my appearance there, the tears he had shed when throwing himself on my chest, I realize that this was a special occasion, a once-in-my-lifetime glimpse of actual "crocodile tears."

8

Looking for
an American Friend

Today, it's hard to believe that before I emigrated from the former Soviet Union, I didn't think about how my relationship with Americans would develop. Even the very fact that these relationships would arise didn't occur to me. After all, moving to another country means living among strangers.

There was only one excuse for this lapse of consideration: there was no time to think about it. At the start of 1974, when I began contemplating such a drastic change in my life, thanks to the efforts of Soviet head honchos to soften up their relations with the West—where else would they get grain to feed the population, on the moon?—an unheard-of, either in my or my parents' lifetime, opportunity to get out of the country sprang up. A window of it—what I am saying, a window! A tiny vent, a crack opened. Knowing the whimsical nature of the country's bigwigs, that crack could get slammed back shut at any moment.

Having settled in the States, at the first stage of our lives here, we, immigrants, lived in a world of our own, kept company with our kind only. We maintained those relationships that had grown in our midst while, waiting for our entry visas to the States, we had stayed in Lido di Ostia, Ladispoli, and other Roman suburbs. Therefore, it was only natural that whole settlements of Soviet immigrants also formed in such American metropolitan areas as New York, Boston, Chicago, Los Angeles, and San Francisco.

None of us knew much about what Americans as people were all about. Thanks to a steady barrage of propaganda, even the most unbiased ex–Soviets had nothing to go by but stereotypical images. For us, the newcomers from the Soviet land, the Americans were hardly more than flickering images of men and women on the TV and movie screens, images filtered by the censors.

We were told that every act and thought of Americans was subordi-

89

nated to business. Every smile was measured in terms of how much profit it might bring. In all Western societies, especially in the headquarters of capitalism, the United States of America, all people were supposed to be beasts of prey roaming the world around them in search of their fellow human beings' blood.

Of course, none of us took whatever the Soviet media delivered at face value. Ever skeptical of propaganda claims, we didn't believe that, in the West, it was a dog-eat-dog world. Yet, coming to this country, we didn't expect to find widespread amiability and goodwill.

In our first encounters with the Americans, they surprised us with their friendliness and benevolence. We found them kind and generous in spirit.

Maybe because of these traits of the American character, I've never felt like a total stranger here. To make us feel better about ourselves, Americans appreciated even our quite inadequate English. To our clumsy attempts to construct a sentence, they would smile and pat us on the shoulder, "Oh, your English is so much better than my Russian!"

Many Americans we met believed each of us knew five other languages. It seemed they were convinced that coming from overseas alone was enough reason to assume that such a person had to be a polyglot.

We also found Americans' readiness to help on the road to be heartwarming. Seeing on the side of the highway a raised hood of a car, they would stop and offer their help, at the very least, to jump-start our stalled engine by hooking it up to the batteries of their vehicles.

Americans turned out to be much more tolerant and respectful of someone else's opinion than we were used to in Russia. Knowing that you saw the movie he or she had seen, the American won't say it is worthless. What if you liked it? It would create an awkward situation. Russians are oblivious to such a prospect. While they would express their disgust with the film, the Americans remain silent or utter a polite "Interesting...."

While we Russians were used to complaining about our lives, when we asked our new acquaintances among the locals how they were doing, we got back a short "Fine!" Thus, while a Russian would say with a sour facial expression, "I've lost my job," an American would characterize the same situation as "I'm between jobs."

It took us some time to get used to the proverbial American smile. In Russia, a smile is reserved for family members and close friends; smiling in public is considered a sign of a person being feeble-minded.

One of the most admirable qualities we found in Americans is their innate, bottomless optimism, and their refusal to stop fighting for a better life. Persistence was their virtue, regardless of the outcome. Their

"Never give up!" motto was a new slogan that went against the grain of our fatalism, the result of centuries of oppression, terror, famine, and war in our homeland. Many of us brought along a deep-seated belief that some mysterious force decides for us what should or shouldn't happen in our lives. Americans we met listened in dismay, when we would run into seemingly insurmountable obstacles on our way to a desirable goal, we would utter with a deep sigh, "Well, it looks like it's not in the cards for me!"

In the world left behind, we used to settle for the minimum. Whereas Americans believed in the proverbial "pursuit of happiness," in our Soviet lives, it was the "pursuit of survival," especially when it concerned any political questions. The second year of my new life, 1976, was the year of the presidential campaign. Gerald Ford ran for re-election, and Jimmy Carter vied for the first term of the highest office in the land. All of us, Soviet immigrants, rooted for Ford. When our American friends asked us why we were so resolute in our devotion to him, they were flabbergasted when we told them that our main reason was that "nothing bad happened during the Ford years, thank God!"

They looked at each other in disbelief and shrugged, "Why not give a new guy a chance?"

One of our first discoveries made by a Soviet émigré was that the Iron Curtain worked both ways. Not only did we know next to nothing worth knowing about America before coming here, but the Americans also turned out to be no less ignorant of our Soviet life, asking us things like "Did you have TV sets?" or "What province are you from?" The very term "province" (*guberniya*) reeked of mothballs: as an administrative term, the very word ceased to exist in the USSR over six decades ago.

The Americans also couldn't fathom why, in times of acute food shortages, we could buy a chicken only if we had coupons redeemable in special stores. Or, if we wanted to travel even to a Soviet-dominated "country of people's democracy," say, Bulgaria, we had to get a character reference from our local Party and the relevant trade union committees.

However, our most staggering discovery was the average American's innocence in world geography. Thinking about how pervasive the geographical illiteracy of many Americans is, I am inclined to think that it all started with Columbus. After all, hadn't he been overwhelmed with joy when he reached America, believing it was the country of his destination—India?

I don't know what causes the weak knowledge of most Americans in world geography. Some see the roots of this phenomenon nestling deep in their collective unconscious, as the innate wish to stay away from the rest of the planet's troubles. Whatever the reason, I still shudder each time I hear things like "Hungary must be part of Russia: people coming from there have the same heavy accent in English."

Some Americans seemed even to be proud of their geographical myopia, seeing it as additional proof of their peaceful nature. They are quite satisfied with whatever land they have; they cast no envious eye on other countries' territories.

One day, I learned about this American handicap the hard way: through public embarrassment. While presenting my first book, a collection of Soviet underground jokes, *Forbidden Laughter*, I set up a sample of them by reminding the audience about the tension between the USSR and China at that time and the possibility of an eventual military conflict between the two countries:

> Question to Radio Armenia:
> "What will happen to the Soviet Union in ten years?"
> Answer:
> "Nothing of notice. All will be quiet on the Chinese-Finnish border."

Although the audience consisted of university students, the joke fell flat.[1]

To credit Americans, some of them were quite insecure about their knowledge of world geography. Once I overheard two men arguing whether Greece was part of Italy or Italy was part of Greece. On another occasion, learning that I came from Russia, an elderly American lady asked me how I liked it here, in my new country.

"Do you find America a much different country than your Russia?" she said.

"Oh!" I replied. "What are you talking about, a different country? It's a different planet!"

Apparently, thinking about all the news reports about space travel at the time, the lady looked at me in confusion and said with some guilt in her voice: "Well, it looks like I should brush up on my geography. Till now, I thought Russia was on this planet."

While my discovery of rampant American ignorance of world geography made me shrug in amusement, one day, my car radio delivered the song "Wonderful World." The lyrical hero of the song admitted that not only he "do[es]n't know much geography," he is equally ignorant of any mathematics, be it algebra or trigonometry. He feels that his knowledge of elementary arithmetic (one plus one), when applied to him and his beloved, is enough to make him happy.[2]

I couldn't believe my ears. The song didn't sound satirical. It didn't make fun of the suitor. It was lyrical in tone all the way through. No hint of sarcasm. I was dumbfounded. What a bizarre way to capture a girl's heart!

Intrigued, I got hold of the rest of the song's lyrics, only to find that the lyrical hero of the song was dead serious about his intellectual innocence of other subjects as well, be it history or biology, any other science, for that matter. Even God damned French they made him take in school.[3]

I was perplexed. Is "I don't know much about anything but I know I love you" a successful pickup line in America? How could any girl find an ignoramus sexy?

True, a female heart could be unpredictable in its choice of whom it might favor. After all, this phenomenon had been observed from time immemorial. As the *Book of Proverbs* of the Old Testament (Chapter 30, verses 18–19) has it:

> There are three things that are too amazing for me,
>   four that I don't understand:
>   the way of an eagle in the sky,
>   the way of a snake on a rock,
>   the way of a ship on the high seas,
> and the way of a man with a young woman.

To my relief, there was at least one stanza of the song's lyrics acknowledging that, on the off chance that the girl prefers an educated young man, the suitor is trying to get better grades:

> For maybe by being an "A" student baby
> I can win your love for me[4]

Soon, I found that, alas, that discovery wasn't an isolated incident. Shortly after coming to the country and making a living as a draftsman in a small electronic company, I applied for the UCLA graduate school in Slavic Languages and Literatures. Preparing for an interview with a professor, I brought with me a book on Old Church Slavonic literature to peruse at my lunchtime. When the company secretary saw the book title, unaware of my intellectual pursuit, she raised her brows: "Ha, Emil, I didn't know you're a nerd."

The word wasn't in my limited immigrant fresh-off-the-boat vocabulary. So, I looked it up in a dictionary of American slang and discovered that it denotes a person seen as intellectual and introverted. (The derogatory term "nerd" was indeed a stereotype which, in time, shed its pejorative coloring and became a term of pride and group identity. It also happened to another former pejorative term—"geek." Nowadays, Best-Buy electronic supermarkets proudly offer their "Geek Squad" services.)

When I encountered that strange phenomenon of being proud of being an uneducated person, I thought it came from my being a greenhorn in a country so different from the one I had left forever. However, after a few years of living in this country, I found I wasn't alone in my discovery. One day, I stumbled upon an article written by my compatriot, the famous writer Isaac Asimov. He titled it "A Cult of Ignorance," stating that not only is there a "cult of ignorance" in America, but "there always has been."[5]

Asimov pointed out that the "strain of anti-intellectualism [...] has been nurtured by the false notion that 'democracy means that my ignorance is just as good as your knowledge.'" Elsewhere in the article, he states, "There are 200 million Americans who have inhabited schoolrooms at some time in their lives and who will admit that they know how to read (provided you promise not to use their names and shame them before their neighbors)."[6]

Almost forty years down the road from my first encounter with the phenomenon, things have hardly improved. According to the 2022 report, literacy in the United States was only 79 percent; 21 percent of American adults were illiterate, and 54 percent of adults in the United States had literacy below the sixth-grade level.[7]

How in the world could such a dismal lack of literacy exist in the country that has invented every technological marvel known to the modern world—the light bulb, the radio, the telephone ... you name it! After all, America isn't some godforsaken land populated by people that worship ignorance.

At first, I dismissed the discrepancy between low literacy and high accomplishment with the thought that, when you have a country with a large population, geniuses will exist, and they will accomplish great things on their own. After all, at the end of the nineteenth century, hardly 30 percent of Russians could read, yet that very country produced Tolstoy, Dostoevsky, and Chekhov, authors whose novels and stories were read around the world.

But the comparison was too simple. It took me some time to realize that the fabric of the country in which I made my home and whose citizen I was proud to become was much more complicated than I thought. America has always been at the cutting edge of technological progress for reasons other than widespread literacy.

Like many other differences between the two societies, the educational systems in Russia and America reflect different core values—the collectivist in Russia and the individualist in America. Whereas in the Soviet Union the curriculum of all years of high school was compulsory for everyone, in America, starting from junior high, there were elective courses, of which every student can choose what he or she is inclined to learn.

Thus, the American approach to education could be represented as an inverted pyramid whose width signifies the ever-increasing demands on the student's upward path toward achieving his or her professional goal. That is why American higher education, especially at the graduate level, is valued on a global scale. It's not by chance that, according to the 2022 U.S. and World Report ranking, "the top 10 best universities globally are predominately schools in the United States, with the UK being the only other country represented on the list."[8]

In Russian secondary and higher education, the emphasis is on discipline and standardization. Russian students must choose their major when they apply to a college, and most of the required courses they must take depend on the chosen major; there are very few electives. So a young person must make up his or her mind regarding their lifelong profession right from the start.

In the Soviet Union, when I was growing up, discrimination against Jews getting a higher education was widespread, and Jewish parents did everything in their power to help their children to get the education that would help them survive. My personal story can serve as an illustration. Upon graduating from high school, I wanted to study literature, but, out of their intentions, my parents forced me to apply to the Odessa Polytechnical Institute. It took me twenty years before I could start all over again by leaving the USSR and emigrating to America. Soon after my arrival, I went to UCLA grad school and earned a Ph.D. in Russian literature.

And cultural conditioning dies hard. The following real-life story of an immigrant is a case in point. Soon after settling in the new country, a middle-aged Soviet musician, a professional violinist, gave up his instrument, enrolled in computer programming courses, and soon became an expert in the field.

The thing was that, back in his homeland, when he was a young boy, his father, a musician, had forced him to take lessons and gain a musical education. Not because of his promising musical abilities, but because his father decided that with at least a secondary musical education, he wouldn't be left without a piece of bread; he could always teach at a musical school or give private lessons.

The man suffered throughout his adult life in the Soviet Union because the music was forced on him and he cared little for it. Once he arrived in America, he made a career switch with no regret.

And yet when here, in America, this immigrant's school-age son showed extraordinary abilities in the technical field—he built a low-cost printer, which won a prestigious prize at his high school—as soon as he graduated, the man took away all his tools and told his son point-blank: "Not on your life! You're going to apply to a medical school. In this country, you should be an MD."

From an American's point of view, the father's reasoning made no sense: doctors who are family practitioners work very hard and often make far less than good engineers. The immigrant father bought into the stereotype of what professions deem most coveted in America, as the following popular joke exemplifies:

> A Jewish mother walks down the street with her two young sons. A passerby asks her how old the boys are.
> "The doctor is three," the mother answers, "and the lawyer is two."

Among other discoveries in the first steps of my American life, I came to realize that the difference between animate and inanimate objects is a relative concept. I have found that, over time, things that are important in our life gain a soul.

For example, this happened with a car. It entered my immigrant life quite early, although I wasn't ready for such a close relationship. Back in my homeland, I could only dream about having a car. In the Soviet social hierarchy of my time, I couldn't even dream about having a car as that was a material object out of reach for people of my social status. Only a big movie star, a famous author, or a highly placed Party official could afford to own a vehicle.

The impression that, in America, cars are a dime a dozen formed in my mind for at least a decade before I set foot on its land. Rereading *One-Storied America* by my fellow countrymen, Ilya Ilf and Yevgeny Petrov, I remembered their perception of Americans as being "born motorists." At the time of the authors' travel across the American continent, the Soviet automobile industry was in its nascent state.

In the same authors' novel, *The Golden Calf*, the protagonist Ostap Bender, a sly operator, stopping in a provincial Russian town, makes a speech announcing the beginning of the automobile era:

> "I am glad, comrades," said Ostap, "to disturb the patriarchal silence of [your] city with an automobile siren. A car, comrades, is not a luxury, but a means of transportation. The iron stallion is replacing the peasant's horsey. Let's set up the serial production of Soviet cars. May our motor rally fight the bad roads and general sloppiness [of our life]."[9]

A few years before emigrating, I learned about the endless highways of America from John Steinbeck's book titled *Travels with Charley:*

In Search of America, translated into Russian. The volume featured the elegiac travel of a lonely man with his dog. They crisscross the country, staying overnight in motels. The reading awakened in me a strange, exciting imagination. Wow, there are so many cars in America that they have hotels for motorists!

In the first steps of my new life, it was hard to fathom how, in the Soviet Union of my time, owning a car was an indicator of prosperity, in America, people used their vehicles to drive up to offices to apply for their unemployment benefits.

Also, back in the old country, your rite of passage to adulthood was considered getting your internal passport. In America, a sign of a young person's maturity was receiving his or her driver's license. One of the first pieces of advice I got from my American classmates in graduate school at UCLA was that it was important to have three people to trust in my new life—a doctor, a lawyer, and ... an auto-mechanic. As the classmate added, "Not necessarily in that order!" There could be situations in which your very life could depend on the person taking care of your vehicle.

When I got my first new car, I invited my American neighbor to look at it. Judging by the models of cars popular at that time, all of them long and wide, a Cadillac or a Lincoln, mine was nothing to write home about. Judge for yourself: it was a Ford Escort.

At first, my neighbor allowed himself a humorous smirk, "Is that all?" But then, as he sat behind the wheel, he smiled a nostalgic smile, sucking the smell of a new car's upholstery into his nostrils. I was surprised. What was there to be delighted about in that odor? For me, the inside of my car reeked of plastic warmed up in the sun. Hardly the aroma of perfume; one could only grimace inhaling it. But, for my American neighbor, the scent evoked sentimental feelings, as if it was the smell of powder, which is used to pre-empt the sweating of a new-born baby's tooshie.

The organization that took care of my daughter, Svetlana, who came to America as a refugee, presented her with a used car. For the transfer ceremony, the vehicle's owners arrived with the whole family. Before handing over the ignition key to Svetlana, they took selfies leaning on the hood, touching the roof, stroking the windshield as if hugging and saying farewell to their good-hearted relative, about whom they would keep fond memories. (I wouldn't be surprised if they keep those pictures in their family album next to the portraits of their deceased grandparents.)

In time, I became aware more and more that, for Americans, their cars are living and breathing beings. They even give them nicknames;

one of my American friends named his Subaru sedan "Bertha" and his Toyota truck "Spike." Because of the uncertainties of life on the road, even atheist Americans pray to a "God of Parking Lots." There are different parking deities around the country; thus, in the Los Angeles area, the name of the parking god is "Murray."

All this knowledge would come to me much later in my American life. But the image of a car as a breathing and living being formed in my mind over the very first years of my life in the new land.

"Buglet"

It's been observed that spouses who have lived together for many years resemble each other not only in character, mannerisms, and habits but also in physical appearance. This is all reasonable enough, but in these hurried modern times, the phenomenon seems to apply more widely.

Take George, for example. He's not married, and he doesn't even have a steady girlfriend. For the longest time now, I've had a strange feeling that he reminds me of someone I often see with him. The same flat nose flared out at the tip, the same way of snorting a bit, just before uttering a salutation. The slope of his bald skull also seemed familiar. At first, I thought I was imagining things, for the man has no brothers or sisters, and I've never seen his parents. To top it off, he's a confirmed bachelor, and, as far as friends are concerned, he's quite a loner.

Nevertheless, whenever his image comes to my mind, for some odd reason, it always seems to double.... One day, when George dropped by, I stepped out to greet him, and it all came together. At that very moment, when he climbed out of his aged Volkswagen, it hit me! I shuddered at the realization that the fellow's mysterious doppelgänger was none other than ... his car!

"Man!" I exclaimed. "How long have you been driving this old wreck?"

He grew quite pale as if I had slapped him in the face. He couldn't believe my audacity, not to mention such personal treachery. He turned around and looked tenderly at his Beetle, which was still grumbling a bit. He then said to me:

"I didn't know you could be so crude.... This Bug, I mean Buglet, and I have been together for a long time now; over ten years. She's not as old as you might think. Remember, you can't tell a book by its cover. Nobody has a car with such a great disposition."

"Disposition!" I thought I was hearing things.

"Of course. She gets turned on the minute you touch her. And oh, if you only knew how she behaves herself on the road in the company of other cars. Dignity. Tact. Manners."

"What are you talking about, George? It's just an old tin car; a candidate for the junkyard!"

"You're a candidate for the junkyard yourself! I've never met a more agreeable vehicle in my whole life. Take your Oldsmobile, for example. Today it starts, but tomorrow—it's dead. Until you kick it between the headlights, it won't even think about work!"

"You keep my Olds out of this," for some reason, I was embarrassed. "One day your VW will play a trick on you, mark my words."

"You'd better look after your Olds," George snarled, and slammed the door as he rolled off.

I knew he was quite offended because I didn't see him for almost a year afterward. Then one afternoon he came to my house in a three-piece suit, looking very serious and gloomy.

"Are you coming from a funeral?" I asked him carefully. "Who was it, your uncle? What a pity! He was such a lively old man."

"My uncle's okay," said George with a voice from beyond the grave. "It's much worse than that."

"Who's died then? George, you've got nobody else!"

"That's true—now I don't.... Now I'm an orphan. My Buglet is no longer with me."

"What happened? Couldn't it carry its weight anymore? Well, time always takes its toll."

"What did you say?" George said tenderly and smiled as if he were daydreaming. "She was so young! Maybe not in appearance, but in her heart."

"Then what?" I asked the man, throwing my hands up in the air. "Don't tell me she left you...."

As I glanced through the window, I spotted a luxurious new Cordoba convertible.

George hid his eyes and said with difficulty, swallowing the lump which had risen in his throat:

"It's all that boss of mine, the greedy ape: 'You're scaring away our customers with that junk pile of yours! I don't want to see it anymore!' I was forced to part with her ... with my dear little Bu.... Bu...," he couldn't continue; his tears were choking him.

I felt sorry for George, with his tender devotion. I said with compassion:

"So, you poor fellow, did you push her all the way to the junkyard yourself?"

"How dare you think such a thing!" George flared up, and his eyes dried in a moment. "I left her in very good hands. At first, I'd visit her every other day, to see if everything was all right. She's a subtle creature, and can't stand any violence."

I tried to pacify the guy.

"There, there, George," I said. "Time is the best doctor. It'll heal your wounds."

"There's nothing you can say to help me," he said. "I'll never forget her. Unfortunately, her new owner moved to another state. But it's all right, we correspond regularly."

"Wha-at!" This was too much for me. "You write to her and she answers? Tell me what she writes. Does she say that she can't live without you?"

"Don't be sarcastic, you dried-up, hard-hearted man. I send her greeting cards on all the holidays. On Christmas ... on Valentine's Day ... on Mother's Day...."

"Mother's Day?"

"Sure."

"And does she answer you? What does she write?"

"You can make fun of me as much as you like. But here," he took out a pack of Hallmark cards and waved them in the air. "Every one of them came with her reply. Her new owner places my cards under her engine for the night, and in the morning, before leaving for work, he puts them under one of her tires. And I see that everything's okay with her. Oil isn't leaking; the tires aren't going bald."

The next day, while I was shaving, I noticed for the first time that my face was a little asymmetrical. My left eye was somewhat higher than the right one. Just like the headlights of my Oldsmobile.[10]

I also got acquainted first-hand with another peculiar American trait—the obsession with celebrities. Knowledgeable cultural critics ascribe this national hang-up to Americans' need to have a bunch of people they admire for their sheer notoriety, the reason Brits adore their royalty. In the country I left behind, nothing of that sort of admiration existed in Soviet people's lives. The aristocracy had been dealt with in 1917, and even treating it in a less than disparaging way was fraught with the danger to be accused of political disloyalty to the regime. Neither did we admire the powers that be. In theory, they were supposed to be our comrades, equal in rights and privileges, devoted to our Soviet homeland.

Of course, there were Soviet movie stars and prima ballerinas at the Bolshoi Theatre. But their private lives were not to be covered, neither in the press nor in any other mass media.

As far as American obsession with celebrities or even celebrities-to-be (regardless of how questionable that "to be" was), I got acquainted with it back in March 1986, after attending the Western Humor and Irony Membership Conference, an association whose abbreviation is a tongue-in-cheek WHIM. A junior scholar at the time, I could hardly be qualified as a "celebrity." Therefore, I was dumbfounded when, upon returning home, I found in my mailbox the following letter, typed out on the stationery of a doctor of podiatry.

The first thought that occurred to me was that the author of the letter had read my mind. My plantar fasciitis began bothering me again, and I thought of making an appointment with a local podiatrist. However, I lived in Santa Monica, California, and the letter arrived from Tempe, Arizona. How come...?

Here it is, as I've found it among my papers.

Dear Emil:

I sure enjoyed meeting you at the WHIM Humor Conference last month.

I would be honored to have a pair of your autographed shoes in my collection along with those of Lyndon Johnson, Vicki Carr, Jamie Farr, and many, many others. I will contribute $25.00 to any charity you specify on your behalf in exchange for your shoes. Would you please autograph your shoes on the soles or inside, whichever is most convenient. A pre-paid mailer is enclosed for you to send your shoes.

Looking forward to having your shoes in my collection.

Thank you for your consideration.

Sincerely,
[First Name and Surname], D.P.M.

That a doctor of podiatry attended the conference wasn't surprising. After all, all conference participants talked about humor, taking the jokes apart and explaining how they work. Or do not. A case in point was my paper in which I compared American and Russian humor and tried to explain why some American jokes wouldn't fly in Russia because of some stark cultural differences. All that could interest not only scholars of humor, but a layperson as well. But putatively putting me on a par with the president of the United States, a famous singer, and one star of the TV sitcom *M*A*S*H*? Give me a break, doctor!

The time came, and a closer relationship between us, the newcomers, and living and breathing Americans, coalesced. Mostly, the interest was genealogical. Many of them were the offspring of Jewish immigrants from Tsarist Russia. Their grandparents or great-grandparents had arrived on the American continent *en mass* starting in the last decades of the nineteenth century and continued until the first quarter of the twentieth. Then, on Stalin's order, the Soviet borders were slammed shut.

It so happened that my first American friend was the man who, on December 31, 1974, shook my hand as soon as, together with my wife Natasha and my one-year-old son Max, I deplaned from the TWA jet and set foot on the tarmac of the LAX. A volunteer of the city's Jewish Family Service, Professor Jules Levin taught Russian at the University of California. He played an active part in my American life. Having learned about my former journalistic career, he invited me to give a talk about Soviet satire, quite a novelty in America. A write-up about the event appeared in a local paper, my first public exposure on American soil.

Jules's interest in meeting me stemmed from his willingness to learn about his family's immigrant past. One day, looking at me with curiosity, he smiled and said: "You know, I catch myself thinking that, if my father hadn't left the USSR in the early twenties, then I would be you now."

Over time, other Soviet immigrants befriended Americans as well. However, soon it became clear that the concept of friendship, ours and the Americans, differed. The following piece written in my first years in America reflects this discovery.

"Looking for an American *Droog*"

Life in America is all right. For us who came from Russia, many of our dreams came true—no state oppression, freedom, and plenty of opportunities. One thing, however, is missing here. We have no American friends (*droogs*), the dear, understanding, and compassionate fellows we left behind in Russia. Rarely do we form close relationships with Americans. If we have "buddies" among the local inhabitants, often the entire conversation consists of "Hi!" "How are you doing?" and "You'll hear from me soon"—and off we both run to our jobs, to a store, to dinner, or wherever. From some of them, I have yet to hear a peep.

We Russian immigrants long for friendship, the deepest interest, and the close attention to each other that we had left behind. Somehow, heart-to-heart conversations occur rarely. They smile a lot, these American devils, and they wish you well until you lose your mind. It is refreshing that they presume you, a stranger, to be a splendid fellow. In Russia, it's the other way around; they assume you're a scoundrel upon the first encounter with you, and you have to work hard to prove that you're all right. Well, give the devils their due: Americans are cheery and well-wishing fellows. That's about it....

I had already given up hope I would find an American friend. But, one day, at a party, they introduced me to a nice man about my age, who was, they told me, keen to meet me. I thought, well, I've heard that before. Now I'll get a few questions about my family, about my job, a smile, a pat on my shoulder, and he'll leave "to add ice to his drink."

However, no, not this time. The guy was truly interested in me. I told him about my family, and he asked about my children's names and ages, and about how well they were doing in school. He inquired about my wife's health. He was curious about how we have adjusted to life in America. He expressed his admiration for how good my (quite lumpish) English is. When I replied it was still a far cry from my Russian, he cheered me up by saying:

"What are you talking about? Between the two of us, you're a polyglot. Your English's so much better than my Russian! All I know is *vodka, sputnik,* and *Na zdrovie.* Ha-ha-ha!"

(I didn't want to disappoint him by telling him his third expression, of toasting, is not Russian, but Polish. The Russians say, *"Budem zdorovy!"*)

I was about to tell him he can live with his Russian without losing much sleep, while I.... However, he already went on asking where I lived, and whether I like my neighborhood. Am I satisfied with the quarters or not? Was my landlord okay with the kids? Is he bothered by the children playing and making noise? Are there any parks nearby to walk to with my family? Are babysitters available where we live so that my wife and I could go to a movie? He asked me about my car, its make, and shape, with care and tenderness we, Russians, reserve for our grandmothers. He's even heard, he informed me, that I write a little.

"How interesting!" he said with awe. "You are the first writer I have ever met in the flesh."

I, of course, was modest and said, yes, I write, but I'm not in the same class as another man in our community, Leikin. He is truly a writer, and I am not at that level.... I do it by the way, here and there, from time to time....

The American insisted. He said it was a bad thing to bury one's talent, no matter how small it may seem. He felt I must find the time to develop it and not allow someone else's success to intimidate me.

In short, little by little, I was relating to this American warmly. What a stroke of luck! I've lived in this country for seven years now and, finally, it seems I have met my true American friend. May God give him health!

It was time to leave, but we still couldn't get enough of talking to each other. The American, as if he was reading my mind, got his card out and extended it to me.

"I'm thrilled I met you," he said with a sincerity that grabbed my soul. "You will hear from me soon. We have a lot of things to talk about."

We shook hands. He turned to leave. Something troubled me, however. Did his American smile, with which I had become so comfortable, vanish too quickly? I brought his card up to my eyes, still smiling. But the smile slipped off my face. Below his name, I read, "Authorized Representative. Home & Auto. Life & Health."

Well, one thing was certain: I had seen a professional at work, no doubt about it....[11]

Published in the New York–based *The New Russian Word* (*Novoe russkoe slovo*), the piece was soon reprinted in Moscow's prestigious Literary Gazette. However, seeking publication in English, I found that the punchline of the story didn't work for American editors. One of them took pains to explain the reason for his rejection of the piece. Unlike the story's protagonist, he guessed right away who the American man in the story was. From his point of view, it was impossible to assume the man was interested in the storyteller as a prospective friend.

It took me a while to see that the editor was right. The very semantics of the word "friend" in Russian and English isn't quite the same. The way the word is used in English means only a "buddy" (*priyatel'*). That is why an émigré acquaintance of mine was amused when his six-year-old daughter came back from the playground one day and announced that she "just made a friend." Back in our homeland, a friend wasn't just a buddy with whom you hang out, go to a soccer game or another spectator sport, or spend your leisure time hunting or fishing. Friendship for the Russians is an extremely important social institution, often even more so than the family. A circle of friends is formed at a young age, in school or college. Often, it is a lifetime attachment. Russians keep friendship in a much higher place in the system of social values than Americans.

There were cultural and sociological reasons for that. Russia's friendship, as it developed in Soviet times, with perennial shortages of things of the first necessity and oppressive state institutions, was a way to withstand the state's pressure and help each other for the sake of survival. As the character in the Russian movie *Adam's Rib* (1991) sums it up, "Communism is when you have a friend who is a butcher." Most times, it was a barter-based relationship. An American woman married to a Russian man sums up what she found through her experience in the following way, "A [Russian] male friend is a brother, a drinking companion, a soulmate, and a bulwark against the outside world."[12] An American observer, Victor Ripp, finds Russian friendship "more similar to war camaraderie than to the Western kind of social friendships—no wonder because Russian life was always a kind of war" (*ibid.*).

In America, it is highly advisable not mixing friendship with finances because of possible hard feelings, resentment, a sense of obligation, awkwardness, and boundary issues. Mostly, that would be incomprehensible in the former Soviet Union. We all tried to help each other survive. To get by until one's payday, there was no other way but to borrow money from your friends. Of course, you'd reciprocate when they were in a tight spot.

Thus, friendship in Soviet life was often a closer relationship than even family ties. In contrast, in America, friendship is presumed to be a respectful association between two individuals, each of whom strives to live up to the mandated self-sufficiency and self-reliance. Such a relationship could be described, to borrow the title of the American bestseller around the time of my emigration, as "I'm okay and you're okay." No matter what, you're expected to stay on your own two feet, to take care of your chores yourself.

The following episode, related to me by a fellow immigrant from the former Soviet Union, could serve as an illustration of that cultural discovery. He was going on vacation. Since their street was to be cleaned the next day, he left the keys to his car to his American friend (who lived nearby) and asked him to move the car to the other side of the street the next day. When the man returned from his trip, there was a ticket on the windshield of his car to pay a fine. When he brought it to his American friend, he just brushed it off, saying off-handedly, "Sorry, I forgot." That's it! The Russian newcomer realized he had crossed the line of American friendship. The episode helped him understand that, for their friendship to continue, when handling his personal affairs, he must rely only on himself. It's none of his American friend's business to take care of his chores. That seemed to be the unshaken foundation of American friendship.

While, like everywhere else in the world, the concept of friendship is dear to Americans, it is often tested by high mobility related to employment. If a branch of the company you work for opens in another state, say, in Texas, and you have to move there, the fact that you have an old friend nearby in New Jersey, well, that's tough luck. In contrast, for a Russian contemplating a much more dramatic relocation, like emigration, having close friends staying behind could be a considerable obstacle.

The concept of sticking to old friendships, often at the detriment of acquiring new ones, was very strong in Russian culture. The Russian proverb "An old friend is better than two new ones" found its way into the work of the famous Russian poet Eugene Evtushenko:

> What's that, new friends?
> It's better—
> A new enemy.
> An enemy can be new,
> But a friend—
> Oh, a friend must only be an old one.[13]

It is also customary for Russian friends to cry on each other's shoulders (the Russian equivalent is) "crying in each other's vest" (*poplakat'sia v zhiletku*), complaining about life's misfortunes and injustices.

While being an asset in everyday immigrant life, in the limbo of displacement, of the uncertainty of daily life in the new land, the institution of friendship was used to fulfill other, not-so-glamorous needs of a fragile human soul, of which the following story makes fun.

"One Should Cherish Friendship"

In emigration, you don't have too many friends. You have to nourish and treasure whatever friendship you might have. Boris and I have been acquaintances for (can it be?) twenty years already. We live in different cities and see each other rarely, but we do sometimes talk on the phone.

A few days ago, he called me and asked, as usual:

"How's it going?"

"Well," I sighed, "Nothing good to report, that's for sure."

"What's happening?" my friend became animated.

"Well, *The New York Times* commissioned me to do an article and...."

"Why in the world do I call you?" Boris asked. "Every time I give you a buzz, you give me grief. Are you truly a friend of mine? Haven't you ever noticed that the words 'friend' and 'friendly' are related? You always get me upset. *The Times* never called me to write for them. Only once they rang me up. Inviting me to subscribe...."

"You didn't hear me out," I said, not to embitter the man any further. "They did commission the article, but I made a mess of it. And they turned it down. They didn't publish it."

"That's better already," my friend uttered a bit more warmly. "Yes, better...."

"Yeah," I added, feeling relieved. "They paid me a kill fee, and that's it...."

"There you go again!" Boris said. "They didn't print your article, but you got paid anyway! What a smooth operator! ... I don't know why I call you! You always have to tell me something rotten. Now you've soured my mood just like that.... Not only my mood but perhaps even our long-term friendship."

I felt he was about to hang up.

"Wait, wait," I cried out, "I have lots of trouble."

"Well, then, what?" he said with little hope.

"The other day, an emigre journal besmirched my name for no reason."

"And so, so?" my friend became animated. "Tell me more...."

"You know, the entire article like a tub of cold water poured all over me.... Even back in Russia, nothing like that ever happened to me."

"And you think this cheered me up?" my friend asked in a gloomy voice.

"It didn't?" I asked, worrying.

"Of course not. Now when anyone hears your name, they'll begin whispering about you."

"So, what's so good about that?"

"The thing is that, at first, they'll ask each other, 'Is he the one whom they cursed in the magazine...' And then they'll forget who did what to whom. The only thing that will remain in their minds is your name. They'll remember it. And do you know what it is when someone's name is repeated often, you idiot? It's called 'fame.' And you try to tell me it's your misfortune. I haven't called you for a month. And now you've killed off the incentive to do it for an even much longer time...."

And he hung up.

I called back right away:

"Sorry," I said, "I didn't do it on purpose. I didn't think you would see what happened to me that way.... I was carried away by emotion. It wasn't that pleasant for me when I read that damn article. I thought my telling you about the incident would cheer you up. Forgive me.... What else? ... Ah, I just got fired," I said. "Now I'm unemployed!"

I heard a dial tone. I redialed and said with alarm:

"Boris, my dear friend, did I make you angry again? Now, I take it, you feel sympathy for me, don't you? Well, what can I do.... It's not so terrible after all. I'll live on unemployment checks for a while."

Again, he hung up. I called him back right away and begged him:

"At least tell me, for God's sake, what did I do this time that made you hate me? Now I'm in real trouble, am I?"

"What's there to explain, you lucky son of a bitch? I've been

dreaming of being let go for a year. To live on unemployment benefits for a while. To get some rest.... To fly off to Europe. On my vacation, there's not much time to enjoy it. What haven't I tried to be let go!
On my job, I stopped doing anything altogether. I walked around the
office with my hands in my pockets. I wouldn't touch any work with a
ten-foot pole on purpose. But my supervisor didn't pay any attention. I
have a long work history; the boss doesn't want to pay me my severance
for firing me. He's waiting for me to quit on my own. In desperation, I
cursed my supervisor up and down. Any other sort of man in his place
would have chased me out right away. That dog knows what I want—
and he doesn't fire me no matter what I do! He only smiles, the worm. I
can't take it anymore! ... And here you are telling me it's handed to you
on a silver platter! You're a lucky dog!" he snarled.

I felt I'd lose a friend if I didn't come up with something dramatic.

"Boris, my friend!" I shouted into the phone. "Wait for a second,
don't hang up on me. Give me time to gather my thoughts. I have lots
of problems. I am sure I'll find one that will cheer you up. OK, I got
it! After all, friendship is the most valuable thing. Y'know, things
between me and Masha are terrible. She told me that no later than the
New Year she's going to leave me."

There was silence from the other end of the telephone. I sighed
with relief.

"You're such a bastard, Volodya," snapped Boris's voice. "And my
hidden enemy. You only pretend to be my friend. Look at you! I can't
get rid of my bitch, no matter what I do. And with you, your wife takes
the initiative. You are a rat, that's for sure."

And he hung up on me for good.

Now I sit and torture myself about what I could tell him to cheer
him up. Emigration is a tough road. There aren't many friends. You've
got to nourish and treasure friendship. I've been friends with him for
twenty years. How many like him do I have here, in America! ...[14]

It turned out that nothing of that sort of understanding of friendship is acceptable to Americans. An emigre colleague of mine shared
with me how puzzled he was when, over lunch, he began complaining
about life's unjust battering, his American friend told him with compassion, but firmly, "Well, the worst thing we can do is to depress each
other."

Another frontier unknown in Russian culture is that conditioned
by privacy. Russian friendship is built along gender lines, and gender
solidarity is taken for granted. In male-to-male private conversations, it
is not unusual for a man to brag about his sexual exploits, to disclose to

another man the intimate details of his encounters with a woman. Such conversations are part and parcel of Russian male socializing.

I learned quickly that any inquiries of this kind are gross trespassing of one's privacy in the new land. When I asked an American friend whether our mutual acquittances were lovers, he stopped me right away and made me aware I had stepped into a no-entry zone: "Come on, Emil, that's none of our business."

Another unexpected pitfall of émigré friendship came from the opened opportunities to realize one's abilities to their fullest in America. Not without malice, Soviet propaganda asserted that people in America find a common language with each other only if they belong to the same stratum of people conditioned upon their income levels. (To some extent, this was true for Soviet society as well.) An immigrant story that developed in front of my eyes made me see firsthand that a considerable difference in earnings could separate two inseparable friends.

Two Russian men—let's call them Yuri and Vlad—were close friends since their college years back in the USSR. It so happened that, having arrived in America, one of them, Yuri, became the owner of a car repair shop, and the other worked for him as a mechanic. Although Yuri offered Vlad a managerial position, the man brushed it off. He preferred working with his own hands, rather than with his head.

They stayed friends. Came a long holiday weekend. They decided to spend it together with their families in a nearby resort town. However, it turned out that all that Vlad could afford was to stay with his family at the local Motel 6, while Yuri could place his wife and their little son at the Hilton. Came the dinner time. One of them took his family to a Jack-in-the-Box, and the other friend to a Smokehouse restaurant. Their paths in American life diverged bit by bit until they each went their way.

The time came, however, when I befriended an American man. He not only helped me to avoid many cultural pitfalls but also taught me what American friendship is all about. He also piloted me in the sea of another cultural territory, the terra incognita of another highly valued human relationship that pertained to finding a suitable mate.

9

"On the bumpy road to love"

As I recall it now, the idea of launching my dating campaign belonged to Marty, my closest American friend.

I needed to look for a new life partner after my marriage broke up. I accept my share of the blame for the break-up, though I think no one is to blame if we stayed together as long as we did by mutual consent.

At the start of that new development, I tried to follow the method of Heinrich Heine, to use whatever literary skills I had to ease the pain. "Of my big sorrows," Heine wrote, "I make little verses, and taking wing, they fly away."

An episode of the American movie *Everything You Always Wanted to Know About Sex* inspired my playful, perhaps facetious approach to lessening the heartache. As a result, the following brief story formed in my head.

"Jerry's Girlfriend"

Out of the blue, I got a call from my American friend Jerry. It had been six months, more or less, since we had been in contact. The poor guy was forever complaining about how much his marriage depressed him, and how there was no way out of his situation. He was sick and tired not only of his career-obsessed wife but of the entire female gender. But I didn't much delve into his family squabbles. In the end, it was his private affair, none of my business. Although I was a willing ear. My family life has also been giving me a headache. The only thing I'd hear from my wife was scolding me either for not doing what I should do or doing what I was told in the wrong way.

And now this call....

"Come on over. It's been so long since we've seen each other. We've got so much to talk about," he said, in great humor.

His life must have taken a turn for the better. Well, thank God, I thought. The last time we met, he'd ended up getting into a frenzy over his wife. Maybe by now, they'd worked things out.

110

"Is there something new with you?" I said.

He burst out laughing.

"I have a truckload of news. Not only had I solved many of my problems, but I also don't even live at my old address. I've moved to the suburbs."

He named a town that was miles outside the city. This surprised me since I thought I knew my friend. He'd always seemed a city dweller at heart.

Yes, Jerry had left his wife and now had a new girlfriend. That was the first thing confirmed when I went to visit him.

"She's calm, she does what I tell her, never utters a word. Not to mention, she's attached to me," Jerry added, happy and a little plumper than I remembered him. He sucked on his pipe and rocked back and forth on his rocker. "No hysterics," he said, "no scenes, no threats to leave me at the drop of a hat. Never a peep of backtalk. Her only shortcoming: she can't cook."

"But that I can do myself, from my army days. In everything else, she's a grown man's dream. Let the young guys have their complicated women with their whimsical streaks. Those guys haven't sown their wild oats yet; peace isn't so precious to them."

I must confess that I was more than a little curious. I tried to imagine what this new mate of Jerry's looked like. I checked around, hoping to see her portrait somewhere. But on the walls, I saw only a few landscapes, only meadows with chamomile flowers.

"Her favorite paintings," Jerry said, catching my glance. "She doesn't like to be photographed. Whenever I think I've persuaded her, as soon as she sees the camera, she turns away. It's a shame since she's cute. What am I saying? She's gorgeous! Huge languid eyes.... But you'll see for yourself soon enough."

"Not to mention the emotional side," Jerry continued. "As I'm sure you know, I've always dreamed of a wife who's what you'd call a 'total woman.' Most likely, I still yearn for the mother absent from my earliest years. At any rate, I got lucky." He sighed in deep contentment.

"I don't know if you'll see what I mean when you meet her. But you're maybe one of the very few of my friends broad-minded enough. You could say I'm one of those pioneers discovering alternative paths. I pave the way to the natural solution to the eternal conflict between the sexes. I strengthen the ecosystem, bringing us closer to nature."

He checked his watch.

"She's never late," he said. "An enviable quality. She never hurries, yet she's always on time."

At that moment, a strange, if remotely familiar, sound rang out in the hall: the tinkling of a small bell. I turned and couldn't believe my eyes. Of course, I expected no ordinary girl; Jerry was eccentric enough that nothing would surprise me. This was just too much. Nodding her head, paying me no attention, Jerry's heartthrob moved right past me. She went up to Jerry, who offered his cheek for a kiss. She missed and poked her thick lips into his ear, which she nibbled. In response, Jerry gave her an affectionate hug and slapped her on her spacious back.

To be tactful, I averted my eyes and looked out the window. An extraordinary sight presented itself. Strolling by the houses were not ladies and their dogs, as you'd expect in the American suburbs, but staid, middle-aged men walking sheep, goats, donkeys, and other domestic livestock on light leashes. The lambs were immaculately clean and wore attractive pink plumed collars.

"You like your coffee black or with milk?" Jerry said, pouring a cup of coffee for me. "At our place, milk is never a problem, of course. Always fresh, with no chemicals or preservatives like milk in the supermarket. You know, I've always been skeptical about politics. But the recent events in my life have forced me to reconsider my views. Those jerks from the local government, those obtuse, barefaced bureaucrats—why should they decide my fate? I've consulted with my girlfriend, and with her approval, I'm running for a seat on our town council. Of course, my chances this year are slight, but, as you've noticed, our numbers are growing here," he said with significance, "are thriving. The scales are tipping in our favor.

"Even in this liberal community, we have more than our share of problems. For instance, while we've accustomed most of the adults to our style of living and sexual preference—some, we know, even sneak a glance at us from time to time in secret envy—the bratty kids still throw rocks at our girlfriends. But that's okay, it's just a matter of time.... One day they'll grow up, get married, and sing a different tune.

"I can't say we've solved all the problems of marriage," he continued. "In our community, the freedom to choose one's partner is far from absolute. Take one of our residents, for example, a solid citizen, the vice president of a body lotion company. He falls in love with a puma he saw in a road-side zoo. He bought it and brought her home to live. But his neighbors told him that it was illegal to keep it; they worry. Though the man swears his puma's always well-fed, and he would make sure it attacks no domestic animals."

I returned to my apartment in the city, thinking about what I'd seen and heard at Jerry's. Of course, he was right about a lot of things. But such a turn was just too bizarre. Besides, I couldn't accept a marriage in which there was no intention of having children. Though it was true, they could still adopt.

My visit to Jerry had so fascinated me I forgot I'd promised my wife to come home early and take her to a new movie. With a pounding heart, I imagined what awaited me, how I'd hear about it all that evening and for at least the next three days. I sighed and recalled that since childhood I'd been enchanted by the natural grace of gazelles.

I wonder: do they breed in captivity?[1]

If you believe the great German poet, his use of his art made light of his sorrows. It hardly helped me. In your midlife, it's hard to fill the void.

"Well, Emil," my American friend Marty said one day as we were resting on the balcony of his apartment in New Jersey, overlooking Manhattan from the other side of the Hudson River. "I think it's time for you to stop sitting on your hands and move on."

He stretched out his long legs, looking at me while we were consuming a delicious Spanish omelet of his own making. Marty was a terrific cook. In fact, after his early retirement, he took private lessons from a French chef and, from time to time, treated me to his meals, exquisite, both to the eye and the palate.

"Almost four years," I said. "I think I'm finally over it. There's no need to rub it in."

"I'm joking, Emil. What I want to say is that I don't see why you don't move on and find yourself a nice woman. You're ... how old are you? Forty-six, forty-seven?"

"Forty-nine in December."

"Okay, forty-nine," he waved his hand as if saying, let's take the worst-case scenario. "Granted, you're not a spring chicken anymore. However, you still have a fighting chance to improve your personal life. You're gainfully employed. Healthy. Not bad looking.... Let me tell you, pal, today a straight, intelligent, and cultured man like yourself is at a premium. You have an incredible variety of women to choose from. There should be hundreds ... what did I say? Thousands of them who want you right now."

And he waved his hand toward the Manhattan skyscrapers. My eyes followed his gesture. There, on the other side of the Hudson River, stood a metropolis packed with hot-blooded, passionate women, just looking for an opportunity to meet me and throw their arms around me.

It made me feel good. I listened to what Marty had to say on any subject, not only on dating. He was my guide through many complexities of the American way of life. He was a voice of reason and common sense. So, if he said it was time for me to move on, he knew best. A general observing the field of the coming battle, I shaded my eyes against the blazing sun and looked in the same direction. I read somewhere in an American magazine the statistics: for a woman over forty, the age I was interested in, the chances of marrying were equal to being run over by a car. It was a cruel way to underscore the plight of women of that age group, but it gave me hope I might save at least one of them from being crushed under the wheels.

I didn't know the first thing about dating in America. Didn't know where to begin. I had been in the country for over ten years, but I'd arrived already married. When I lived in Russia, the Soviet Union was still going strong, and dating was a simple matter. Since we had little space on our own, we'd meet girls in the streets, have dates with them in city parks, and make love in hallways. Here, in America, all my youth experience was of no use.

I didn't even know where to begin. I had been introduced to my ex-wife by mutual acquaintances. My social circle in America was limited. I was no longer young enough to follow my old country's way, where it was quite acceptable to just run up to a young female in the street and say, "May I introduce myself?" And I understood that in America, a female accosted that way would call the police for protection.

So, I didn't even know where to begin.

"Oh, c'mon!" Marty said when I expressed my dismay. "Here," he threw me a copy of *New York Magazine*. "Look at the personals. Trust me, there are hundreds of appreciative women waiting for you."

I scanned a few pages of the ads.

"Marty!" I said. "What a pleasant surprise! I can't believe it. They all want me. Look, I fit their requirements. They all want a man who is cultured, caring, thoughtful, successful...."

"No, Emil," Marty said in the voice of a doctor telling his patient that his biopsy showed positive. "You're not successful."

"What do you mean?" I said. "I came to this country with a hundred bucks in my pocket. Now I live in a co-op building with a garage. I got my American Ph.D. in Slavic literatures from the University of California. I published three books.... I..."

"Spare your breath, Emil," Marty said. "'Successful' in America means making good money. Trust me on this. You're not successful. Yes, you're a published author, but your books are scholarly. Are any of them on *The New York Times* bestsellers list?"

At this moment, I recalled a chat I had with an American middle-aged man sitting next to me on the Santa Monica beach. When he learned that I was a fresh-off-the-boat immigrant, he asked me about my plans in America. I told him I applied to UCLA grad school to study Russian literature. He sighed and said with sympathy in his voice, "I see ... you want to be poor...."

"Look at the brighter side, Emil," Marty continued. "You're free from worrying that a woman is interested not in you, but your money."

That's what I like about America. There is always room for every kind of person, even in matrimonial affairs.

That was how the whole thing started. Marty becoming my love guru was like winning the lottery for me. I couldn't wish for a better advisor because he was perfectly qualified for it. Unlike me, a Russian-born foreigner, he was a red-blooded American and knew American women. (I'm tempted to say here "better than me," but it wouldn't be true; I knew zilch.)

Besides, he practiced what he preached. For the time I knew him, after his divorce, he twice lost girlfriends to the vagaries of life and female hearts. Each time, it took him only two weeks to empty his heart of break-up bitterness. He poured it out from his system, as decisively as, in the car shops, they pour out old dirty oil from a motor and replace it with fresh oil. He'd soon find another lady friend.

I studied personal ads in magazines. Marty helped me to understand their lingo. I scanned them, often getting excited as I read the profile of a prospective lady. Every one of them seemed to be the one.

"Not so fast," Marty cautioned me. "Hold your horses."

And he poured cold water on me. He warned me that a lot of catfishing was going on in these ads. For example, he explained to me that, if a woman states that she is "cuddly," there is a good chance that she is fat. "Romantic" could mean "needy and clingy," and I should better stay away from her as far as I could. "Old-fashioned" might stand for not caring about sex; she may allow her lover to touch her once in a dark blue, or even black, moon. "Outgoing and fun-loving" could denote either annoying and talkative, promiscuous, or both. "Open-minded" could signify being desperate, ready to throw herself at any man that fate would send her way. "Spontaneous" may well turn out to signify that you would never know what to expect from her, and "provocative" could read just one thing: she is capricious.

Seeing that I was becoming discouraged, Marty stopped and laughed: "The truth of the matter is that, alas, men aren't better in that respect, either. There's a lot of catfishing in their ads as well.... But let's not be negative. I'm sure there are plenty of good women over there. Why not try to meet somebody in person? Then there would be no need for guesswork. Keep your eyes peeled, Emil. You might get lucky that way sooner than you think."

When I started dating, I failed miserably. The main reason for that was that I brought with me a culturally pre-conditioned attitude toward the female gender. As I mentioned already, the last time I dated, I was in my twenties and took to dating as a romantic adventure, not even thinking about what would happen after the first date. Being a romantic fellow, I felt then that a young woman expected me to show my affection for her very early, at the first opportunity, to hug her and maybe even give her a little kiss. Now, already in my late forties, I dismissed this strategy as inappropriate.

Yet, the problem lay deeper. The thing was that, in my old country, romantic relationships were expected to be patriarchal. From the very first encounter, you were to show that you were an alpha male, taking care of the woman along the lines of old-fashioned chivalry. You should open a door for her and pull out a chair for her. When going upstairs, you should be one step behind her, and going down, a step ahead, in case she loses her balance. When dining, you were to pour her water when needed and, by all means, she shouldn't fill up her wine glass herself. Also, you're expected to be a gentleman and pay for dinner with a woman. It didn't obligate her to be intimate with you. The reason for such a cultural situation was simple: the buying power of women in Soviet society was, overall, not on par with that of males.

Way before stepping on the dating warpath, I realized that I was on unfamiliar cultural terrain. Over the first years of my academic life, attending scholarly conferences in America, I'd rush to give my female colleague a helping hand in handling either a stack of books she purchased from the publishers' booths at the conference or getting into her winter coat, holding it up for her. Most of the time, the reaction was one of raised eyebrows. One of them, knowing my background, smiled and told me I should relax: she wasn't handicapped and capable of taking care of herself.

In the first steps of my dating campaign, I also made many mistakes based on my hang-ups, my preconceived notions, and even prejudices of which I wasn't aware. Every time I recall the following episode of my dating life in America, I shudder in embarrassment.

As with others, on our first get-together, we met in a café.

She was tall, broad-shouldered, fair-haired, and gray-eyed. To melt the ice of meeting with a stranger, we briefly told each other about ourselves. In response to my story, she told me she was born in Dusseldorf, her marriage to an American man brought her to the States, and, as it was in my case, her marriage proved unsuccessful.

When she ended her story, she smiled. And something must have triggered a reflex in my brain. I decided not to see her anymore.

It took me some time for the reason for such a drastic decision to reach my consciousness. It had nothing to do with the real woman I met but, as I understood much later, everything to do with her being German and her look fitting the stereotype that had been lodged deep in my consciousness from my early childhood days.

I was only a few years old when the war with Germany broke out. I still remember the whistling and howling of bombs during the air raids and hiding with my mother in the bomb shelter of our building on Deribasovskaya Street in Odessa.

Then my mother and I took the train and, for several months, fled from the German troops rolling toward the city. On the way, our train was bombed, and my mother was wounded. Decades later, I can still see her face, with blood running over it.

When the war ended, I learned not only that my uncle, my father's younger brother Lazar, had died on the Kursk Bulge, shot by a German sharpshooter, but also that my grandfather Uri, on my father's side, who failed to flee from the city of Minsk where he lived, was bayoneted by German paratroopers.

No less tragic was the fate of my grandfather on my mother's side, Wolf, who, together with other Odessa Jews, was driven into a barn and burned alive. My aunt Judith, my father's older sister, and all four of her children, my little cousins, perished in the Minsk ghetto.

I already knew that post-war Germany denounced its Nazi past and recognized and accepted its historical responsibility for wartime atrocities to a much greater extent than Russia did about its bloody communist rule.

However, I couldn't help it. The fact that the woman was German, and her appearance fit the image of a "blond beast," the Nietzschean term the Nazis interpreted as his endorsement of the racial superiority of the German Aryan type, was my brain's deciding factor. That image was ubiquitous at the time of the war and years afterward in all Soviet war movies. The woman sitting in front of me in that café resembled those images.

Later, I felt ashamed of it. The woman was born after Hitler shot himself, and here I was blaming her for the faults of her nation and punishing her with rejection. I never was able to get rid of my Jewish complex and call her. It's a pity. She could have been the one with whom I'd spent the rest of my life. Well, to tell the truth, I was afraid of that very thought.

Perhaps, after I met the German woman, in a knee-jerk reaction, I swung in the opposite direction and answered the following ad I spotted in the personals of *New York Magazine*. It read, "Soviet Jewish woman,

45, a painter with eclectic interests, is looking for a man whose key attribute is intellect."

This was refreshing. I sensed a kindred spirit. She was independent. She didn't mimic American ads with all those phony "vivacious," "cute," and "leggy"—all the "meat market nicknames," as Marty characterized them.

I didn't expect the woman I was looking for to be beautiful. I was wary of an attractive woman. She could be spoiled by the easiness with which she attracted men and, therefore, could be as flat-spirited as day-old open soda water in a bottle.

I sent a note with my telephone number to the woman who placed the ad. In a week, on Saturday around 5 p.m., she called.

"My name is Rima," she said. "I got your letter today. I liked it, and I'm calling you right away."

Then she informed me that, for four years, she has lived with her boyfriend. They are still under the same roof.

"I ate his potatoes and wrote my book," she said. "The first three years we had a beautiful relationship. It was when I began working on my book that things got sour between us. He is a man of limited mind. He expresses no interest in my writing.... Now he wants me out of his apartment. It was he who paid for the ad. It was too expensive for me. Now the case is in court. They would have to kick me out. I'm looking for an apartment."

"What kind of book are you writing?" I was curious. "A novel? A non-fiction book?"

"Hell knows. I've shown it to someone. He read and told me that this is an *ex-po-se* or something like that."

"Wait a minute. Aren't you a painter?"

"Yeah, I am. But I wanted to write something to understand what was going on, and I got involved. Now it's finished. It's about a hundred fifty pages."

"Well, what do you plan to live on? You're a painter. Do your painting sell?"

"No.... I have my style, of course. But American art galleries want something similar to those painters they sell well. My work is original. So nobody wants them. I've made around a hundred of them. No, I have other ideas. Some time ago, I worked in real estate. And I learned you can make good money if you buy foreclosed homes. I could make this money and write.... Also, I'm thinking of renting an office and telling people I'm a counselor."

Her frankness was startling.

"Well, it's not that easy to make them come to you," I said. "How will they know you exist?"

"I understand that many won't. But there will be some who are glad to talk to anyone. If I make a thousand business cards and give them to the doormen of the adjacent buildings, I think I can get about ten clients."

"But it's not a reliable income, as far as I know."

"Yeah, I know. But I don't care. It's not for the money. Let them pay me little or nothing at all. I'd hear them out and write a book. I kind of began enjoying writing books."

"Well…"

"I have other ideas. I learned Congress has fellowships—like thirty-five thousand bucks for someone like me who wants to write and has no means. I'm in the process of finding out how to get one of these fellowships. I'll apply and get one."

The conversation was entertaining. The admixture of the woman's shrewdness and naivete amused me.

She was talking far too long for my taste, and I felt I should try to bring the conversation to some closure.

"What do you expect from a man you're looking for?" I said.

"Money," she said with a slight snort. "I want them to support me while I write. I have ideas for two more books."

"Wait a minute," I said, quite amused. "Didn't you say in your ad that you are looking for a man with intellect?"

"Yes, but I thought that, if he is smart, he's already made his money."

"Well, Rima," I said, amused and entertained by the conversation and feeling almost sympathy for this frank and unabashed user of a woman. "I'm not in the category of a man who has money. I have just a regular salary."

"Take out a second mortgage on your home," she said with an already familiar slight snorting.

I laughed.

"Listen," she said. "Maybe we can be just friends. I've put some extra pounds on lately."

Before hanging up, I asked: "Were you ever married?"

"Oh, officially hundreds of times. Men needed exit visas from Russia to Israel, then from Israel to the States…." She spoke in a jocular tone. "In reality—never."

She was referring to the early 1970s, the first time when the Soviet Union, the country that locked off its citizens for several decades from the outside world, allowed some people to apply for emigration. To save political face, the powers that be made believe that people would never even think of leaving the glorious Soviet Union if not for their need to join their relatives. Therefore, the Jewish ethnic minority, the "majority of which lives in a capitalist country," could apply for emigration. Many Russians were ready to pay substantial sums of money for bogus marriages with those lucky single men and women of the lucky minority. I remembered the Soviet-era underground joke, "A Jewish wife is not a luxury, but a means of transportation."

There were other reasons, to quote a famous American song, I "never met [other women] on the bumpy road to love." They all stemmed from the fact that I was still a stranger in a strange land. Despite nearly ten years of living in America, I failed to read cultural signals and got myself into embarrassing situations.

The following episode is the best illustration of my wake-up call. After many months of hesitation, Marty talked me into placing an ad in the *New York Review of Books*. Scanning personal ads, I learned something about the cultural differences between Russia and America. According to the ads, all Americans, without exception, are, in alphabetical order: "accomplished, beautiful, cultured, dynamic, enthusiastic, first-class (also 'a real first class'), generous, humorous, independent, jovial, knockouts, loveable, multifaceted, nurturing, outstanding, passionate, questing, reliable, successful (they vary from simply 'successful' to 'very successful,' to 'extremely successful,' to 'exceptionally successful'), 'terrific,' 'upbeat,' 'vibrant,' 'wondrous,' 'youthful,' and 'zestful'—to name a few."

You cannot go wrong with these people. No matter whose ad you respond to.

As to a Russian personal ad, it may well begin with "From the outset of my life, I was down on my luck. I was born with one leg longer than the other, so if not careful, I end up walking in circles. I lost my father when I was four and my mother when I was seven. Twice I fell victim to fire and flood. Last summer, I was thrice struck by lightning, and a mad dog bit me." And so on ... the Russians appeal to a compassionate soul.

Of course, I composed my ad along American lines. However, I didn't want to exaggerate any of my qualities. American men didn't have any problem doing it. One man's ad in *NYRB* began with "Incredibly Gifted...." Give me a break, mister! The rule of truth in advertising was something that I felt responsible for. I wrote, "DJM, attractive, intelligent, stable, non-smoker, 47, physically fit, my children grown, seeks a woman of similar qualities between ages 40 and 45."

(I hasten to note that the mentioning of my intelligence was based on my self-assessment *before* I undertook my search for a mate in America.)

Two weeks later, I received half a dozen letters. One of them, without a photo, intrigued me and stood out in comparison with the others. It was typed on both sides of a small sheet of blue-lined paper. Here it is in its entirety, with punctuation and spelling preserved:

Dear Guttenberg (Great place for a published author to live.) I live 1 mile from Brooklyn Bridge, easy parking, convenient?), Often published (I have 4 published books, non-fiction, I hope?), European (I've visited Europe & St. Thomas: 7 & 8 times, 1–4 months & 2 weeks each, respectively). I'm fluent in German, English, Spanish, and Body Language. From '91-now, I've been in Atlanta 7 times. I made my only long weekend trip in 94 for a college exhibit. It was too rushed. I'm laid-back. Summer '95, my 2nd show, 2 weeks, was more relaxing. In 92, I was in Montreal. In '94, I went from the Dominican Republic to Florida.. I prefer the Dominican Republic: San Domingo, 6 trips; Santiago–1. I made virgin trips to Central & South Americas. I love Puerto Rico: Ponce & Mayaguez twice. I made the 16th trip in July to San Juan. I loved Panama City, Panama. I started in '97 in Salvador. After 13 years of war, they're at peace. In mid–May, I am off to Guatemala. All non–European trips were about 2 weeks. Professor (more in common), smoke-free, grown kids. Hopeful plus. Warmly humorous and hotly sensuous (Unlike some younger women, I am no tease. I am responsible for it. That is how I have so much fun, no worries) seeking with intriguing NYRB ad (since you never give your looks at all-precise height? Age? Weight?) for a woman (Me, I hope, depending strictly on your answers to the above?):

I'm clean, curvy, cute, single, slim, Barnard female WASP, 44 years, 36C, 22", 32", 110 lbs., 5'7", natural light blond hair. I want a healthy, caring, kind, honest, reliable, and financially successful man. Discreet sensual fun assured. I live in Long Island City. The best view of the East River is from my forest- or garden-like bedroom, fresh-cut flowers, music, me, candles, green carpet, curtains, walls. I laid, made, painted them, and finished light oak furniture's virgin wood-great hands.

I changed from banking to my 1st career, teaching. It's worth the pay cut, freeing time for my NYU MBA, Mom, decorating & hopefully you. You sound like the most fun of THE 4. My stepdad died in 1980. I spend some weekends in Amherst with Mom. I'm a good daughter. Thank heaven for USAir—hope they don't crash again.

Please send the day phone #, since I can call days, teach nites: Cecilia Ferder, [her address]. Don't worry about your work #. I give pleasure, not embarrassment. If brief talk clicks, we'll make a date at once. I never send it to strangers. That's worse than bars which I always avoid.

Love and lust, (signed) Cecilia.

Something in the letter sounded strange. But, although in places the style was too terse and abrupt, and I spotted a few non-sequiturs, it was extraordinary. Besides her being at times humorous and a bit self-deprecating, an attractive quality in all human beings, I was overwhelmed with the intimacy and sincerity offered from the outset. "Love and lust." Wow!

However, I was not sure of my impressions. Though it has improved over the last few years, my command of English was still not quite the same as that of a native speaker. It's not the words' semantics, but their temperature, so to speak. When upon arrival in America, I got my first job as an assistant in an engineering lab, my supervisor cursed me back and forth for failing to understand some of his instructions. But his curses did not affect me. He shouted, "Dummy," "Blockhead," "Fathead," but I didn't feel offended in the least. I just smiled in response, which enraged him even more. Of course, since then my English has improved, but, in matters of importance, I felt I need to double-check my assessment of English in the ad with a native speaker. Just in case...

So, I called my love guru, Marty, and read him the letter.

He heard me out and said, with respect and admiration toward the author of the letter in his voice: "Okay, Emil. Don't screw up this time! Here's my advice: Call her right away and set up an appointment."

Knowing that my rule for a blind date was to meet at a coffee shop for a cup of coffee, not so much to save money, as not to become stuck in an open-ended evening having dinner with someone who, in a few seconds, turns out to be a complete turn-off. Uncharacteristically for him, Marty sounded a bit patronizing: "This woman deserves special treatment. Think of a very nice place, not a cheap coffee shop. She's worth it. She sounds accomplished, witty, and classy. And what openness! No game playing. If I didn't have [he mentioned the name of his current girlfriend] in my life, I'd be interested in a woman like that!"

Something in the letter, however, still sounded a bit too strange for my Russian taste. But what do I, a foreigner, know about this great country? I should do what the locals say.

Two days later, around 5 p.m., before leaving for the La Guardia airport for my late evening flight to Chicago to give a paper at the annual Slavic Studies Conference, I called Cecilia. Her machine picked up my message. I left my number. She called me right back.

She sounded like her letter—energetic, sophisticated, with a bit of strain in her voice, characteristic of businesspeople. I attributed it to her vocation as an instructor of classes on business transactions, as she informed me when we began talking. She spoke at a brisk pace as if reading a prepared text inflating her voice to add cordiality. That's what I thought. But Marty's voice was still in my ears, "Go for it, Emil. Don't fuck it up."

I opened my conversation with Cecilia with a weather filler.

"It's a bit chilly today," I said.

"Yes, it's cold," Cecilia said, with little inviting notes in her voice. "In weather like this, like to have a man to keep me warm."

It was a bit too forward for my taste, but I was keeping the course prescribed by Marty. I set my mind to set a date with her. Since the area where she lived was unfamiliar to me, I asked her whether she knew a nice place near her home where we could meet. She paused for a moment and then added with intimate aspiration: "I'm a good cook. Why don't I cook for you? We can have a nice dinner at my place."

And she described her apartment in detail—about the wallpaper with flowers and other decorations of her own making....

Wow! That was more than I ever dreamed of. A woman was so sure of her charms that she wants me to skip the boring and stressful blind date ritual, and go straight to a close and cordial relationship, as it should be between adults who have been around the block a few times. This offer of intimacy made me melt. Finally, when I was already dog-tired of American dating games as if to answer my prayers, a woman comes along, who is the very embodiment of domesticity and familial warmth. Tasty food and intimacy, in the highest sense of this word.

I promised Cecilia that I would call her to set up a time as soon as I returned to New York. She agreed since she also wanted to ask me a few more questions.

I arrived at La Guardia airport and found that my flight was delayed because of a snowstorm in Chicago. I had enough time to call Marty. I told him about my conversation with Cecilia.

"I'm going away for a few days to see my cousin in Gainesville, Florida," he said. "After you see her, call me to tell me how the whole thing went for you. I'm sure you'll have a helluva good time. You lucky dog!"

I returned to New York on Thursday at around 3 p.m. and called Cecilia. First, her machine answered, but then she picked up the phone. She recognized my voice. In the same business-cordial tone, she said: "I want to ask you a few questions, Emil. Do you mind? No? That's what I thought.... First, what do you prefer for dinner, meat or fish? I'm more in favor of fish, but if you want..."

"I love fish," I said, already foretasting an evening with a refined woman with a maternal concern for a man's stomach. It was so unlike other American women I met who considered cooking for the man in their life slavery and the steepest moral degradation.

"Fine," Cecilia said and added, in the same breath, as if it was a matter of equal importance as to what kind of food I prefer. "You don't mind my asking whether you have any social diseases?"

Since the question caught me by surprise, at the first moment, I didn't quite understand what she was talking about. What social diseases did she mean? Abnormal shyness? Morbid tendency to close up from an interlocutor? Fear of crowds? But because, when asking this question, Cecilia lowered her voice a bit, I realized what diseases she was concerned with.

I felt blood rush to my face. The woman was so straightforward.... At last, I met a grown-up, without hang-ups, a true woman who did not count the number of dates before going to bed with a man of her liking. During our first conversation, when she invited me to her home and talked about dinner, I have to admit that the possibility of other pleasures of the flesh, besides home-cooked food, did flash in my mind. But now the lady was leaving me no doubt she was talking business, and she didn't want to give me a hard time. After all, she wrote in her letter, "Unlike some younger women, I am no tease." She was consistent; I had to give her credit for that.

"No," I said.

"That's good," Cecilia said. "I also assume that you use latex prophylactics?"

Here I felt I blushed even more. "Well," I said, "if it's necessary..."

"Well, it is," Cecilia said. "And may I ask you my last question? I won't take it personally if you say no."

At this moment, I still couldn't imagine what question she could ask me that I'd say no to. But I was wrong. She had one: "It'll be two hundred dollars, please. Cash, of course. Any problems with that?"

I couldn't talk for a while. After a long pause, Cecilia asked, "Are you there?"

I was dumbfounded. Finally, I was able to utter in a coarse voice: "No, thank you. I'm not interested."

"It's all right," said Cecilia in the same cheerful business tone she maintained during the entire conversation losing no bit of enthusiasm. Not a shade of disappointment. "I don't take it personally. Goodbye."

It took me full few days to come to my senses. In my search for a woman in my life, I never considered seeking the company of a representative of the oldest profession. I never understood some men's fascination with it. I always considered the whole institution of sex for pay humiliating for men. I thought myself attractive enough not to resort to buying a woman's body. Maybe my libido was low, but, no matter how beautiful and fresh she might look, a prostitute had never turned me on. Just the opposite. The very idea of having sex with her was as appalling to me as any other senseless physical exercise. I was looking for a full-fledged relationship, not just sex.

Especially embarrassing for me was that the incident proved that, after living in America for over a decade, I had failed to recognize a woman who wasn't looking for love.

A few days later, Marty returned from his Florida trip, and I told him about Cecilia. He paused for a second and then laughed: "Why didn't you tell her you usually charge for sex yourself?"

"How is it possible that a Barnar graduate, with an NYU MBA, an author, a professor, a world traveler, has such a sideline?"

"What's so surprising?" Marty laughed. "It happens to some people. She caters to educated men only. It's her cut of the market.... Two hundred bucks, home-cooked dinner included? Not a bad deal. In time, when you become her steady customer, she might give you a discount," he chuckled.

I reread Cecilia's letter in disbelief. How could I be so naïve as not to ask myself a logical question: how does a woman offer "love and lust" to a stranger? Now some phrases in her letter got another, more revealing meaning. "I'm on the laid-back track." Her mentioning "teaching nights" on "business transactions" became clear.

Besides, there were some obvious buzzwords, which, in my excitement, I didn't pay attention to. Now I recalled that when I read in her ad "I'm clean," it sounded a bit strange to me. Doesn't everyone in America take showers daily?

And there was that total giveaway phrase "discreet sensual fun assured" that I had seen in *New York Magazine* ads for massage parlors, which, according to the TV program *Hard Copy*, are often euphemisms for underground bordellos. (I paused for a moment, asking myself how come Marty didn't spot it, but then I recalled I read him the letter over the phone. He could have missed it.)

In the background of these straightforward buzzwords, Cecilia's mentioning "great hands" concerning polishing and finishing sounded almost poetically suggestive.

But some other aspects of the letter were still puzzling. Why did she spend half of her letter describing her travel to Central America? To imply that she had been around not only a block but also the globe? That she was as hot as the weather in those equatorial countries she visited? Why did she mention that her apartment is rent-stabilized? Letting me know that she isn't rich, and that's why she has to charge for her services? Why tell me that she's a good daughter? To make me feel that two hundred bucks for a dinner with a woman with a golden heart is a bargain?

Then again, why did she disclose her real name, telephone, and her address right away? Wasn't she afraid of being arrested for practicing an outlawed profession? Or did I miss the latest news, and it had been legalized already?

I'll never get the answers to all these questions.

The incident with Cecilia made me realize that, when it comes to the American dating culture, I was still as blind as a newly born kitten. To stay out of trouble, I should seek the company of women from other cultures. I live near the great City of New York populated by humans of over a hundred nationalities. There, at least I won't make the mistake of assuming I know something about another woman's cultural background, as she might not be aware of mine. Terra incognita versus terra incognita, so to speak.

So, I responded to an ad on the *Match.com* site placed by a lady of Polish background. I informed the lady that I'm Jewish and come from the most Jewish city in the former Soviet Union, Odessa, now Ukraine. Knowing the proliferation of Catholicism in Polish culture, I thought it was a kiss of death.

To my surprise, she found it intriguing and suggested getting together for a brief hello. To spare both of us from the pain of rejection, I invited her to come to my lecture at the college. My class on Russian cinema and society was sizable, with nearly fifty students of a wide range of ages, including retirees that took the course as auditors. The Fall semester had just begun, and I didn't know yet who was who in the classroom.

So, I invited her to come over and sit through the first part of my double-time class. If whatever she would see wouldn't make her leave during the intermission, she was welcome to come up to me and introduce herself.

She did as I suggested. And she came up to me during the break and introduced herself. I offered to have a cup of tea in the nearby French bistro after the class....

As you, my reader, hold this book in your hands, we have celebrated our twentieth anniversary.

PART III

Discovering Self in America

10

Law as a Carriage Drawbar

An early step in adjusting to an unfamiliar environment is to find something recognizable, something to trigger your memory of things past. Moreover, although when leaving my home country, I thought I'd never don my satirist's cap again, it didn't take too long before I pulled that cap back down to my ears.

One day, looking over a new issue of a Russian-language immigrant newspaper, I come across a few ads that puzzle me. I pick up the phone and called the editor. He knows me: I contribute to his paper.

"Sorry to bother you with it," I say, "but I'm dying of curiosity. I cannot figure out what a 'business marriage offer' means. An offer of a joint venture? Here's another one, 'Looking for a sponsoring husband'?"

"No, Emil," the editor chuckles. "These ads are marriage proposals. If a foreigner wants to settle here, one of ours, a Russian immigrant with citizenship status, will file for him or her all the needed papers. If they agree on the dough, of course."

"Wait a minute," I say. "As far as I know, what you are describing to me can get you in trouble with the law in America. It looks like these ads offer to commit a federal offense. It's called 'sham marriage' which could get you up to five years of jail time and a fine of up to $250,000. Other criminal charges may also apply, such as fraud to obtain a visa, harboring an alien, or making a false statement. By the way, all persons who participated in arranging a sham marriage between an alien and a U.S. citizen are also subject to penalties as well."

"Yeah?" says the editor after a brief pause. "Well, I don't care. The paper states that the publisher is not responsible for the paid ads."

Ads of this kind appear in the Russian émigré papers from time to time. Such blatant disregard for the law sounds bizarre, but it is hardly surprising considering the attitude toward the law the ex–Soviets brought with them. Double-dealing, even outright theft of state property, was the daily occupation of a considerable part of the Soviet population. Cheating the state was not a hobby, like collecting stamps or playing Chinese checkers. Almost everyone who was not too lazy was stealing from the state.

However, it would be wrong to assume that Russians are pathological thieves and cheaters. They are open-hearted and honest in their private lives, with their friends and family, but they have no qualms about cheating, giving and taking bribes, or stealing when dealing with the state. Since the state machinery was seen, to borrow the term from a different political context, as the "enemy of the people," the violators of the law did not see their actions as either dishonest or shameful. As if to say, what else is the state for if not to be the subject of deceit?

There were good reasons for that kind of attitude in Soviet times. "Penury doesn't know any law," says the old Russian proverb, a paraphrase of the Latin saying, "Necessity has no law" (*Necessitas non-habite legem*). Often, for many Soviets, there was no other way to survive but to cheat.

Suffering from overwhelming poverty, people stole from the state everything that wasn't nailed down. They filched and socked away anything of any value from their workplace. These kinds of small-time thieves were called "pilferers" (*nesuny*). The people stole from the state, believing that, no matter how much they steal from it, they still won't get their worth back. I still recall a cover of the satirical magazine *Crocodile*: a young worker leaves his factory, a car tire wrapped around his chest. The caption says, "I take what belongs to me. Don't all the factories and plants in our country belong to the working people?"

It would be wrong to assume, however, that such an attitude toward the law by the newcomers to America was the heritage of Soviet times only. An old Russian saying expressed a skeptical sentiment toward the very concept of the law: "The law is like a horse carriage shaft—it would turn wherever you want it" (*Zakon—chto dyshlo: kuda povernul, tuda i vyshlo*). Because, in the country's whole history, it was the state that had held the reins of power, people learned how to finagle their way around government control.[1]

Russian legal nihilism has long historical roots. Until the abolition of serfdom and the reform of the court system in the second half of the nineteenth century, the law did not protect the interests of the vast majority of the country's population, the serfs. The jury system introduced by Alexander II existed only until the October 1917 takeover of power.

For the duration of the Soviet regime, with its kangaroo courts, when a case was decided by three government-appointed officials, it became impossible to prevail against the state during the hearing. (When testifying, there was no swearing on the Bible and asking God for help: any religion was considered "opium for the people," a drug of choice, so to speak.) The law enforcers carried out their masters' orders.

The Soviet-time legal nihilism hardly changed much with the collapse of the communist system. In the mid–1990s, determined to learn Russian at the level of a native speaker, an American student of mine rented an apartment in Moscow for a year. He was flabbergasted one day when, out of the blue, his landlord demanded he pays extra for his room.

"Why?" the student asked. "Have I broken something?"

"No, no," the proprietor said. "It's just the dollar rate against the ruble's gone up."

"Wait a minute," the student said. "Didn't we sign a contract with an agreed rate?"

The landlord shrugged: "Well, yeah, you wanted me to sign some paper, so I did. But now pay up."

During one of my visits to Moscow around that time, I saw that even common sense didn't make the Russians respect any rules and regulations. I was flabbergasted when, seeing me struggling to lock in the safety belt, the taxi driver just waved his hand and advised me not to bother with it.

"Just throw the belt over your chest," he said, making a face. "I don't want to give a traffic cop an excuse to stop me for a violation of those damn safety rules."

A recent memo for Westerners coming to Russia to engage in business activities alerts them to the fact that the Russians have a "complicated attitude toward the law." The memo informs the foreigners that, despite the posted warnings about the prohibition against walking dogs in certain park areas under the threat of a considerable fine, they might see plenty of dog walkers right under these postings. The same goes for puffing cigarettes under the sign "Smoking is prohibited here." To protect the lives (or at least the limbs) of Westerners, the memo also advises them not to take it for granted that the cars would slow down when they step on a marked pedestrian crossing.

But that is concerned with everyday life. In business, giving a bribe to grease the bureaucratic machinery is assumed to be part of the mode of operation in Russia. Thus, my Russian émigré acquaintance revealed to me that a budget for an architectural project includes a kickback, called the "permission fee expenses." They could run up to 25 percent of the project cost.

It would be wrong to assume that Russians are ashamed of their proclivity for breaking the law. Many of them take pride in their nonchalant attitude toward the law; they see it as a manifestation of their innate free spirit. On this account, they consider themselves superior to Westerners. Recently, an émigré friend of mine expressed his dismay when quoting a recent letter from Russia from his old pal who always refers to Americans as being "law-abiding bobbleheads" (*zakonoposlushnye bolvanchiki*).

The Russians perceive their opposition toward any law or regulation as part of the national character, which this popular joke illustrates:

> "How do you make a Russian jump from a bridge?"
> "Just hoist a sign over it, 'Jumping from this bridge is prohibited by law.'"

When I arrived in America, like many other ex–Soviets, I brought with me the customary *blasé* attitude of my homeland regarding any regulations and prohibitions. As a UCLA grad student, one day I drove a visiting professor of our department around the campus. At one point, my passenger looked at me, dumbfounded.

"There was a stop sign over there, Emil," he said, looking back and checking whether he had not been mistaken.

"Ah!" I waved my hand. Sort of, no big deal....

The man looked at me in disbelief. From that moment on, he braced himself, becoming wary regarding his safety.

Former Soviet citizens arriving in America brought with them the only paradigm of the relationship between them and the state they ever knew. They absorbed it with their mother's milk. Even if they were aware of Thomas Paine, the American political activist of the eighteenth century, and his pronouncement informing the colonists that "in a free republic, the law is king," it would hardly impress them. Paine's edict, which echoes Cicero's, the ancient Roman orator's and state leader's dictum "We are slaves of the law to be free" (*Legum servi sumus ut liberi esse possimus*) would fall flat on their ears. "Slaves of the law? Who— we?" "Oh, no! ... We aren't slaves to anyone and anything anymore. We're free at last."

An acquaintance of mine, a freelance journalist who had moved to America in the post–Soviet era, talking about the difficulties she had to overcome, said that she does not receive much help from the Americans. "In America," she said with disdain in her voice, "everything must be by the letter of the law, but ours [Russian immigrants] do help. Semi-legally, but they help."

That is, if the law prohibits doing something, then the desire to help should justify overstepping that law. By using the word "semi-legally," she brushes aside the very concept of law, like shooing away a fly, or even better, a wasp on a hot day, when it tries to land on your sandwich. It never occurs to her it is inconceivable to do something "semi-legally," just as it is impossible to be "semi-pregnant."

One day, sitting in a Brighton Beach café and waiting for a friend to join me, the thought crossed my mind that, for some ex–Soviet newcomers, America was a modern-day Klondike. At the nearby table, two Russian men, a middle-aged father and his teenage son, were dining.

At one point, the father, a tall fellow with thin whiskers, dressed in a suit jacket, yet wearing outsized leather pants and army boots, looked around and pulled something out of his jacket pocket, wrapped it in the table napkin, and showed it to his son. Right at that moment, a glaring ditty of the Russian cabaret repertoire died for a few seconds. The pause was long enough for me to hear the father's proud voice: "Well, see what I just got, sonny.... A six-shooter.... Chrome-plated, mind you.... Look at it! What a beauty! A piece of art, isn't it?"

I doubt he had any criminal intentions in his mind. He enjoyed his gained freedom of doing something he couldn't even think of in his past Soviet life.

Feeling grateful to the country that gave shelter to me and my family, I feel ashamed reading in the papers about many legal trespasses committed by my fellow Soviet immigrants. It is hardly surprising, however, that they fell back into their old habit. They couldn't help but see any state as a cow that, if they approach stealthily, they could milk to their hearts' content. From time to time, American newspapers published news stories, some more embarrassing than others, of Russian immigrants' flagrant violation of the law. Although the police nicknamed the financial shenanigans "Russian mafia" activity, at least initially, they were unorganized. The police's headache, such as the "Odessa mafia," sprouted in the Brighton Beach area of New York City in the mid–1970s and metastasized later into San Francisco and Los Angeles. (Or the Armenian crime group that developed in the Hollywood area of Los Angeles and the city of Glendale.) These fellows were involved in the heavy stuff, such as extortion, fuel and credit card fraud, murder, kidnapping, and narcotics trafficking.

I am talking here though about the run-of-the-mill fraudulent activities reaping the benefits offered by the American government to refugees running from the Communist regime, be it housing for low-income families, subsidized by the city or state, or SSI (Supplemental Security Income), or food stamps—social services unheard of in their homeland socialist state.

To avoid taxation, they worked for cash. It hardly registered in their consciousness that, as the expression "the state are we" goes, all these generous handouts are paid, in fact, by their hosts—the American people.

The protagonist of my story, which appeared on the pages of the *New Russian Word* in New York, is a Russian immigrant who came to America convinced that his Soviet-grown "black-market businessman" talent would find better use in the capitalist society.[2]

As irony has it, one sign of adjustment to a new society is committing a crime specific to that society. One day, my local TV station showed one of our own, an ex–Soviet immigrant, a doctor, being taken away in handcuffs by the police. The man was arrested for being involved in medical insurance fraud.

That episode inspired me to write the following story titled "How I Became an American." It seems I was compelled to turn the tables and level the field. Or was it some weird, defensive impulse to make a point that one of our own was involved not in any "Russian emigres'" crime schemes publicized in the country, but in an indigenous one in which he couldn't ever be involved before stepping on American soil?

The thing is, that while there was no shortage of things ex–Soviets did in their homeland to fight back against the state that had its hands in our every pocket, the crime of milking medical insurance didn't exist under the socialist system. The simple reason for that was that, on the books, medical service was free. Besides reminding the reader of Margaret Thatcher's pronouncement, "There is no such thing as public money; there is only taxpayers' money," it is worth taking a quick look at what that "free medical service" looked like.

In the Soviet Union, if you were sick, despite outstanding specialists in certain areas of medical science, Soviet medicine, designed to protect health and extend the life of the builders of communism, was limping on both legs. For an ordinary citizen, it was often an insoluble problem to see a good doctor, buy scarce medicines, be admitted to a health resort, get baby food, or treat one's teeth under anesthesia.

The free medical care cost a pretty penny. If you were admitted to a hospital and wanted to be treated well, you had to bribe every step of the way—to have clean linens, to be assigned to a reputable surgeon, etc.

They performed surgical operations using old technologies and primitive tools. Many died waiting for the scheduled heart surgery, and disabled people with crutches and prostheses had to stomp on foot to the fifth floor. Often, because of the shortage of hard currency in the state, the only piece of advanced medical equipment bought in the West could be found only in a government hospital.

I am not even talking here about the horrendous cost of lost human lives caused by failing to inform patients about the X-ray doses they received during their treatment or the psychiatric hospitals where healthy people were turned into people with disabilities.

All this knowledge made me think of "the innocent abroad" character who drives the story, which appeared in the New York–based *The New Russian Word*.

"An Incident in a Bank, or How I Became an American"

I don't know how it happened, but a door in our bank, a massive door with a vault lock, the door that led into the safe deposit box chamber, this door began to fall to the floor stretching out its steel springs. Being next to it, I reached out my arm to brace it, attempting to return the colossus to its former, upright position. My arm was of no help, and I braced it with my shoulder.

The door continued to tumble slowly, one might even say, gracefully. The door was hanging over me a few inches from my nose as I descended to the floor. I wanted to scramble out from under it, which would not have been hard, but just then somebody ran up and whispered into my ear:

"Stay there!"

I obeyed out of surprise. I stayed on the floor and went limp. Stretched to the limit of its springs, the door rested on its vault lock wheel and could fall no further. It covered me like a blanket, with the upper edge tucked under my chin. I looked around. The entire staff was looking at me, mouths agape. They all whispered among themselves; I could only hear some chatter:

"What a lucky dog! Wouldn't you know it! Just rolled into the States from his God-forsaken Russia and such a windfall right into his lap! The sheer luck of these immigrants! I wish I could renounce my citizenship and re-enter the country as a refugee...."

I couldn't fathom what was going on. What was there to envy in all of this? The bank floor was made of marble; it wasn't particularly comfortable. I was about to lean on my elbow and crawl out, when Linda, a tall, slim beauty, whom I had long admired from afar, broke away from the crowd, dashed over, and slid under the door.

"Move over," she said, "there's plenty of room for two."

I did not know what to think. I felt my face searing from her nearness. My tongue turned into a molten lump....

"But ... why?"

"For the same reason as you."

I didn't even have time to open my mouth before our supervisor ran in and saw the picture—two of his tellers lying under a door, with only their heads visible. He gasped, clasped his hands to his head, as he always does when desperate, waved his hands in the air like John Travolta, and ran to the telephone.

Meanwhile, the beauty whispered hotly into my ear:

"Do you have a lawyer?"

"A lawyer? ... What for?" I asked, my ears burning from the general idiocy of the situation.

"You won't get much by yourself," she said. "Find a good lawyer. I can recommend mine, Mr. Stickman. That's even more convenient since the accident involved the two of us...."

The supervisor came tearing up to us. He ran around us in quick steps. First, he lay on the floor to the right. Then he did it from the left side. He looked for any visible space between the door and our bodies. Suddenly he roared:

"Get up!"

I strained and scraped my shoes against the floor, trying to get out from under the door. But the beauty grabbed me by the tie, pulled me toward her, and whispered:

"Don't you make a move, silly! He's trying to take you by surprise."

She rolled her eyes and groaned. The supervisor grew even paler and ran for the first-aid kit.

The beauty called after him:

"Call an ambulance! I'm dying! My back's broken!"

The supervisor froze in his tracks and did not make it to the first-aid kit. His breathing, at last, resumed. He clutched at his heart, rushed towards the phone, and called an ambulance. His voice sounded like he needed to be hospitalized himself.

The office had come to a standstill—everyone was too excited: say what you will, it was a diversion from our dull bank existence. Had a robber come in at that moment, not only would he have met no resistance, but they would have filled his sack and shoved him out the door, so he wouldn't keep them from gawking at the spectacle unfolding on the floor.

The ambulance arrived. They gently removed us from under the door, like a cake from the oven, the beauty from one side, and me from the other. She whispered to me in farewell,

"You've got broken ribs and a dislocated hip joint, understand? Stick to that."

I felt awful. A healthy man has got himself stuck in such a crazy situation. It was time to put a stop to this nonsense. As they carefully laid me on the stretcher like a porcelain soup tureen, I lowered one leg to the floor. The paramedic picked it up and lifted it back, saying:

"You don't know your good fortune, man. You're a recent arrival in America and haven't figured things out here yet."

Either he read my name tag, or he guessed by my face, but the paramedic said this so heartfelt that I thought, *Who knows! I've crossed half the globe. Probably the germs aren't the only thing different here. Even the concept of happiness could be different....*

I sighed and went with the flow. If the quickest path to happiness in this country is to do as the locals do, then they know best, and that is the way it should be....

They took me off to the hospital, and I was X-rayed from all sides.

"I have disturbing news," said the doctor, entering the ward. "Your skeleton's in perfect shape. It's good enough for a classroom model.... But don't despair. Besides the skeleton which can be examined, you have the nervous system. It's complicated to isolate problems there."

As I pondered whether to rejoice or grieve at having an adequate skeleton, Linda rolled into the ward in a wheelchair, bandaged from head to toe. Only one of her mascara-laden eyes was visible. Seeing her in such a pitiful state, my heart skipped.

"My God," I said, "how did all that happen? Did you fall out of the stretcher?"

"Wait until you fall out!" She said from under her bandages, her one eye on the door. "I rocked the stretcher so much, not only did I fall down the steps, but I also took down the paramedics too, these two big, muscular guys. That's them, on crutches, out in the corridor. Not a day passes that I don't get flowers from them in gratitude...."

In the morning, I went to work. I had not even sat down when the phone rang. Mr. Stickman called the same lawyer whom Linda had recommended when we lay on the floor.

"Congratulations!" he said.

"Thank you," I said, "I'm glad it was just a little scare."

The lawyer lowered his voice and whispered:

"Keep it down over there! Are you out of your mind?"

"I'm okay," I said, not without some pride, "both physically and mentally."

"Mentally—I doubt it!" He bellowed into the phone. "Will you shut up already? Insurance companies have their ears everywhere. They'll report on you in a second. Listen to me carefully. Because you fell on the floor, you have disrupted sleep, aggravated by headaches and lumbago in the small of your back."

"But I've...."

"Shut up!" he barked. "What are you, a Martian? Ah, you're from Russia! Well, it's about the same thing. You're in a free country now!

You don't understand all your rights and opportunities yet. I'll send you to the doctor. Say what I told you to say, and everything will work out. I take forty percent."

I decided I had enough of it. This whole comedy was becoming tiresome.

"I'm not going anywhere!" I said and hung up.

It was time to stop being a wimp.

Just then Linda called. Tears in her voice and peculiar breathing, in which I spotted vague promises, she whispered:

"Why are you betraying me? Didn't we agree to stick together? I've depended on you so much. I said to myself, 'He's smart and sweet.' Come on, go to the doctor, what harm can it do? Please, do it for me!"

I melted. All resistance evaporate in the warmth of her charms. She talked me into it. I went.

On the way to the doctor's office, I followed the jolting movement of a weird bumper sticker on the back of a ratty old Buick: "Hit me, I need the money!"

In the reception room, I got into a conversation with another patient. She was wearing a thick neck brace. This prevented her from nodding her head, which gave her a proud, I would even say regal, look. She looked down at me.

"So, you've hurt your neck?" I asked.

"My neck's a trifle," the lady said. She unzipped her collar, put it in her purse, and reached for a cigarette. "It's bothersome, just a hassle. Your neck," she repeated, "forget it. You won't make much on that. I've got something better than that. Total repulsion towards sex."

"Towards what?"

"As soon as that car struck me, something inside me got displaced. As a result, I lost my sex drive. Now a man means no more to me than a fire hydrant on the sidewalk. They're the same. Oh no!" she said dreamily. "They won't get off cheap with me. A lousy two or three grand won't cut it now."

"Is it incurable," I asked, "this indifference to men?"

She looked at me, elegantly tipped her cigarette, and asked:

"What kind of accent do you have?"

"It's Russian."

"I see…. I've read in the papers that back in Russia you hadn't even known what sex was. You can't understand what a loss it is."

"Well, that's not entirely true." I felt embarrassed. "The population somehow has been growing…."

"An increase in population," the lady said, "has nothing to do with sex. I would even say," she squinted, "that it works in inverse proportion…."

As soon as I entered the examination room, the doctor began kneading my head and probing my stomach, saying:

"Well, now, partner. Haven't been here long and you already know your way around. You understand what's what. I've always said that immigrants are America's hope, her fresh blood."

"So, what we have here," he intoned, giving me time to absorb the information, "first, you have a severe migraine. Second, you wrenched your left shoulder ('one is enough,' he noted, 'no need to overdo it'). Third, partial memory loss (you don't remember the details of your fall). Fourth, nocturnal hallucinations. It is dangerous to salivate at night. You could choke. In fact," he summarized with some solemnity, "you are nearly in a vegetative state as it is, for which I heartily congratulate you. We'll start with ultra-violet heat therapy, the artificial sun, so to speak. We'll rejuvenate photosynthesis, boost the chemical processes...."

As he spoke, I understood less and less what was happening to me. My body felt numb. I became duller by the minute. My light-green corduroy pants turned into some thick and moist stalks. They reminded me of celery from the farmer's stand in my neighborhood in Brighton Beach. A family of ants ran on it. I tried to move, but I could not. I gathered whatever was left of my will and jerked my leg up from the floor. Bursting the parquet tiles, some roots showed from the soles of my shoes. I freed the other leg. With the roots scraping the floor, I dragged myself towards the door and out of the doctor's office.[3]

The time will come, however, when the newcomers will lose their innocence. They will not only excel at that peculiar American crime game but come up with their own, quite elaborate schemes. At the time of this writing, the Southern District of New York and the FBI indicted ten of my compatriots for five-years-long swindling of the healthcare system by billing for no-show cases, where aides provided no actual help to patients, conspiracy to commit mail, wire, and healthcare fraud, and to violate the Anti-Kickback Statute by billing Medicaid for home-health and personal-care services not rendered.

11

Blacksmiths of Happiness

As was often the case when I lived in Southern California, the inspiration for writing the following piece of mine came from reading the *Los Angeles Times*.

"In a Baseball Cap and Sunglasses"

Some time ago a story appeared in a paper regarding a certain John Smith. As a result, my entire life has been turned around.

Mr. Smith, it seems, would put on a baseball cap and dark sunglasses, enter the bank of his choice, and take a place in line. When his turn came to approach the teller's window, he would smile, say "How do you do?" to the teller, and extend a large sheet of paper across the window to the teller, on which he wrote something like this:

Please wrap up one thousand dollars in this paper. My pocket is heavy with a gun of a considerable caliber. I have been in a good mood since early this morning, and should you do anything to spoil this, I may unintentionally pull the trigger. I am the person to do it, believe me.

Sincerely yours,
(Illegible signature)

After a minute's hesitation, the teller would pack up the demanded sum, saying, "Thank you for dropping by; have a nice day," and then would call out, "Next in line!"

In a short period, in such a quiet and intelligent fashion, Mr. Smith had walked out of thirty-six banks with about forty thousand dollars.

He informed reporters that his decision to resort to this business came about because of some unfortunate circumstances. His marriage was on the rocks, he had trouble at work, and he would smoke, in secret, some junk that was harmful to his health.[1]

Coming from a country of legal nihilism, the country in which they compare the law to a horse-cart shaft, free to turn in any direction of one's liking, the ways the law was practiced in America came across to us, newcomers, as strange, bordering on bizarre. The American system of justice was preoccupied with being as exact as possible. It took great care to ensure that the punishment does not over-weigh even for a bit the gravity of the crime. The sentencing often cited the perpetrator's despair caused by his poor social conditions. The careful administering of the law, and its charitable character, was a cultural novelty that many of us, the ex–Soviet newcomers, had a problem digesting.

Americans took it for granted that such treatment of the law was universal. It opened to me quite early in my American life. Back in 1978, after two full years of living in the new country, I was startled when, watching the newly released American film *Midnight Express*, the main character, an American college student caught smuggling drugs out of Turkey, says to his jailers in bitterness, "Don't you have any sense of mercy? Are you pigs?"

Mercy? I thought. What's that? You broke the law, pal. What else did you expect when they caught you? A paid vacation in Hawaii?

It took me years to understand my reaction at that time. I gradually realized that I came from a culture in which the concept of mercy wasn't part of its political agenda. The attitude expressed by the saying "Moscow doesn't believe in tears" had been used for centuries on end. It was part of the country's history from medieval times on, from the time of the rise of the Moscow principality when a large tribute was collected from other Russian towns and principalities. The towns sent petitioners to Moscow with complaints of injustice. Such petitioners were often punished with extreme cruelty to frighten the dissatisfied. Often, the Moscow tsar himself carried out cruel punishments, seeing in the complaints of the petitioners an act of popular discontent with the policy of centralization. This gave rise to several proverbs and sayings about the cruelty, bribery, and injustice of the Moscow rulers, their officials, and the poverty and lack of rights of the common people. "Moscow does not believe in tears" was the most popular of them. From that time on, Russian rulers made sure that people did not forget it and knew this expression by heart.

No sense of empathy was ever developed in the Soviet era either. In Soviet culture, there was not even a concept of compassion toward the less fortunate. Schoolchildren were taught that every Soviet person is the "blacksmith of one's happiness." Kneeling buses, street sidewalks accessible for wheelchairs, parking spaces for handicapped (one day, I overheard "an American would rather excuse invading a foreign country than taking a parking space for handicapped")—all these things were puzzling for the Soviet immigrants. Even a minor physical irregularity, like that of Peter Falk, the star of Columbo, a TV series highly popular in its days—he had a glass eye, the result of his childhood disease, could produce condescending smirking. No wonder that, in the memoir of his American life, one Soviet immigrant, a well-known writer in his homeland, characterizes the ubiquitous care about the less fortunate in America as odd, and considers it an "American obsession with deformed bodies."

It should come as no surprise, however. A few years after the end of World War II, dubbed in the Soviet Union as the "Great Patriotic War," its invalids, the war-time vets—legless, with amputated hands, former tankmen with burned-up faces—were swept away from the streets of Soviet cities. Since the state, which had sent them to the battlefield, didn't take care of them, they had no choice but to panhandle at railroad stations, markets, in front of cinema theaters, and other public places. And there were a lot of them: according to statistics, two and a half million disabled people were discharged from the army, nearly half a million of them one-armed or one-legged.

Soon after the October 1917 takeover of power, the cultivation of pitilessness had begun by calling out the enemies of the revolution, whether they took an active part in the struggle against the Bolsheviks or just expressed doubts about whether it would benefit the country. The very social standing not only of you but even your descendants was often enough to consider you as being an enemy class-wise. "To judge with whole severity of the Soviet law!" (*Sudit' so vsej strogost'iu sovetskogo zakona!*) Such a call to action often made the headlines of Soviet papers in Stalin's times. Since the interests of the state were always considered paramount over that of an individual, the government's suing anyone meant convicting. Generations of Soviet people grew up in a society of intransigence and intolerance, on the unquestionable subordination of private life to the interests of the state. Therefore, despite loud statements, socialism, which was allegedly built in the USSR, was not humane. No wonder the attempt to give it a "human face" was suppressed by tanks rolled onto the cobbled squares of Prague in August 1968.

Without realizing it, we brought with us culturally imbued indifference about whether the punishment exceeds the crime. It is known that, in Stalin's time, a peasant could be given years in prison for a few ears of wheat picked up from a collective farm field and a blue-collar worker for being late for a factory shift.

So, it was hardly a wonder that, back in 1977, we, ex–Soviet immigrants, couldn't believe that no harsh punishment was administered to a man who put in an embarrassing situation not even a regular governmental official but the president of the United States himself. Interpreting for Mr. Carter over his official visit to Poland, a State Department translator made a couple of gaffes. When addressing his audience, President Carter said, "When I left the United States," the interpreter rendered it as "When I abandoned the United States." "I'm happy to be in Poland" became "I'm happy to grasp Poland's private parts," and "I praise the Polish constitution of 1791 as one of the three great documents in the struggle for human rights" was "Your constitution to be ridiculed."

As we learned from the press reports, since the Polish language wasn't among the most frequently used by the State Department, the translator wasn't even a full-time employee, but a part-timer working on a contract. After several of his missteps, an employee of the American embassy in Poland replaced him. End of the story....

So, what punishment for the embarrassment of the president of the United States was brought down upon the hapless interpreter's head? No contract resumed? That's all? Ha! We, ex–Soviets looked at each other in disbelief. In our home country, in Stalin's time, they would shoot the jinxed perpetrator of such an international scandal. Or, if he were lucky, at least banish him to the gulag for years. At other times, an interpreter to any government official was appointed out of the best in the country. A contract, my foot....

In everyday life in America, the ability to forgive one's trespasses is part of being human. It is assumed as a given, as a matter of course, that the forgiven deserves a second chance, and has the right to a fresh start. We, the newcomers, couldn't believe it when an NPR station reported about some "work release program." Prisoners work outside of their place of confinement, coming back only for a night's sleep? I'm not even talking about such an oddity as a "house arrest." Isn't it a contradiction in terms? They interviewed a theatrical director who staged a Shakespearean play behind the prison's bars as part of the inmates' rehabilitation. Ha, as the Russian saying goes, "Only the grave can straighten the hunchback." ("The leopard cannot change its spots" is its American counterpart.)

Apparently, by the time I came across that article in the *Los Angeles Times*, my Soviet-bred disapproval of the American attitude toward criminals had accumulated enough emotions that, after a short while, the following story was formed in my head. Admittedly, I push the issue over the top in this piece. But the piece drives home the point that you can get away with committing a crime in America. (Though in a convoluted way, making fun of it, the story also reflects my admiration of American entrepreneurship.)

So, upon reading the reported list of the bank robber's reasons for committing his crime—his marriage problems, his troubles at work, and his smoking habits, harmful to his health,

"Oh, no!" I said to myself, " I get headaches from tobacco, too, and I know there's no way I'm going to quit smoking.... Only yesterday I had a run-in with my boss.... As for my married life, the hot pre-weekend battle about whose elderly relatives, hers or mine, were to be taken to the country for some fresh air already takes place...."

Feeling an incredible similarity between my fate and that of Mr. Smith, I went out and bought a baseball cap and put on a pair of dark sunglasses. Bearing in mind that Mr. Smith was arrested only because his last haul comprised new bills which attracted the suspicion of the police, I added a post-scriptum to the note I had prepared on a large piece of paper:

"P.S. To avoid any misunderstanding, please, no crunchy bills."

Having prepared everything down to the last detail, I walked into the nearest bank and took my place in line. After waiting for what seemed like an eternity, with my heart pounding away, I walked up to the teller's window and unfolded the large note. I had designed it to hold a thousand dollars. Everything went as smoothly as greased lightning.

The teller, after reading my request, smiled so sweetly at me that one would think he was the recipient, and I was the donor. Then he corrected a misspelling that he had found in my message, eliminated an unnecessary comma, and added two which I had failed to include. He put one big stamp and two small ones—one round and the other triangular—on the note and then signed the request. Afterward, he looked me over and, begging my pardon, straightened out the collar of my shirt.

"Drop by more often," he said, as he concluded his maneuvers by banding the package together with a blue strip of paper.

Just before the exit, unable to restrain myself, I turned and looked back. There was no limit to what I expected to see—police officers with machine guns, helmeted soldiers with tear-gas grenades, and even the Attorney General of the United States, in person. Only what I saw....

A hefty young lad was approaching the teller's cage after me. He was wearing sunglasses. And his head was covered with a baseball cap, the same type as mine. The teller, smiling in the same fashion as before, was stacking packet after packet of bills on top of a piece of wrapping paper. Next in line was a heavyset cashier from the nearby supermarket. She was wearing a baseball cap and sunglasses. From behind her, there emerged a thirteen-year-old boy wearing the same uniform. An aged blind man whom I have seen and helped across busy intersections had only to add some headgear to his outfit. Since he never removed his dark glasses....

I felt as if I were going out of my mind. I rushed out of the bank. The first thing which caught my eye was a newsstand booth with a poster ad in the window. It read:

GOING TO THE BANK? DON'T FORGET TO BUY
YOUR GENUINE SMITH SUNGLASSES HERE.

There was a line leading up to the booth. Shoppers, one by one, joined the line from the nearby sporting goods store. A sign of flashing lights over the entrance announced:

A BASEBALL CAP IS NOT MERELY HEAD-WEAR.
IT'S A SYMBOL OF SUCCESS.

An adjacent stationery store boasted:

TAKE HOME THE WORLD'S GOLD
IN OUR FIRM'S HEAVY-DUTY PAPER.

Maybe I am dreaming, I thought to myself. I closed my eyes and opened them again. A window of the lawyer's office next to the bank carried an advertising sign too:

NEWEST TYPE OF SERVICE FOR ILLITERATES—
COMPOSITION OF NOTES ACCORDING TO SMITH:
KWOLITY GARANTID.

Someone tapped me on the shoulder. Surprised, I swung around, barely able to avoid trampling a dachshund wearing a baseball cap. The dog was on the leash, which was held by the general manager of the bank I had just cleaned out. The banker was wearing a T-shirt with a half-portrait of Mr. Smith. He smiled kindly at me.

"I have a request," he said. " Would you be so kind as to tell all your friends and neighbors to keep our bank in mind? You'll make a nice commission for every robber you send to us."

"I understand nothing," I yelled, feeling as though the entire world was going crazy. "How can you be interested in people robbing your bank? I don't get it."

"You see," said the bank manager, straightening the sunglasses on the dachshund's nose, "banks are being robbed, anyhow. Compared to previous methods of robbery, Mr. Smith's is easier to take and much more humane. Nobody is shot, no beatings, no holding of hostages at gunpoint. Just to compensate cashiers for mental damage, we're obligated to pay sizeable sums of money. But a bank that has been held up gets good advertising, both through the press and television. The number of depositors increases (deposits are insured anyway!)."

"But you'll never have enough cash stored up that way," I cried out. "Everybody will be glad to bite off more and more."

"Unfortunately," the banker let go with a sigh, "far from everybody. In a day or two, we are introducing a bill in Congress, whereby sums of stolen money will be subject to income tax. As you no doubt noticed, we register the payment and your picture," he added. "A clerk snapped a color photo of you as soon as you came into focus. You'll be needing a photo I.D."

He pulled a neat little packet out of his pocket and extended it to me.

"The first copy is free and any additional ones are at a significant discount. This is an added privilege for customers. Payments like the one made to you will be written off as expenses for charitable causes. This should calm your anxiety about what advantages we get from the entire operation. So then, be a good fellow, stick around the neighborhood and drop in."

"Without fail," I promised out of politeness, at the same time feeling rather perplexed.

"Well then, from my thousand bucks, the tax law will snip off something like seven hundred at the end of the year. Then inflation works on the rest. Let's take into consideration the rate of rising food prices, along with that of gasoline. My insurance companies, as sure as green apples, will have to raise my premium payments, since my new business increases the strain on my nerves. This way," I estimated, "it looks like my entire profit comes out to be the cost of a baseball cap and sunglasses."

Thinking over the twists of fate, I strolled through the park where children were taking pony rides. Out of pity for one of the ponies who had to work in the scorching sun, I covered its hard-laboring brow with my baseball cap and attached the dark sunglasses in front of its eyes.

The pony whinnied in gratitude.[2]

12

"Save Kisa!"

"Blame It on Uncle Sam"

One day I got a call at the university. A charming female voice asked: "Did you know any tigers while living in Russia?"

"Only superficially," I said, trying to figure out what this was all about. "Just 'hello' and 'goodbye.'"

"Can you suggest a name for a Russian tiger? You know, we mean a domestic name. Nothing official."

"Well," I scratched the back of my head. "It's hard for me to think of a name. Let me be frank with you. Even if I had ever met a tiger, something made of stainless steel was always between us—a cage, a grating.... Things like that."

"Didn't you know any Russian tigers who were not dissidents?" The caller sounded surprised.

"In Russia, everybody's under suspicion."

"That's some totalitarianism!" The woman got mad. Then she made another attempt. "Haven't you run into a tiger socially on some occasion? At a friend's house or somewhere else?"

"Russians prefer cats over the tiger for catching mice."

"A tiger is a cat," I was reproached. "Only somewhat bigger. Please give us a Russian name for a cat?"

"Murka," I mumbled. "Kisa...."

"Kisa! Terrific! Easy to remember. That's very important," the woman was thrilled.

Why should one remember a cat's name?" I was amazed.

"We're organizing a campaign to save Siberian tigers. We already have a female tiger from the city zoo that we photographed from the waist up. Such a cute, gentle puss! You would be tempted to pet it...."

"Possibly," I said after some hesitation. "It depends on what you want me to pet. If it's just a portrait, I'm your man. But the original.... I don't feel like committing myself to it right now."

"We have to give the tigress' name a Slavic flavor," the caller

147

went on meanwhile, "so it'll be clear right away who we're protesting against. How does 'Save Kisa!' sound in Russian?"

"*Spasite Kisu!*"

"Terrific!" the woman exclaimed and hung up.

The call didn't surprise me. Americans, I have learned, protest a lot, and often. It seems against everything. Against windfall profits and underpayments.... Against the rise of prices and the decline of public morals.... Against freezing some funds and reviving others. Having been brought up under totalitarianism, I've never been happier than when I see people with placards in their hands. They're as much a part of the urban landscape as those dollhouses of McDonald's.[1]

The above is the opening of my satirical piece, written and published in English translation in the *Los Angeles Herald Examiner* in February 1984, nine years into my American life. The phone call is not invented. A graduate student at the Department of Slavic Languages of the University of California at Los Angeles, at our department secretary's request, I answered the incoming call.

If only I had stopped at the retelling of the conversation with the calling lady, leaving it in my memory as a humorous episode! But, alas, in my piece, I go on to scoff at and bring up the very idea of public protests to comic absurdity:

That's why I wasn't at all surprised when, recently, while running in the pouring rain, which had inundated Los Angeles, I noticed that my acquaintance Jerry carried a poster. Only he didn't hold it in front of him, as any self-respecting demonstrator would do, but over his head.

"Are you protesting against something or protecting yourself against the rain?" I asked.

"Both," said Jerry.

"What are you protesting against?" I asked, ready to go.

"Against the rain," he said.

"What?!" I came to a dead stop. "Against the rain?"

"Precisely."

"Against which one? This one, or against any rain in general?"

"Don't make an idiot out of me. There's an average amount of rainfall per square inch in Southern California. Any deviation from the norm is a crime against the population. What's going on now."

He pointed with his chin (his hands were busy) toward the seething streams of water along the sidewalks.

"They shouldn't get away with it."

"Who's they?"

"Who! The government, of course."

"But excuse me." I was puzzled. "Isn't rain a natural phenomenon?"

"Yes, a week per year for the Los Angeles area is natural. But a month is an outrage, a malicious act."

"I agree. It's hardly a joy," I said, holding back my running nose.

"But what can you do?"

"Fight them!"

"Well, what about other natural phenomena, then?"

"Oh, don't worry. I've already protested gusty winds in March. It's true, however, that my calculations were off the mark somewhat. I made my placard too big and was therefore blown onto the roof of a bank on Wilshire Boulevard.... But it did me good: many more people saw me. I even got into the papers, which is a big success for any demonstrator."

"Do you protest often?"

"I try at least once a week."

"What if there's no cause?"

"Oh!" Jerry laughed at my naivete. "Don't you worry! There's no shortage of causes."

"What are you protesting next week? Do you have your plans already?"

"Sure," he said. "We're going to protest unrequited love."

"No kidding," I said. "And who's guilty?"

"It's clear who. The government."

"You love the government, but it doesn't love you?" I thought I must be going out of my mind. "You just got through cursing it up and down!"

"Are you crazy?" Jerry looked at me as if he had never seen me before. "Who loves the government in this country? Even if it's the best one, you must learn the good American tradition. No, the situation is like this: An acquaintance of mine fell in love with me, but I don't care for her too much."

"Pity. Why not?"

"Her eyes are brown, and I only like blue-eyed girls. I can't do anything about it. That's the way my psyche works. Dark eyes frighten me. It's a Freudian complex."

"You poor thing," I said. "But what does the government have to do with that, after all? How can it possibly influence your friend's eye color?"

"It can, and a lot," said Jerry. "Her mother had a boyfriend with blue eyes. If my friend were his daughter, we would now be together, there wouldn't be any suffering. But the government drafted the poor fellow into the army and her mother had no choice but to marry another guy—with brown eyes. This can serve also as a protest against the military draft."

I was about to leave when I realized:

"Wait a minute, wait a minute! It is *she* who is unhappy. Why are *you* protesting?"

"First, I'm doing it out of solidarity. Second, she works all day long and attends school at night," Jerry said. "Isn't it a dog's life if one doesn't even have any time to protest a bit here and there?"[2]

Rereading this story now, after living several decades in America, I scratch the back of my head trying to figure out where did it come from then, in 1984. It was less than a decade after arriving in America. Why I felt like ridiculing the very idea of public protests? Now it seems incredible I could even think of mocking the very institution to which I owe my freedom. In the end, as I understand it now, thanks to that institution, I had received a lifetime present—the opportunity to emigrate from a country in which I, like other Soviet Jews, had been captive and treated as a second-class citizen. A suddenly opened possibility to escape then, in the mid–1970s, seemed unbelievable; we, Russian Jews and non–Jews, were all hostages of the Soviet system. If it were not for the public protests of the 1960s and 1970s in America and other democratic countries, which spearheaded the lawmakers' political demarches in favor of the freedom of emigration, the very movement for freedom of Jewish emigration from the Soviet Union would never materialize.

As I realized it much later, if it were not for that grassroots movement, I would never get near America. After all, it was started not by the American government but by most ordinary people. At least at its first stage, it was not public figures, not congressional representatives and senators, who took part in it but ordinary people—students at American universities, housewives, pensioners, blue-collar workers, including religious people—not only Jews but also Christians of various denominations, Catholic nuns, among others. I learned about it much later, after living in America for several years and making friends with one of those Americans who considered it their moral duty to fight for the freedom of emigration from the USSR—Si Frumkin.

Why did it happen that way? Maybe because never in my past Soviet life I have done something out of the pure sense of duty, as a citizen of my country, and I have the right, guaranteed by the constitution, to give feedback regarding the way the country is governed, to show what needs to be corrected. After all, what the form of legal public protests is for?

As I now understand, then, as an immigrant living a few years in the country, the ironic attitude to the protests, to the sporadic appearance on the streets of men and women with posters was incomprehensible because, in my Soviet life, I had done nothing *voluntarily*.

Oh, the word itself was familiar to me. It was often used in my Soviet life. But, pronounced by the representatives of the authorities, most often by your immediate superior, it was invariably understood as *voluntarily compulsory*.

Indeed, voluntary in form, but compulsory, depending on the place you occupied, had been such activities, as attending or conducting political information briefings, studying the genius works of Comrade Brezhnev, the foundations of Marxism-Leninism, sitting in at various meetings of the Party officials and senior executives.

The same was concerned with a trip to the collective farm in the fall to help with the harvest, or sending your subordinates there, signing up for a government loan, and joining and paying membership fees to *DOSAAF* (Voluntary Society of Army, Aviation, and Navy Support), and, if you are an engineer or scientist, to the STS (Scientific and Technical Society, *NTO*), to the Red Cross, and other "voluntary societies." Refusal to be appointed a police helper (*druzhinnik*), to buy government loan bonds, to attend a work-for-the nation-day (*subbotnik*), or a demonstration organized by the authorities was fraught with at least deprivation of bonuses, and sometimes job dismissal.

No wonder I met the American custom of volunteering with puzzlement. Who, in his right mind, would want to do it?

Back in my home country, there was no opportunity to volunteer, to do something out of such a natural human feeling of empathy and compassion. Soviet ideology left no room for helping people that in America come under the umbrella of being "less fortune." Of course, there were plenty of less fortunate in the USSR, but they could not be considered such for ideological reasons. The role of luck in life was not recognized.

As far as public protests are concerned, by the time I arrived in America, I knew only about only two of them in my old country. About one of them, which had taken place in the city of Novocherkassk, I learned through the grapevine. In 1962, in the Russian city of Novocherkassk, workers of one of the local plants walked the streets protesting their low wages. They were met with the deadly fire of the Soviet Army and the KGB. (It became public only thirty years later, after the collapse of the Soviet Union.)

I learned of another demonstration of protest, this time against the Soviet invasion of Czechoslovakia over the jammed BBC broadcast. The

protest lasted just a few minutes before the police and the KGB arrested
a handful of intellectuals gathered on the Red Square, holding up a
poster that read "For Your and Our Freedom."

No wonder the only thing we could do with my friends and colleagues was to gather in the privacy of our Moscow apartments and
trade many underground jokes:

*Here, in the USSR, we have freedom of assembly, procession, and
demonstration.*
Over there, in the West, they have freedom after *assembly, procession, and
demonstration.*

A Soviet sparrow flew to the West.
*"What? Are things that harsh in Russia in terms of food?" a Western spar-
row asks it.*
*"Oh, no," the Soviet one said. "We have plenty of it! Nowhere do they scatter
as much grain on the road as over there."*
"So, why are you flying in here then?"
"I crave chirping a bit."

As to elections Soviet-style, we all knew well Comrade Stalin's pronouncement that served as the guidelines for those in power after him,
"People who vote decide nothing. People who *count* the votes decide
everything."

The elections were conducted in full correspondence with the
Soviet constitution, that is, all people in power were elected through
direct and secret voting. There was little wonder that, the next day, all
the loudspeakers in the country solemnly reported that 99.97 percent of
votes were given to the "candidates of the bloc of Communists and non–
Party people, which expresses the inviolability of the moral and political unity of Soviet society."

There was little chance for you to skip the show and avoid voting.
Toward the evening of the voting day, a boring-looking man knocked on
the door of your apartment and asked, begged you to go to vote. He was
not allowed to go home to have dinner with his family. At his place of
work, he was appointed an agitator, that is, he had to ensure everyone in
his precinct voted.

The very word "democracy" frequented Soviet papers, but hardly
anyone knew what it meant. Of course, it was easy to understand that
this is when the people are in power. In Soviet reality, this meant that
you were told when, what, and why something was going to take place.
And you had no choice but to follow the rules. In the interests of the
whole Soviet people, of course...

An ordinary Soviet person was quite often an opportunist, an
adapter. Otherwise, how else could he survive in a system in which

every step was proscribed or directed? It seemed strange to volunteer to take part in any, even local, government. The question always arose, "Why do you need this? And what will you get from this?" And so on.

Once, talking to my American friend, I expressed surprise that he was running for the office of a cooperative on the shore of the lake where he lived. And he did this to volunteer to be part of the cooperative board. When I asked him why he needed it, he shrugged, "Why, to let someone who God knows how qualified to do it? A token lesson in what democracy is all about, which never reached my consciousness before."

Recently, rummaging through my archives, I came across a clipping of my story published in translation on the pages of the *Los Angeles Herald Examiner*. For a long time, I wondered how it could be that the editor of an American newspaper published my satire on the holy of holies of democracy—public protests. Is it possible that he agrees with me, a native of a totalitarian country, in which very few of them ever took place and were never publicized?

Then I realized that, by changing the neutral title of my story "Save Kisa!" to "Blame it on Uncle Sam!" the editor lent my satire a truly American character. Do not shift the blame onto the government for everything you could handle yourself, pal! Your life is in your own hands. As an American acquaintance of mine expressed it, "The government should be not seen or heard. They should just take care of stuff." (That explains my puzzlement when I learned over the TV program that the current country's president asked the networks to give him some time to talk to the nation during the broadcast of a Super Bowl game.)

This archival finding once again convinced me of the wisdom of the story from the *Pentateuch* of Moses. It took me a long time to see that it was a waste of time to bring people who grew up in slavery to the promised land.

13

"How Much for a Dozen of Insults?"

My gradual acquaintance with America let me realize the direct connection between the economic system and politeness in society at large and, even more so, between two people.

Once, while leafing through the Sunday insert of the *Los Angeles Times*, I came across a cartoon that puzzled me greatly. A "sandwich man," that is, a fellow with advertising boards hung on him—middle-aged, stooped, deep bald patches, thick-lens glasses—carried a billboard that read, *"Insults—25 cents."*

My first reaction: Jeez! They monetize everything in America, including epithets. In my old country, there was plenty of swearing around. Free of charge.

The cartoon brought to the fore of my consciousness the fact that somehow I didn't notice that I heard people cursing to a significantly lesser degree than back in my Soviet life. It looked like I got used to such a paucity of cussing rather quickly.

Of course, the effect of a foreign language was also at work here. Cushioning of semantics, softening of the emotional impact. After all, profanity in your native tongue is much more effective and carries more angry energy. Thus, to a Russian speaker's ear, the English "fuck" doesn't sound as offensive as a comparable swearing *yob tvoiu mat'* (mother-fucker). In everyday American life, people often use expletives just to express annoyance with themselves, when something goes wrong or they can't find the right word scanning one's brain.

Looking at the newspaper cartoon made me realize that, though I've already lived for about ten years in the new country, when I walked in the streets, no one pushed me, snagged me, or, even more so, insulted me. If someone passing by accidentally touched me with his coat's sleeve, I immediately heard the apologetic "Sorry!"

From this discovery, it naturally followed that, in America, people rarely reach the point where they forget about regard for each other. After all, if you stoop so low that you insult others, you don't respect yourself foremost. The impersonal character of the Soviet economic activities provided no room for human dignity. And where would the self-esteem of a Soviet citizen come from? Soon after moving out of the country, it slipped out of my mind that everyday existence in my homeland was hardly void of rudeness, boorishness, and indignities. At every step on the streets of the Russian cities, one could hear the vilest curses. And this is understandable. You needed to discharge your anger, to relax your emotions, overwhelmed by a life filled with annoyances. At least verbally, you had to relieve your frustrations borne by the perennial lack of the first necessities and the constant need to overcome insurmountable bureaucratic obstacles. Considered unacceptable in polite society, the abusive language was appropriately termed as "street [or square] cursing," [*ulichnaya (ploshchadnaya) bran'.*]

Although swearing is the most democratic phenomenon—after all, everyone is capable of it—in a working environment, dressing down another person (or persons) was an advantage for those in power. It was invariably the prerogative of those in charge. After all, they dubbed the Soviet economic system the "command economics," and you don't rule the roost whispering....

Russian jokelore of the time expressed the relationship between the superiors and their subordinates accurately: "If you are my boss, I'm the fool. If I'm your boss, you are the fool." "Yesterday, I had an exchange of opinions with my manager. I stepped into his office with my opinion, and I left it with his."

The abuse of authority by low- and mid-rank bosses in Soviet institutions and their impudence concerned powers that be. They fought the arrogance of the supervisors through public condemnation. I remember a caricature on the cover of *Crocodile*, the country's main satirical instrument. It depicted a certain boss yelling into the telephone receiver, his mouth looking like a street loudspeaker. From it, swearing and insults gushed directed at his subordinates. In many institutions, the periodical so-called "Weeks of Improving the Culture of the Working Environment" (*Nedelia kul'tury proizvodstva*) were held, during which they tried to use administrative means to fight the arrogance and boorishness of everyday interactions.

One of the few topics open to public criticism was the incivility of certain administrators. Not once, they asked me as a satirist writing for the capital's newspapers to address in print the discourtesy of certain supervisors. Of course, the targets of press punditry were some

small bosses, as we, Soviet satirists, joked among ourselves, those ranking "not above the building manager" (*ne vyshe upravdoma*).

Most often, they publicized the issue in the newspaper Labor (Trud),
the instrument of the All-Union Central Council of Trade Unions. At
least, in theory, it was to serve the interests of the working class. Thus,
they published one of my satirical columns calling the public attention
to the rudeness of some Soviet managers, though of a lower rank, of
course. About one of them, an incredible rumor spread:

> It spread quickly, like a fire in the steppe, among the workers of
> the Housing and Maintenance Office of the Frunze district in our cap-
> ital. People didn't believe their ears: according to an eyewitness, the
> head of the establishment, Comrade Ukladchikov, said hello to his
> subordinates. Their boss's rudeness and shouting, his cynical jokes
> made them sick daily.
>
> But rumors, alas, remained such. As before, greeting no one,
> Comrade Ukladchikov only grimly lectured the employees:
> "You address me in the wrong way, as 'Nikolai Ivanovich' and
> 'Nikolai Ivanovich' again."
> "How should we call you?" his subordinates asked.
> "I'm not Nikolai Ivanovich to you. To you, I'm Comrade Director!"[1]

In this column, I mention another manager, Comrade Smorodinov,
the head of one of the local technological management, who also fla-
vored all his oral communications with traditional street language. He
ruled with the help of shouts, threats, and swearing, from which everyone hid, but avoiding it was impossible:

> Perhaps, it was the manager's pain for the entrusted transporta-
> tion management that manifested itself in such a peculiar way? Maybe
> Comrade Smorodinov's stern adherence to principles took such unat-
> tractive forms? No! It was just the easiest thing in the world for him
> to cut off a subordinate in mid-sentence, shout at him, and curse him.
> "Well, why can't I call worker names if he is really at fault?"
> Sidorov shrugged.
> Even belonging to the weaker sex didn't save one from the cavalry
> charges of the taxi commander. It was easy for him, not at all embar-
> rassed, in front of everyone, to insult a female employee with hints far
> from ambiguity.[2]

In the conclusion of my column, I had to make the point of my
write-up as plain as possible: "The ability to achieve top results, to force

out monthly working plan fulfillment, even with the help of humiliation and insults, is hardly high-quality doughtiness. We should consider excellent only a leader who is deeply alien to petty tyranny and rudeness."[3]

Common folks understood the straight talk interlaced with curses much easier than the official Soviet vocabulary, contrived and highfalutin, the language of *Pravda* editorials. They rarely took it seriously, letting the bombastic jumble of propaganda clichés go in one ear and out the other. Swearing served as a popular way of expressing emotions that conventional words could not adequately vent. Therefore, a large range of vile speech was used as a means of meta-communication.

The phenomenon was hardly new in the Soviet era. Back in the nineteenth century, in his *Writer's Dairy*, Dostoevsky notices the ability of the core Russian obscenities to express a wide spectrum of feelings and notions. After observing the behavior of six young workmen on the streets of St. Petersburg, he "became convinced that it is possible to convey all thoughts, sensations, and even all deep reasonings by using only [obscene language, which,] from time immemorial, had been found and accepted throughout the whole Russia."

He concluded that, with the help of "only one noun, forbidden to be used in front of ladies [...], without saying a single another word, [six fellows he observed] repeated that favorite word six times in a row, one after another, and they understood each other fully."[4]

In my time, I was convinced of these observations' accuracy. After I graduated from the Odessa Polytechnic Institute, they sent me as a young specialist to work as a foreman at the Kyiv Assembly Management #2 of the Ministry of Gas Industry. I had a team of locksmiths under my command, and my responsibility was to document monthly their labor and submit the paperwork to the payroll office. I describe this incident in a short humoresque below. Everything in it, as they say, is "drawn from nature." I just give all the characters fake names. The episode in actual life helped me learn what it meant to "speak in a language which people understand."

I should explain one phrase in the piece to the American reader, the one that is easily understood by a native speaker of Russian. Everyone in my home country knows the expression "to cuss someone out using three-storied obscenities [*pokryt' tryokh-ehtazhnym matom*]," that is, subject a person to a stream of earsplitting expletives. You can metaphorically match the strength of profanity of this expression to an uppercut in boxing. In the story, as a tongue-in-cheek way of describing such speech, I compare the prolonged verbal abuse produced by the character to paragraphs of Leo Tolstoy's prose known for their length.

In the humoresque, with the help of the meta-language of cursing, the protagonist's experienced colleague reproaches the workshop foreman for his unnecessary swaggering, a desire to show off, to flaunt his power to the rookie engineer. Something like saying to him, "Stop playing the fool...."

They could interpret the story as a mockery of the working masses, for whom swearing is the most understandable language. But, at the time of its publication, in the early 1970s, a "campaign to improve the culture of everyday life and working environment" was going on in the country.

"Magic Words"

A rookie supervisor Pashkin, a recent college graduate, stood in front of the foreman of locksmiths Poddubny and trembled. His first month on the job has ended. He had to submit the foreman's completed work-order paperwork to the payroll, which the man had to cosign. As he had used to do before his school exams, Pashkin had sat through two nights, calculated all that the crew has done, and double-checked the numbers. Now he took the stack of papers to the workshop, to the foreman.

"I won't sign it," Poddubny said right away.

"Why?" Pashkin was struck dumb.

"I just won't. That's all!"

"What do you mean? Without your signature, Sergei Ivanovich, the accounting won't accept it! The entire crew would get no payment!"

"I don't give a damn!" Poddubny said calmly. "You didn't include all work produced. I won't sign!"

Pashkin turned pale:

"Sergei Ivanovich, you haven't looked it over yet. I included every job done."

"I already know that it is sheer nonsense in your papers. All-out rubbish! I won't even take it in my hands," answered Poddubny and pointedly hid his palms under his armpits.

"Listen, Sergei Ivanovich!" begged Pashkin. "Well, do you want me to read it aloud, and you'll tell me whether anything is wrong?"

Pashkin grabbed the top page of the work-order stack:

"Transporting pipes up to two meters long at a distance of up to ten meters...."

The foreman yawned, stepped into his office, and began calmly changing his overalls.

Desperate, Pashkin rushed to the phone.

"He doesn't want to sign it!" he said as cheerfully as he could to his friend Venichev, also a recent college graduate who had worked in the department for over a year already.

Five minutes later, Venichev came over to the workshop. He approached Poddubny. Then, as if forgetting something, he returned to Pashkin:

"Here's a lesson for you: how to negotiate with him. Listen and memorize."

Venichev thrust his hands into the pockets of his raincoat, took in as much air into his lungs as he could, and, without pausing, poured out a protracted, three Tolstoyan paragraphs long passage.

From such a solid chunk, Poddubny's sallow cheeks gained color. He turned to Venichev, and his whole appearance expressed keen interest in what the man was saying.

Then, the second portion of words of the same thickness followed. Poddubny smiled kindly.

The third charge, fired by Venichev, cheered the foreman up. Laughing, he slapped Venichev on the shoulder:

"Well, I got it, I got it! Let me sign them!"

Shaking his head in satisfaction, the man took to scribbling with the pen.

"It's outright trouble with those Pashkins," he said, handing over the signed paperwork to Venichev. "They don't know how to talk to people. What only do they teach them in the colleges!"[5]

All this prehistory of my acquaintance with the language of insults in my homeland makes understandable my amazement seeing that caricature in the American newspaper depicting a man with a billboard announcing the price for a dirty word. The following story inspired by that cartoon, published in the Russian daily paper *Novoe Russkoe Slovo*, in the first years of my time in the new country, could serve as a record of my attempt at adjustment to life in a culture so different from the one I had left forever.

"How Much for a Dozen of Insults?"

I was in a foul mood that day. I didn't understand exactly what was bothering me, but I couldn't shake off my gloom. I grabbed a cap and a windbreaker, hoping a little fresh air would help. Although it rarely does....

The first thing that caught my eye—I almost collided with him— was a man strolling quietly along the street with a cardboard poster hanging from his neck. The sign said, *INSULTS—25 CENTS; $2.50 A DOZEN.*

I must admit, I've gotten used already to the freakiest forms that free enterprise takes in America, but now I was a little taken aback. It was too much. Also, it was unclear whether the fellow was selling curses or buying them. His face had all the marks of culture, and intelligence—a thin, aquiline nose; tender, nervously twitching lips; and attentive eyes which seemed ready to hear out his interlocutor politely. If such a man could insult, it could happen only in a state of extreme irritation. By the same token, he didn't look like a masochist fixed to pay cash for invectives hurled at him. Unable to contain my curiosity, I caught up to him, walked alongside him for a while, almost in step, and at last, brought myself to ask:

"Excuse me, are you selling insults or buying them?"

"Bug off, blockhead," he said, took a quarter from his coat, and deposited it in the breast pocket of my jacket.

"Look at that!" I was astonished. "He even pays!"

Meanwhile, the fellow with the sign continued his way.

Probably some kind of nut, I decided.

By this time, the man had reached the corner and turned around. In a few minutes, we were face to face again. Reaching for me, he hissed out of the side of his mouth:

"Why are you staring at me, you hippo?"

And just as deftly, his hand slipped another coin into my pocket.

"Listen," I caught up to him and took him by the sleeve of his coat, "what's with you? Are you nuts?"

"You're nuts yourself, ugly face!" he said, freeing himself. "Your mother had you in a streetcar! May you see the worms in your dreams! Scum, child molester, rotten growth on the body of humanity! A cockatoo in a green tie!"

Dumbfounded, I looked myself over—where did he get the idea about a green tie? It was a gray pinstripe.

As if he guessed my thoughts, the man corrected himself:

"Okay! I beg your pardon, a cockatoo in a gray tie. Pinstripe."

Then, he matter-of-factly pulled out a dollar bill, extracted three-quarters from a mound of change in his cupped hand, and slipped it all into the side pocket of my jacket, since I covered my breast pocket with both hands.

"Hey, hey, buddy," I said, "mind what you say! I see the loony-bin is missing you!"

The fat man's face gained color, and an incomprehensible spark ignited in his eyes, which to this point had surveyed the world indifferently.

"And what misses you is a good club!" he declared, putting his palms on the hips and looking me up and down. "Because you cut out from the same stuff."

He took out a dollar and, businesslike, inquired:

"Have you got the change, you ... cretin? Eh, you owe me fifty cents."

"Who gave you the right to insult me?!" I said.

"No one gives it to me. I buy it, you, a miserable parasite! A mental midget!" he said after a pause, pondering something. "There," he smiled peaceably, "now there's no change needed. We're even."

"Maybe we could have a drink," I suggested, pretending to take everything that had passed between us as a refined joke. "I'd like to chat with you a bit."

The stranger looked at me for nearly a full minute, then abruptly wheeled about on his heels and started down one of the little uptown streets, where there are a lot of small snack bars.

When I caught up to him—he moved rather quickly, glancing at his watch from time to time—he had removed the cardboard sign from his chest, hiding it in his well-made overcoat. Altogether, the man produced an entirely respectable impression. Had it not been for the scene so recently enacted, I'd never have believed I could squander good daylight hours on this dull-looking and quite conventional gentleman.

We went into a cafe and ordered beer and hot dogs.

"Have you been cursing for long?" I asked, fishing for an opening.

"About two weeks..." he sighed. "Two weeks..." he added pensively.

"Did anything drive you to it? Something out of the ordinary?" I said carefully.

"Out of the ordinary?" he looked at me with the pain of a man who knows the suffering of the world. "God forbids! Everything is ordinary. Too ordinary. I've felt like cursing, you could say, for as long as I can remember myself. From the moment I let go of my mother's hand, everything's gone wrong. And what about you?"

For the first time, he looked at me with some curiosity:

"You never get that way?"

"Well, it happens," I faltered. "No getting around it."

"It happens! Ha! My dear sir, I only have to open my eyes in this world, to remember where I live and who I have to deal with, and I want to howl on the spot."

"Well, then howl to your heart's content," I said.

"Ah-ha-ha-ha!" the stranger burst into a deep guffaw interspersed with coughing. "To my heart's content! But at whom! Tell me, in the time we live in now, who can you just like that, wholeheartedly send to hell? No one! That's the point! You can't even come close. Your wife? But try it! That'll cost you a bunch! A lot more than a quarter! She'll pout for a week; she'll ruin your mood for a good two more. You'll be deprived for at least a month of those few marital pleasures purchased at the price of your freedom. And you only wanted to let off steam.... Lay it onto your kids? That's not so easy these days too. Take my neighbor: he's a truly decent man, no monster at all; he gave his children a college education.

And what happened? The darling kiddies schemed among themselves and sued him for a poor upbringing. It turns out he hollered at them for this and that when they were teenagers. He had good reason, the usual things.... And now, see, if you can believe this, they have frustrated sex lives because of parental repression. It's boring, they say, as the morning exercise program on the radio.

"Without drive and imagination.... God damn them!" the stranger fumed. Then he smiled:

"At least I can utter it free of charge."

"And in business?" he continued, sipping his beer. "Tell me, who can you rail at to purge your soul? ... Your secretary? Do you know how hard it is to find a good secretary these days? Oh-ho-ho! ... Or a customer? Oh, no, no! ..." he shook his head in feigned fright. "Even if he's a certified idiot, you can't. Mental incompetence is an insufficient cause. The customers are always right. Never mind whether they give you ulcers daily...."

"So, you wind up having to relieve your soul on lunch hour." He glanced at his watch. "I've got to go," he smiled.

They brought the check. I reached for it. The stranger beat me to it.

"I'll pay," I said, "after all, it was my suggestion."

And I laid my money on the table.

"That's silly," the curser fidgeted, extracting his wallet from his pocket. "No one invited me. This is my lunch hour. I always come here."

For a while, he struggled to exchange his banknote for mine. I tried to insist. He resisted desperately and kept endlessly placing his banknote over mine. His stubbornness enraged me.

"You ass!" I blurted out, surprising myself. I rarely lose my self-control. "Douchebag!"

By inertia, I added a half-dozen other choice words, threw the money on the table, and ran out.

Oddly enough, I suddenly got relieved and quickly started for home.

On the way, a thought struck me. I even chuckled in satisfaction. Whistling merrily, I pushed my cap back on my head and turned into the first stationery store I came upon. I felt like finding a large sheet of cardboard there....[6]

Rereading this piece many years later, I see some traces of my Soviet background. While the case of grown-up children suing parents for poor upbringing was in the news in America at the time of writing, the comparison of boring sex life to gymnastics lessons over the morning radio was not American, but Soviet-time program.

14

"Footmall"

The following dystopian satire on America, written back in 1985, sums up my vision of the country after the first ten years of settling in it. It is part of my second story collection in Russian titled *The Lost Boy and Other Stories* (*Poterialsia mal'chik*) issued by the publishing house Moscow Worker in 1993. The place of publication carries an unintended symbolism in as much as the newly formed state called "the Russian Federation" imagined itself, by a sheer change of the state attributes (the emblem, the flag) and its constitution, to be miraculously cured of the pestilence of its Soviet past. The story betrays its author's Soviet conditioning. Perhaps, to a much greater degree than other American stories, it proves beyond a reasonable doubt that the biblical caution, expressed in the *Book of Numbers*, that people born in slavery who are over twenty years old cannot shed the mentality they were imbued with from the cradle.

To begin with, the story pokes fun at American consumerism, a staple of Soviet propaganda in my time. In the same vein, the author tries hard to make the reader believe that all that preoccupies all Americans is a material acquisition, and that their lives are devoid of any spirituality. From that standpoint, in America, a shopping mall substitutes for a recreation park, and buying a new piece of furniture is a good enough reason for a holiday-style celebration. Such ordinary human emotions were unworthy of a highly conscious human being—a Soviet person.

While the story reflects the author's puzzlement over the huge, disproportionate, in comparison with other public events, popularity of spectator sports, especially football and baseball, in America, it also reflects the author's bewilderment at the feminist movement in America, the pronounced desire of women to take their destiny into their own hands. American feminist Betty Friedan's declaration, "No woman gets an orgasm from shining the kitchen floor," reflected her call to reject the plight of modern women and their confinement to traditional roles. The open discussion of a woman's right to sexual fulfillment in America bewilders the narrator who came from a culture in which such an issue not only never entered public debates but has also been on the cultural taboo list from time immemorial. In the Russian culture of the time, a woman's pleasure in lovemaking was considered almost indecent and not expected.[1]

The political trend affected the American pop culture of the time. In the movie *American Gigolo* (1980), Richard Gere plays a man who considers it his civic duty to help to satisfy women sexually. In one scene, he says with a compassionate sigh that a wealthy man hired him because his poor wife was deprived of having an orgasm for four whole years.

That movie blew my Soviet immigrant mind. Wow! Unbelievable! What a country!

The story betrays its author's bewilderment regarding the abundance of pets in America. This very human need to seek the companionship of domestic animals existed, of course, in the USSR as well. But there were much fewer of them because often there was nowhere to keep them. Most of the population was huddled in communal apartments, not the most convenient place to keep your dog or cat in comfort.

Another surprise for the newcomer was the quite relaxed educational demands in American elementary and middle schools in comparison with the rigorous Soviet education programs. It felt that, in contrast with the Soviet ones, American children have it overly easy. (I address this newcomer's myopic vision in Chapter 8.)

The story also reflects the puzzlement produced by the striking contrast between the American sphere of entertainment, mostly TV and cinema, and the culture left behind. Because of their mandatory ideological functions, called to help to shape a "true Soviet person," that is, a highly conscientious builder of the future of the whole of humankind, communism, Soviet TV and Soviet cinema never aimed at providing the viewers with pure entertainment, never pursued strictly commercial aims. There were several good Soviet comedies, but they were always imbued with the proper socialist morality and educational messages. None of them ever aimed at evoking such primitive emotions as horror. For horror's sake, of course. (I'm tempted to comment that there was no need for such movies; the real-life horror of several years of Soviet history rivaled the most chill-producing episodes in American movies belonging to that genre.)

The story also reflects the difference between American and Russian cultures in their attitude toward natural gifts. In Russian culture, it is assumed that talent itself is of indisputable value, its conscious cultivation is not needed, and the practical application of talent is not that important. An excellent illustration of this cultural stand is the nineteenth-century Russian story titled "The Left-Hander" (*Levsha*) by Nikolai Leskov.

The story is about one-upmanship vis-à-vis the West. In response to a skillful English handiwork, a miniature mechanical flea, so small you have to examine it under a microscope, a flea that can dance to music, an illiterate Russian artisan shoes this flea. And the implication of his nickname, the "left-hander," is that he does it with little sweat. In the Russian language, to express an undemanding job, they say, "It's no big deal. It can be done with one the left hand alone" (*odnoj levoj*).

Although once being shoed, the mechanical flea lost its ability to dance, it doesn't matter. What does matter is that, in comparing inborn talents, the Russians proved capable of beating the pants off anyone.

In Russian consciousness, talent is not to be discovered or developed. It is either there or not. Period. Thus, in my time, there was only one literary institute in the Soviet Union. The competition to be accepted there was fierce. In that respect, I recall an episode that took place at Hunter College in the late 1980s. The Soviet Union was still going strong, and a delegation of Soviet writers visited our college. When they learned that, in our English Department, students could choose the concentration in creative writing, they asked how fierce the competition among the applicants was.

"What competition?" one of our English professors shrugged. "Any student can choose it."

"What do you mean, any?" the Soviet visitor was flabbergasted. "Who told them they have a talent?"

"No one," my colleague replied. "At the end of the first semester, students find out if they should continue. Whether they have what takes to pursue creative writing."

Finally, and most important, is the following story's plot. Its protagonist keeps moving in circles, having no aim in mind. This circular movement betrays the author's bewilderment regarding the aimlessness of the American way of life. In the time of my Soviet adulthood, the 1960s, hardly anyone took seriously Nikita Khrushchev's pronouncement that the "current generation of Soviet people will live under communism." An underground joke of the time debunked it: "Communism may well be on the horizon, but it's known that the horizon is the line between the sky and earth which moves away as you approach it."

If you ask an American what he would like to achieve in his life, in most cases, he will say that he tries to live his life so that he would leave this earth a little better than it was before he appeared on it. That's all. No grandiose designs. Yet, the propagandistic drumming aside, the cultural expectation of someone who grew up under the Soviet system was that history has a vector, that it moves in a certain direction, to some future destination.

"Footmall"

It was one of those days when I didn't know what to do with myself, or what to live for. I threw my growing-stout fifty-year-old man's body into a car—it even squeaked under me, as if I had broken its backbone—and rushed away from home. I drove without thinking, at random, with no plan, and soon I darted out onto the expressway that ran through the city.

All eight lanes worked at full capacity. There were hardly any passenger cars ahead. Enormous trucks, their covered bodies resembling the mammoths' backs, flooded the highway, slowly, but without respite, pushing in the same direction only they knew of. Among them, from time to time, like dinosaurs, floated car haulers with multi-tiered pyramids of automobiles, both brand new ones, barely covered with road dust, and used ones, chewed up by the road, going for scrap, under the dull blow of the press. Rumbling of the engines, panting, noisy, like the sigh of a giant, emissions of brake air. Heavy labor, wheezing, sweat, stubborn movement forward—the space crawled under the car wheels....

Not knowing where I was going, I kept to the far-right lane, so as not to be drawn into a long-distance haul, in an unknown direction.

In this manner, I crawled through the city center. Looking around, having nothing else to do, I noticed someone waving his hand at me. It was Bill, my neighbor, a businessman. Amazing, energetic fellow! Whenever I would meet him, he was always in a hurry. On business. The cars drifted; I pulled down the window.

"How are you, Bill?" I shouted.

"I'm busy as hell," he smiled, his face contorted from torment. "And here, just look at it! We're barely moving...."

"When are you coming back?"

"I don't know for sure. Not too soon...."

The movement quickened, and Bill, waving goodbye, began switching lanes, each time winning a few yards of the road until he disappeared behind the truck bodies.

"Where should I go?" I thought, sighing. "It's time to decide on something. I shouldn't roll on like this forever just because everyone is rolling somewhere!"

About ten minutes later, having reached the exit from the city, I approached an overhead sign. Each lane now became a separate road with a number and the name of a destination point.

I wrestled with myself over where I would go when my gaze came upon a freshly painted arch segment on the far right. Instead of the road number and destination, it stated, "FOR UNDECIDED."

Some road workers' practical joke, I grinned.

Spurred on by curiosity, I moved to the far-right lane.

"EXIT ONLY," flashed a poster on the shoulder.

And the bounding lanes of the lane began veering to the right, away from the mainstream of the highway. Taking the ramp, I noticed I wasn't alone. A long line of other cars followed my suit—a used Buick, a brand-new Porsche, a heavy Rolls Royce, a green Buglet, a student's joy, and a trendy, squat, like a dachshund, Pan-Am sports car....

The roar of the freeway subsided a bit. I drove along the small settlements separated from the road by a row of souvenir shops. Realizing that it doesn't matter where to exit from the road, I pulled under one of the countless arches decorated with a poster with flashing lights.

"Welcome to Nowheresville!" *"A rather strange name,"* I thought and stepped into the first souvenir shop. The shop was like any other. I bought a postcard with a view of the town, *"Nowheresville is the joy of a suffering heart,"* and a children's T-shirt with the inscription: *"My grandfather visited Nowheresville and brought me this stupid thing."*

I moved from one shop to another until I realized I had circled the town. Through the side door of one shop, I walked into a square. The first person I saw was a cyclist. He pedaled as hard as he could; the spokes glittered, merging into a solid gleaming disk. Yet, he moved a tiny distance. At first, I thought it was some kind of new training bike model. However, an electric panel flashed on the handlebars, *"People and dogs, beware! I may crush you!"* From time to time, the cyclist pulled the bell lever.

I looked around the square and saw a lot of dogs. In Nowheresville, they adored them. They sat with their masters in a café. And not just at their feet, but next to them, in special chairs. Some specimens in straw hats and sunglasses sipped their dog cocktails through a straw. I am ready to swear I noticed a spark of passion in the eyes of one Saint Bernard, who sat on a chair opposite his owner, a youngish woman who gazed at him with an adoring look. The damned Bernard, too, looked at her and, it seemed, smiled carnivorously, patting her graceful hand with its claw.

In one of the small cafés, I noticed a pretty tennis player in a short skirt with a racket in her hand, who was drinking a milkshake. The girl smiled at me, and I smiled back. I sat down next to her and ordered my favorite cocktail, the Brownian Movement, a mixture of lemonade and flower syrup with an ounce of the finest pure alcohol. The tennis player moved up to me and whispered with a sweet smile:

"We'll get married tomorrow. My name is Letha."

"Phili...." I was about to introduce myself, but she beat me to it, saying that if I didn't mind, she would call me Ralph. In memory of the first puppy in her life.... She always called all her husbands that way, she added, smiling.

I had nothing against it. Ralph, so be it, Ralph.

We finished our cocktails, and Letha held out her hand to me:

"Let's go."

"Where?" I asked, rising after her. By that time, I didn't care where to go with Letha. Just to be near her.

"What do you mean, where? I just said it. To marry."

"You said—tomorrow...."

She smiled.

"It's tomorrow already," she said.

"Well, okay, let's call it 'tomorrow,'" I said, looking around in search of a clock.

"Don't waste your time," Letha said. "Here, in Nowheresville, we prohibit clocks. Not even the sundials. To avoid any accidents...."

"What'd happen if you look up time?"

"Nothing special. You wouldn't be able to live here. You'd start doing stupid things and go crazy."

"What do you mean, go crazy?"

"Go back to the Road," she said.

"How can you live without checking the time once in a while?" I said.

"It's possible," Letha said in her sweet little voice. "Since childhood, I have never known what time it is. Did it have any adverse effects on me? Well, look at me. Do I look like an unhappy woman?"

Indeed, I thought, admiring Letha. Next to her, I did not want to think about time.

We were married in a quick ceremony. The robot dressed in a toga in the presence of two robots-recorders pronounced solemnly:

"Do you swear, the Alien from the Big Road, to give Letha, your lawful spouse, at least a dozen orgasms a month, three of them per week until death do you part?"

"I swear," I muttered, wondering how many orgasms I would have to work out per year and whether I would have any vacations.

"Do you swear, Letha, to deliver to Ralph, your rightful spouse, the pleasures of his choice at least once a month, until death do you?"

"I swear," said Letha coquettishly.

Hand in hand, my newlywed wife and I strolled around the town. In the center of Nowheresville, there was a huge stadium with covered stands. We peeked into it. They loved spectacles in this town. The stadium was packed to capacity. The score on the "WE" and "THEY" tableau exceeded several million. At the moment we entered, the score was "11, 078.657: 8, 768.987." I thought the scoring system in Nowheresville was strange. Every score was worth hundreds of points, and maybe thousands.

"Nothing of the kind," Letha shook her shoulders, reading my thoughts, as if they were typed on my forehead. "A goal is a goal. Just the game never stops, and the score grows. One team replaces the other without interruption."

"Why?"

"Why not?" Letha said. "They take a break for the teams to rest. If the teams change, then there's no need for breaks. People pay money to enjoy the game, not a break."

"Well," I said, "doesn't the audience get tired?"

"When they get tired, they leave, and others take their place. Always like this...."

Along its outer perimeter, the stadium was filled with shops, large and small, hundreds of them. However, all other institutions and service offices were there, too. It was logical, since, as I understood it, the stadium was the place where the Nowheresvillians spent most of their lives. The entire structure was called "Footmall," which comprised a stadium and a shopping mall.

Among others, there was a furniture store. The locals would buy an armchair, carry it to their home, which looked like their neighbor's home—a house with a garage for two cars—and invite their neighbors. They would come to look at the armchair, gasp, shake their heads, congratulate the hosts, and consume meat bought at one of the Footmall's shops. They roasted the meat by the pool on a grill.

I talked with Letha about this and that, wandering around the Footmall. I couldn't take my eyes off her charming face. When I looked away for a moment, right then, wrinkles sprouted around her eyes and lips. When it happened for the first time, it scared me. I asked her what was going on.

"Nothing special, honey," she said. "We, Nowheresville's women, grow old if our men stop paying attention to us."

"But it was only a minute...."

"What's a minute?" Letha said. "Haven't I warned you? Not a word about your road people's time. Here, a minute or the eternity, it's all the same."

All the next day (in the town, thank God, at least there were sunsets and dawns) we fussed in a small garden around Letha's cottage, then went to the stadium again, and, in the evening, stopped by at a local school.

"What is here in the daytime?" I asked.

"A special school," she said. "They teach children how best to kill time between childhood and adolescence. In an ordinary school, they teach such nonsense. Many parents prefer to sign up their children for classes in this school. At least, the boys and the girls don't get bored here."

I heard some noise and giggle behind one door. The class time of the senior group was ending. Out of curiosity, I peeked inside. Along one wall, there were a bunch of teenagers with bows in their hands. At the opposite side of the room, a teacher, bare to the waist, stood looking around and scared.

"In our town, they become teachers on court orders," Letha said. "The judge's verdict spells it out, 'To work as a teacher in a local school for such-and-such term *pro bono.*' For serious crimes, they give them life sentences. But criminals prefer capital punishment instead."

"Could that be that you have the death penalty?" I asked in horror.

"Well," Letha said. "The highest measure is an Expulsion to the Road."

In the evenings, they offered classes for ungifted adults on the same premises. In the town, they believed that if you did not have a natural talent, it wasn't a big deal. You could substitute talent with the evening classes on your favorite subject. I didn't have a talent in photography, and Letha—in drawing. So we signed up for the classes. We had the same instructor. He was a very pleasant person who was convinced that the idea that possessing at least some talent was a primary requirement for getting involved in the arts was one of many prejudices inherited from distant epochs, which does more harm than good to humanity.

"Talent is just a matter of time," he said.

He convinced us. Not only did we get imbued with it ourselves, but we also converted our neighbors to our faith. We invited them to see our work. In the corner of the frames with our drawings and photographs, I showed how many hours, in my old sense of time, Letha and I put into our pieces.

"What a hardworking couple you are!" our neighbors said in admiration.

Once I returned from the stadium a little earlier than usual, as I entered the living room, I heard loud sobs coming from our bedroom. I rushed there.

It was Letha's sobbing. She stood with her back to me, with one hand pressed against the wall, and crying. I wanted to approach her and ask what happened, but at that moment, she screamed. I chilled with horror. Letha screamed a few more times in the same terrible way. I was about to rush to her and ask what had happened when, with no reason, she stopped screaming and squealed, like a little doggy that you stroke behind its ears. The screeching thing turned into good-natured, iridescent laughter, and, with her head thrown back, she roared.

My goodness, flashed in my mind, *the poor thing has lost it. But why?*

At that moment, Letha pushed off the wall, and the laughter stopped. Without looking back, she went into the bathroom and began splashing there. I was already at the bathroom door, ready to knock when she almost hit me with the door that opened. Her facial expression was the embodiment of calmness and composure.

"Letha!" I said, looking into her eyes. "What's the matter?"

"What happened? Why are you asking?"

"I just came in and...."

"Ah," Letha laughed, "I've just recharged my nervous system."

Seeing my bewilderment, she remembered:

"Oh, yes, I keep forgetting you're from the Road, that you don't know what's E.P. Don't they have such a service in the town you're from? Come here," she took my hand and led me to the wall. "Do you see it?"

Looking closer, I saw a small piece of plastic.

"Give me your finger," Letha said, grabbing my hand. "Not this one, the index one."

She pulled my finger to the plate. It rang out, taking it inside. The finger penetrated the shaggy walls inside the plate.

"Now close your eyes and relax, relax. Otherwise, it won't work," insisted Letha, patting my back.

I relaxed, and a weak electrical current ran through the epidermis of the finger. My spine muscles tightened, and an unspeakable fear seized me. A huge, stinking city cesspool monster appeared before my eyes. It stretched its hideous paw straight to my mouth, trying to tear it apart. Out of surprise, I opened my eyes and jumped off the wall, pulling out my hand.

Letha burst out laughing.

"What was it?" I asked, looking in amazement at my life companion, whom I trusted until this point.

"This is the E.P."

"What kind of monster is this?"

"Again, they show monsters to men only!" Letha got angry for the first time. "What male chauvinist pigs they are! ... For us, women, they show only ugly dwarfs.... Well, that's okay. I'll write to them today, damn bastards."

"To whom will you write?"

"To whom, to whom.... To the head of EPC, the male chauvinist pig."

"I understand nothing.... What's that EPC?"

"It's the Electronic Pleasure Cable. And its director of programming deserves to be hooked not on to his cable, but the high-voltage electric one.... What a bastard! What an arrogant male chauvinist!"

"What are these electronic pleasures?"

"You've just begun enjoying them and stopped right away, you little fool."

"You call it pleasure?"

"Oh dear, the Road still sits deep in you.... Back there, where you come from, they had driven it into your head that only positive emotions give pleasure."

Letha told the EPC history. Scientists have long established that the greatest pleasure for the inhabitants of Nowheresville was the alternation of impulses, which, through a direct effect on the brain, make a person feel compassionate, fearful, and jolly. Then, they synthesized these pulses and created generators, which, based on their basic configurations, produced a myriad of variations. Everyone could receive a charge of these wonderful impulses in the comfort of their apartment by connecting to a city network of electronic pleasures for a small fee.

From that day on, nothing remarkable happened to me. I lived the same way. I went to the same school, sometimes refreshing myself with the help of EP cable. I led that kind of life for a long time. Maybe for a year, maybe for two. And maybe just for a week. The climate in Nowheresville never changed during my stay there. It was a solid warm summer with no rain and too much heat. If a cloud appeared over the town, a squadron of aircraft would take off into the air. They were guided by housewives who had completed evening aerobatic courses. They lifted into the sky some device, resembling a slotted spoon, dragged it to a cloud, and pulled it along, away from the town....

I could not stand it any longer. I rushed to my car and dashed about the town in search of the exit gates. I found them and rushed along the narrow road that went along the town's borders.

I wanted to go back to the freeway. But to no avail. The traffic around the town was one-way; I couldn't find the entrance to the freeway, no matter how much I looked. I had already decided in desperation to turn off the asphalt, to dash across the field, but I realized it wouldn't work. My car was a lowrider, and it was a potato field, with thick leafy tops. I looked at the freeway, on which cars rushed, disappearing behind the horizon. I wanted to go back, to any meaningful movement, which had some starting point and moved to some finish…. But, alas, I couldn't do anything—I drove a lowrider…. I wish I had a dune car, squeezed between huge tires, and I could dart forward without caring about any roads.

I looked at myself in the rearview mirror. And I saw how ridiculous it was. I wore a shirt with a tie and a three-piece suit…. Here, you need shorts, hair grown to your shoulders, tanned neck and arms, and eyes wild from excitement, from intoxication with one's life. Where to get it all, where to get it!….

I was driving and driving, but to my surprise, I was in the same place. I found that, in the Nowheresville area, they built a circular road like a Mobius strip. I made endless loops that brought me back to my original point of departure. The landscape around did not change; it only moved in a circle. The angle of view was now larger, now smaller, but it was still the same. It was all the same….

At some turn, a horrific thought that I wouldn't be able to return home seized me. That I wouldn't ever be able to do it….

Suddenly, I spotted a familiar car among others. It was Bill's, my neighbor's, red Mustang. He got excited seeing me and waved his hand. We had parted, I recalled, on the freeway, in the same way—waving at each other….

"How come *you* are here?" I shouted, driving alongside his car. "You drove off on some business, as I recall. And you shouldn't have to return soon…. How have you wound up here?"

"I can't understand it myself," he said with a shrug. "I stayed on my route all the time. I couldn't have lost my way. I checked out the road signs on the way to be sure I was on the highway I needed…. I've taken care of a lot of business. At point A, I met Mr. B. In town C, I made business arrangements in town D. After reaching it, as soon as I'd managed my affairs there, without wasting time, I went to town E. I stick to my route all the time. I checked the map. The road went along, until it gradually narrowed and turned into this whirling, damn it! … It seems I'm here for the third day already…. I was here yesterday. And the day before yesterday," he said, looking around.

For the umpteenth time, we drove around the Footmall on a wide circle….[2]

IV

The Road
to Americanization

15

"Comrade Millionaire"

In time, not only did I discover my hang-ups and the cultural biases I brought along without even being aware of their existence, but I also found out things about my new country's cultural peculiarities as well. And I found out my road to Americanization is long and not always straightforward.

"Did you read that piece in the *L.A. Times* the other day?" an American man asks me one day. "About buying a baby buggy in Moscow? Quite amusing, isn't it?"

I pluck up all my courage and utter as modestly as I can: "Not only did I read it, but I also wrote it."

September 1977. As my fate had it, upon immigrating to America two-and-a-half years earlier, not only had I settled with my family near Hollywood, but I also had a short romance with it. More to the point, a one-night stand.

The Cold War was in full swing. Therefore, like the pebble ricocheting on the water, my Soviet satirist's career made a few touchdowns in America. The *Los Angeles Times* published a few of my satirical jibes at the Soviet way of life that I couldn't help but write back in the Soviet Union, knowing beforehand they wouldn't pass the censor's smell test. The latest of these publications was one that appeared in the op-ed pages of the *Times* on July 7. The piece, originally titled "The Wheel," is autobiographical. I had written it back in my Moscow days when expecting my son Max's arrival in this world, and I stood in line to buy a baby buggy at the Children's World department store in Moscow; shortages of goods of first necessity in the Soviet Union were endemic.

A few days after the piece was published, I attend a reception organized by the city's Jewish Family Service. On the occasion of the Jewish new year, they attempt to bring us, newcomers from another planet called the USSR, into the fold of the American Jewish community. Perhaps those who respond to the call to come down to meet the newcomers might give them a helping hand in their first steps in the new land.

After all, no Jew should forget that once upon a time, his people were also strangers in a new land.

Together with a few other former compatriots, I circle the tables loaded with snacks of endless variety. Although I'm long over the first shock of American supermarkets—you get used to good things, don't you?—I still marvel. "Good God," I say to myself, "where does all this cornucopia come from? Why so much of everything?" Some stuff, especially exotic fruit, like avocado, mango, or kiwi, I see and taste for the first time in my life.

As I'm trying not to give away my bewilderment, I find myself next to a middle-aged man, dressed in a navy-blue blazer and a pair of beige trousers. Though of small stature, he is powerfully built, his big head tight-fitting his body. His large, bulging eyes make him look not just attentive, but inquisitive.

(As I'll learn much later, the reason Berle attended the reception was that his parents were Jewish immigrants from Russia who had come to America at the turn of the twentieth century. So, he was curious to see how the new crop of newcomers from the land of his parents look. I encountered this American curiosity before, that imaginary time travel. My first American friend, Dr. Jules Levin, who, as a volunteer for the Jewish Family Service, had met me and my family as we first arrived in Los Angeles, told me sometime later with a smile, "Do you know, Emil, what I think as I look at you? If my parents hadn't left Russia in the 1920s, when it was still possible, but stayed in the old country, I'd be you!")

Guessing by my clothes—I'm still wearing the leather jacket I'd bought in Rome where, together with others, I stayed waiting for our entry visas to America—that I am one of the new arrivals, the man watches for a while with discreet curiosity my clumsy attempts to place a slice of lox onto an open bagel with cream cheese. When I'm done, he extends his hand to me with a friendly smile: "Hi, my name's Berle. And yours?"

For a moment, I'm startled. Since I know already the name of a famous American comedian of Jewish descent, Milton Berle (I'm not aware yet that his last name is a shortened version of Berlinger), I assume Berle is a Jewish name, and my old country anxieties kick in. How come a man uses his Jewish name in public? Back in Russia, if your given name was Jewish, like, say, Boruch, you would be sure to introduce yourself to a stranger with its closest-sounding Russian equivalent—Boris. When, at the height of Stalin's anti–Semitic campaigns, my younger brother was born, my parents gave him the Russian name Vladimir, instead of the intended Welwl, the Yiddish variant of Wolf, in honor of our grandfather on my mother's side. While our father's real name was Abram, back on Odessa streets, my mother would call him "Arkady."

When I give the man my name, his eyebrows raise in surprise: "Did you say Emil?"

I nod. The man looks somewhat lost. He thought he was attending a reception for Russian-born Jews, not for Frenchmen. We've just met, and I haven't told him the whole story of how, being born Samuel, I first adopted "Emil" as part of my pen name, and getting used to it in time, upon arrival in America, I made it legal in my naturalization papers.

Berle and I have a small talk. He asks me how long I'm in the country, where I came from, and things like that. When I tell him I arrived from Moscow, he asks me that question about the piece in the *Los Angeles Times*.

When I tell him I wrote it, Berle says, "Is that so?" and gives me a big friendly smile.

We part. He makes another circle around the snack counter, from time to time stopping and chatting with other immigrants. When he stops near me again, he says: "Have you read about the Christina Onassis scandal in the papers? What do you think of it?"

Shortly before our meeting, the papers had been filled with high-society gossip about a romance between Christina, the heir to her late father's, the Greek magnate Aristotle's, $500 million shipping, financial, and industrial empire, with Sergei Kauzov, a representative of Sovfracht, the Soviet ship-chartering agency, in Paris. While the papers state that U.S. intelligence sources think he "may have KGB connections," for anyone like me, who was born and raised in the Soviet Union, such careful suppositions are a laugh. But of course! They charge anyone in that position abroad with espionage tasks.

I tell Berle I find it hilarious that Christina wants to marry a Soviet citizen and make her home in the Soviet capital. (Even before that event, I've often scratched my head about how little Americans knew about life in the Soviet Union, never mind the ultra-rich Onassis' daughter.) I chat with Berle a bit more, and before leaving, he says: "You know what, Emil? If you come up with an idea for a movie based on the Onassis story, give me a ring. If I like it," he adds, "I'll make sure you'll be commissioned to write the script."

He hands me his business card, gives me another of his big warm smiles, pats me on the shoulder, and leaves.

I look at his card. It's simple, yet elegantly designed, stating that the man's surname is Adams, and he is president of his firm—the Berle Adams Company.

The next day after meeting Berle, I put my brain to work. Looking back at that episode of my life, I realize that I had a romantic notion about the writing profession and the way Hollywood operates in particular. Now, I say to myself, "OK, man, here's your chance to build your writing career in America. If you fuck up, you have no one—no one!—to blame but yourself." (By that time, I'm already aware of the fact that the worst thing that could happen to any human being is when you have no one—not a single other person!—to blame for your failure.) Here it is, Mr. Emil, your golden opportunity. As the American saying has it, "either shit or get off the pot." If you fail, stop even thinking about calling yourself a writer!

For three days, I'm hardly a pleasant presence in my family. In the evenings, after dinner, when my three-year-old son Maxim is in bed, I rush out to the streets and pace along the sidewalk in front of the house in which we rent a one-bedroom apartment. It is of little help, and I began making circles around the block. First, I go south, to the intersection with Oakwood Avenue, then I turn right onto North Spaulding, make another right onto Rosewood, and go back to our Genesee. When I reach our house, I think of our landlord, an elderly Polish Jew who, after spending a few years in Stalin's gulag and surviving it by a miracle, remembers only a few phrases in Russian that he recites to us thinking it would please us to know he knows some words of our native tongue. He memorized only the camp guards' swearing directed at him and other prisoners, like *eb tvoiu mat'*, the Russian equivalent for "motherfuckers," and some other choice phrases. When I asked him in whose honor our street, Genesee, is named, he told me that, as far as he knows, it is the name of some Native American chief. I'll learn in time that he might have made it up, that the name means "Beautiful Valley." But, now, gearing up to meet the new challenge in my American life, pacing the sidewalks of neighboring streets in my frantic attempt to come up with a story makes me think of the only Native American I know about. It's Chingachgook, the hero of James Fenimore Cooper's novel, the tribal chief in *The Last of the Mohicans* and *The Deerslayer*, which I read in Russian translation back in my youth. Thinking of him makes me feel that, like Cooper's character, I have also stepped onto the warpath.

I juggle around in my head the elements of the springboard story. To avoid being sued for libel, I make the Greek citizen Christina Onassis into an Australian one of Italian descent, Karina Gasperetti, the surname of my classmate; at that time, I attend the UCLA grad school for Slavic studies. She's also the only heir to her late father's ... er ... uranium mines. Kauzov becomes Kozlovsky, the name of a journalist writing for New York's *New Russian Word*, whose criminal reportages I read with interest. (I'm not aware yet that it is a poor choice, that, to avoid the risk of being sued for defamation, Writers Guild of America lawyers advise not to use even the first letter of a real person's name.) In terms of a conflict, I make Kozlovsky hope to defect to the West, which, unbeknownst to Karina, makes their interests clash. Kozlovsky is a good-natured man who craves freedom, not Karina's money.

For me, the whole notion of a multimillionaire woman wanting to live in the Soviet Union is so bizarre that comic situations pop up in my head. The gist of the story I come up with is that around the time Christina's character falls for the Russian, the man contemplates defecting to the West, and Christina's desire, after marrying him, to settle in Moscow, threatens his plans.

(It's little wonder that a defector plot is on my mind. High-profile stories about Soviet citizens escaping to the West are galore. In 1974, the year I left the USSR, ballet dancer Mikhail Baryshnikov jumped off his theater wagon while touring in Canada. Two years later, military pilot Viktor Belenko flew his MIG-25 to Japan, pianist Yuri Egorov prolonged his Roman holidays indefinitely, and, following a chess tournament in Amsterdam, Soviet grandmaster Viktor Korchnoi made his smartest off-board move refusing to return to his Soviet motherland.)

In hindsight, perhaps it was good that I didn't know any details of Kauzov's appearance. Otherwise, it would be too tempting to use them as fodder for comic exploitation. As known from the social media of today, the man was balding, his "mouth glisten[ed] with gold teeth," and he had a "glass eye that he now and then calmly remove[d] and replace[d] in public." Any comedy writer would give an arm and a leg for such props. What a ball I could have with them! It'd feel natural to suggest his KGB-designed artificial eye is equipped with a mini-camera, and his gold crowns have built-in semiconductors that allow him, by clutching his molars, to send his reports to the Moscow Center in Morse code. On second thought, my ignorance was for the better. Such a character's features would make him look like a villain, not a man who is fed up with the Soviet system and looking for an opportunity to escape, a part I wanted him to play in my storyline.

After a few rewrites, I brace myself and call Berle. He invites me to talk about it over lunch in my neighborhood, at Canter's, the famous Jewish deli on Fairfax Avenue, just a few blocks from my home.

The night before I meet a Hollywood producer, I sleep poorly. What if I fail my fortune test? What if, when crossing the Soviet border, at customs, they stripped me not only of Soviet citizenship, but they also confiscated my sense of humor, which, unbeknownst to me, they put on the long list of things forbidden to be exported from the country? What if, when I read my notes to Berle, he would just give me a standard American smile of politeness, only that?

The time of the lunch arrives. I order a pastrami sandwich with a pickle on the side, but I can hardly eat it. My mouth is too dry. I'm nervous. I get hold of myself and read my plot outline to Berle.

To my great relief, he chuckles several times.

"Good work, Emil!" he says when I finish. "Now we have to rewrite it the way they are accustomed to in Hollywood…. There's a certain format to it…. When can you come over to my office to work on it?"

And he gives me another of his business cards.

For the next ten days, I visit him on the third floor of a shiny, glass-covered, multi-storied building overlooking Sunset Boulevard. I was aware of its name before I arrived in America. They screened the eponymous movie at the House of the Journalists in Moscow. Together with my fellow Soviet journalists, I watched, my heart pounding, the famous flick with young Bill Holden and Gloria Swanson. Now both the street and Berle's office look quite ordinary. Perhaps only the paintings on the walls (one of them, as I made it out, is a Picasso) of his office make me think that its owner hardly struggles to make ends meet.

We work. Berle's secretary retypes my scribbles. I just write down Berle's suggestions. In all fairness, though we came up with a full-fledged movie treatment that bore my name as its author, Berle's contribution is so significant that, if he would suggest signing it with both, his and my, names, I wouldn't object. Though the overall plot outline was mine, Berle gave me much feedback and background information on the Onassis character. For example, how the hell would I know what motivates the Karina character to want to live in the Soviet Union of all places? I fled the country at the first opportunity, and she wants in? Go figure! It was a mystery to me. Who in one's right mind would want to live in the USSR while so many people dream of flying the coop?

But Berle suggested a plausible scenario. When she meets the Russian, Karina is intrigued. She recalls her college professor's lectures on Marxism. What a wonderful way to live! A state in which all people share everything, like members of one extended family. A country where she will be accepted for her worth, not for her wealth. Karina is eager to learn more about Russia. She buys books on Russian culture, watches documentaries about Russia, buys Russian records, and has dinner only in Russian restaurants. She plans through a friend to meet Kozlovsky on a business matter. The friend has them meet in a Russian restaurant, of course.

When working with Berle, I learn bit by bit that his company distributes American TV shows abroad, and he is producing a movie, *Brass*

Target, based on a controversial account that General Patton was assassinated by a bunch of American *no-goodniks,* not that he died in an automobile accident. Despite having a great cast, including Sophia Loren, John Cassavetes, and Max von Sydow, Berle is concerned the movie might not make much money. That fact alone has made me feel that the man is well-positioned in Hollywood, and I should take working with him seriously. Deep down, I'm at a loss. How can he worry about movie success? The mere presence of Sophia Loren in the film impresses me and makes me feel in awe of what Berle is doing.

(In hindsight, it was a good thing that I knew beans about the man at that junction in my life.) Before setting up his little company, Berle Adams (born Beryl Adarsky) was the co-founder of Mercury Records and an MCA executive. In his business, he not just rubbed shoulders and breathed the same air but also worked with a megastar of his time, Glenn Miller. I knew the man through the *Serenade of Sunny Valley,* a Hollywood movie shown in my hometown's, Odessa's, theaters after World War II. Berle booked road dates for Glenn, as well as for Nat King Cole, the Andrews Sisters, and Jimmy Dorsey, among other American performers whose music and songs, as a youngster, back in my Odessa years, I had admired, catching them on my father's imported short-wave Grundig radio receiver. Later on, Berle signed a stand-up comedian, Bob Newhart, booked him into clubs, and soon sold *The Bob Newhart Show* to NBC, which won a Peabody Award and an Emmy nomination. He was also the MCA agent for Jack Benny, Rosemary Clooney, Eddie Fisher, Dinah Shore, Norman Lear, Charles Laughton, and Alfred Hitchcock. He talked Marlene Dietrich into starring in a revue. There were many other superstars he worked with—Neil Diamond, Elton John, Olivia Newton-John, Danny Kaye, Gene Kelly, Fred Astaire, you name it. So, my ignorance about all of Berle's credentials is true bliss. If I knew even a small portion of his background, it would be too intimidating for me. It would freeze my mind.

Once we finish with the treatment, we agree to title it "Comrade Millionaire," and Berle tells me he'll be in touch. "Let me make a few phone calls," he says.

A couple of weeks pass by. Since I haven't heard from him, I assume that's the end of my Hollywood romance. Yet, comes another Monday, and Berle calls me asking whether I'm free for lunch this week. We'll be joined, he explains, by the vice president of Twentieth Century–Fox in charge of television. The man asked about our proposal and would like to discuss the possibilities.

It's too hard for me to believe that somebody that high in the famous studio's hierarchy has nothing better to do but discuss over lunch my whimsical treatment based on high-society gossip.

I don't sleep well that night. Just in case I don't get it right, I don't say anything to my wife about the forthcoming meeting with Hollywood biggies. I don't want to be embarrassed later that I failed the test of fate.

I'm full of apprehension. Well, I try to cheer myself up. After all, why won't I get my lucky break in Hollywood by a sheer lineup of luck and circumstance? When I finally close my eyes, I have a recurring dream. Like in a film loop, it runs infinitum. Bill Holden's character in the *Sunset Boulevard* movie sneaks up to our Genesee apartment, hides beyond the cypress in front of the house, and, at the right moment, jumps into our window, shouting into my face, "Don't mess with Hollywood, Emil! Get it straight from the horse's mouth: they'll eat you alive! ... They'll shoot you in the back, and you'll wind up like me, in the pool face down."

I wake up in horror. I'm relieved at the first thought that comes to my mind: we don't have a pool in our backyard; we can't afford such a place yet....

Finally, the morning comes. I drive up to the restaurant at the Beverly Hills Hotel. As I approach it, I realize that, as a UCLA grad student, I hardly can afford the valet parking. Never mind the embarrassment. Brand-new Mercedes and Ferraris roll up to the hotel entrance—and here I come in my ancient 1966 Dodge, its left side dented in two places....

Berle and I are joined by a tall, polished man in his early forties. The ease with which he and Berle communicate with each other makes me feel they have worked together for ages. They talk and talk, hardly paying any attention to me. As I munch on my Caesar salad, they discuss "Comrade Millionaire" from every angle. Since I put so much heart into the story, I feel awkward that the gentlemen talk about my work without asking me anything. They talk aloud about how the line of action is to be changed and what characters should be doing.

Finally, they acknowledge my presence and ask only two questions. One is who would be good to cast for the part of Kauzov's character.

I name a young actor popular at the time, Michael Moriarty. Though he is Irish American, his appearance fits the overall image of Kauzov, especially his balding hairline. What about Christina?

I don't know where I get the guts to do it, but I utter: "Natalie Wood."

The men exchange glances and reply almost in unison:"No problem. We can approach her."

Wow, what power men I am dining with! Boy, oh boy!

Before we part, Berle explains to me what should happen next. They will send the treatment to all three TV networks—CBS, ABC, NBC— and, if any of them express interest, they would place their production order with the 20th Century–Fox. In that case, Fox will contract me to write a script with Frank Waldman.

I thought I'm hearing things. What? With Frank Waldman? To write a script with a seasoned scriptwriter who, most recently, authored scripts for the hilarious Inspector Clouseau and two highly successful movies of the Pink Panther series?

I ask Berle in dismay: "Why does a writer with such credentials need me?"

"No, no," Berle shakes his head, "he'd need you. I bet he doesn't know a thing about Russia. He can't do it alone."

In a few weeks, however, it is all over. Since Berle and the 20th Century man saw our project as part of the "Movie of the Month" series popular at the time, the TV networks they approached were preoccupied with much more substantial subjects than a mindless love affair of a super-rich woman with a Soviet playboy. Instead, they turned to one of the much more important themes, the permanent threat of a nuclear station meltdown (*China Syndrome*).

Though the story about my flirtation with Hollywood seems anticlimactic, it led to two important developments in my American life. The rejection didn't crush me. It did a lot of good for me in the long run. First, I learned a lot about how the La-La-Land operates, thus saving myself from a lot of heartbreaks. I realized it was a huge gambling enterprise, a super-casino where every single day zillions of wannabe scriptwriters search for the golden key to fame and fortune. Though later some producer bought an option for my "Comrade Millionaire" treatment for half a year and it earned me some money, the episode didn't suck me into the Hollywood frenzy. I was about to finish grad school; I had a family to feed and couldn't sit and wait until fate smiled at me. Second—and this development was very important for me as an émigré writer always in danger of being stuck in his past, in his homebound memories—my experience during the time of working with Berle Adams led me to write my first piece on American material. It pleased me that the *L.A. Times* found it good enough to appear on one of its op-ed pages:

"Let's See ... a Socko Ending to This Disease Might Be..."

One day, I went to the dentist. My right molar was killing me. A nice-looking (they don't hire any other kind) assistant put me into a chair, hung a paper napkin from little clothespins under my chin, and turned on the light overhead. But the dentist was nowhere to be seen.

"Where is he?" I asked.

"Don't worry, he'll be just a moment," the assistant said. "As soon as he can hide the body."

My jaw dropped.

"Thank you," said the assistant, pulling up her chair. "We'll do some cleaning in the meantime."

Oh, God! I thought. *What am I doing here? Who recommended this guy?*

Gradually I came to my senses and asked, somewhat cautiously: "Whose body?"

"Of an auto mechanic."

"Atta boy!" I said, a bit relieved. "They deserve whatever they get."

"You think so? Dr. Roger was hesitant to kill or not to kill."

"No doubt about it! The minute you spot an auto mechanic, shoot with both barrels! For all the hassle they give you."

"But then he'll lose his line," the assistant said with a tone of concern for her boss.

"What line?"

"The plotline, of course."

"Is he writing a novel?"

"No, a movie treatment."

I live a few blocks from Hollywood. The view over the mountains is splendid; here and there I can see palms and cypresses. Lately, the air has even been clean. It's lovely and a far cry from Moscow left forever behind.

But I recently discovered that the entire area is infected with a dangerous disease. Its symptoms are nervous agitation, insomnia, dizziness, and hallucinations, which take the size of gold bullion the size of a suitcase, sliding down the Hollywood hills. There is no cure, though some relief might be found by moving, with one's entire family, away from Southern California.

The name of the disease is *screenwriteritis*. In Los Angeles, everyone writes scripts—journalists (it seems as though God himself commands it when a typewriter is always at hand), grocers, housewives, and taxi drivers. Every server in town is a budding screenwriter who makes a living in the meantime by serving flaming omelets.

It doesn't matter with whom you strike up a conversation in Los Angeles. You find out he has either just started writing a script or has just finished one and is starting another. Talk abounds about things called "shared credits," "separated rights," "development funds," and the altogether mysterious "step deals." It isn't rare to hear assurances at least five times a day that Bo Derek of the movie *Ten* fame has shown interest in a script, that she has agreed to risk her career and be filmed fully clad.

I've noticed that at American parties (where the drinks are so diluted that you don't even have to sit down to drink them) you must be very careful what you talk about. Even if it is as trivial as your misadventures during your last trip to your nephew's wedding in Cleveland, how you missed your plane and boarded the wrong one—to Bangkok by mistake.

"Did you tell this to anyone else?" someone asks. "Good, then keep your mouth shut. It could be an excellent comedy. I'll send you the first draft of an outline tomorrow. I will be your co-author."

And he disappears, rushing off to his typewriter.

At one of those parties, someone told me a horrible story: Every morning a ten-ton mail truck enters the gates of one of the largest Hollywood studios. Choking and sputtering exhaust fumes, it worms its way well inside, then backs up to a receiving bay on a huge, specially designed machine. Stuffed manila envelopes fly into the bin—thousands of envelopes containing outlines, treatments, and fully developed scripts. Growling, the machine puts its steel jaws to work, grinding envelopes to pulp within minutes.

"Why are they doing this?" I cried in despair.

"So, they don't go bankrupt, spending all their money on script readers," came the answer. "It's impossible to read that much material. And there's no way to stop the flow."

"Does anybody know about this?"

"Everyone, I think."

"And they continue to write?"

"Yes, they keep doing it anyway...."

Still digesting the peculiarities of my life in the new land, I was about to raise a plastic glass of whiskey to my mouth when I felt the gaze of a beautiful young woman on me.

I have to admit, I harbor no illusions about my looks. I don't remind people either of Cary Grant or Gregory Peck. Any resemblance to Woody Allen is due only to a similarity in height and hair color; I don't even wear glasses. I could never win the heart of a woman just by standing there, my mouth shut.

But the beauty kept looking at me and even started to breathe heavily. I turned around. Was I blocking her view of a rock star?

I looked back, feeling as though someone was pouring a thin stream of water down my collar. The woman's chest was heaving; she was breathing faster and faster.

Maybe she needs oxygen? I thought. *It's stuffy in here. Perhaps I should take her out onto the balcony....* But then, who knows, maybe there is something in my face, some magnetism....

She walked up to me. She touched my elbow and turned me toward her. Her eyes were shining. I just stood there, still unable to figure out what I had done to deserve this attention.

"Listen," she said, sounding passionate or at least breathless. "I know you're from Russia and see our life differently.... Like, in another way.... You know, unusually.... That's terrific!"

"What do you think is so outstanding about that?" I utter, flushed from the excitement of the moment. "'In another way,' you say. So what?"

"What are you saying?" she said. "This is extraordinary, this is marketable!"

"What?" I asked again. I stared at her; maybe the beauty had drunk too much.

But, no, she said soberly:

"Your impressions about America have a market value. They are a commodity—salable."

"What do you mean, salable? Who buys impressions about America?"

"Producers," she said. "You little fool! We'll write an outline together. I have an enormous number of acquaintances in the movie world, and I'm sure this will work. Put down your glass, don't drink anymore." She led me to the door. "Don't wait any longer; go home right now and try to recall everything that has amazed you about America. Remember," she said, helping me into my car, "it's marketable."

I went home—alone, half-sober, and rather angry. I could not sleep. I jumped from my bed, stretching my hands out in front of me like a sleepwalker, and rushed to my desk where my typewriter sat, uncovered from the previous day. My fingers found the keys on their own and began to fly over them. "Alexis in America. An outline. All names and events are fictitious...."

All at once, I felt agitated. Dizzy, too. My room was filled with patches of emerald, and an unbearable brilliance emanated from the Hollywood hills, radiating down. Then, there it was.... Sliding down toward my home was a gold bullion the size of a suitcase....[1]

16

"Disappearance"

The story "Footmall" captures many sides of American life as seen through the eyes of a person whose world outlook was informed by Russian culture and the Soviet educational system. As to an American proverb, quoted earlier, "It's easier to get a country boy out of the country than to get the country out of the boy," I came to realize that the proverbial "country" still sat in me.

Apparently, in parallel with all this, another process had taken place, the slow, subconscious process of the author's Americanization, bit by bit adopting a new system of values, another kind of human relations, and a unique organization of living. Published after a decade and a half of emigration, the stories included in his collection *The Lost Boy* (Moscow: Moscow Worker, 1993) gradually move into the realm of magic realism. In other tales, the author tries to comprehend his own life without attachment to its specifics, its realities.

Symbolic in this sense is the story "The Loss," in which its protagonist, an author of Broadway vaudevilles, discovers one day that he has lost his sense of humor, which disqualifies him from his line of work. This happens to him, not because of some sudden onslaught of depression, but because of his new, deeper look at life, which he finds not funny at all. And he realizes that his former ability to make people laugh was only a way for his psyche to deal with life's vagaries.[1]

In another story, titled "One Day," the narrator attempts to relive his entire life retrospectively squeezing it into twenty-four hours.[2]

This departure from the former writer's view of life, from his former persona, was noticed by the author of the introduction to the collection, a prominent Russian literary critic, Lev Anninsky. As they say, "On-lookers see more than players"; this observation is suited to this case.[3]

In the collection, which includes both satirical stories from the Soviet era and an assortment of them written in America, the critic notes the process of the author's gradual leave-taking from his Soviet satirical past, the upshot of which is rendered in the story "Disappearance." One day, the protagonist's loved ones disappear one after another, together with other familiar people and places. This transformation culminates with the loss of the hero's face. All this takes place against the background of a seemingly smooth life, secure, devoid of any unsolvable conflicts. Commenting on this story, the critic evokes the title image of the novel by Lewis Carroll, popular at that time in Russia: "Loss of one's face, *realized* as such, in a certain sense, is already an attainment of one's face, even if, to achieve it, one has to cross all borders, get into the world behind the looking glass, and make sure that is gone.[4]" Back then, when the book was just published, still wandering in the wilderness of my American life, I dismissed this insight as a figment of the critic's imagination.

Now, at an even greater distance of time able already to look at what came out of my pen many years ago with an open mind, with detachment, I can't help but concur with the critic's insight.

"Disappearance"

Half an hour had passed since Bill had returned from the movies. He and Maud had gone there—he in his car, she in hers—right after work. Bill parked in the garage and put the kettle on, expecting his wife to come in any minute. It surprised him she wasn't home yet, but decided it must be because of one of Maud's little quirks: she was always trying to find some new route home from the movie theater. She had driven around in circles and was now making her way through traffic somewhere on the far side of town.

Bill turned on the TV and sat through the news—a teachers' strike, a small fire at the spaghetti factory, and a girl of twelve's disappearance. Most likely, it was the usual story—she was abducted by a daddy who had missed his little girl since the family break-up. Divorce, divorce.... Everything was going well between him and Maud. Soon, they would have been married for fourteen years. Fate is a funny thing. "Never assume you're spared forever from a prison ward or beggar's cup," as his Russian grandmother used to say. There are no guarantees—well, that's obvious. No, with Maud and him, everything seemed to be all right; they often phoned each other from work and went to the movies together. Their boy, Patrick, was already thirteen, a big kid. He sounded to be happy at Lawrence, the boarding school they had chosen for him.

"I have to buy him that new album for Christmas," Bill thought. He couldn't remember the name of the rock group his son liked. "I must ask Maud."

He looked at his watch again. An hour had passed, but his wife was still not home. Bill worried. Panicking would be silly. Something had happened with the car. Her Camry had been tuned up, but you never know about automobiles. Bill had an engineering degree, but to him, a machine was no less complicated than a human; it could be just as unpredictable. There was always the chance that something wouldn't work. Yet Maud's automobile was almost new; plus, it was Japanese. Bill had consulted Consumer Report's latest indexes for reliability when he picked his wife's new car. But nothing's perfect, it seems. Probably, as he was pacing the floor from corner to corner, Maud was trying to call him. Maud always called him first if there was a problem. His wife, a calm woman, got nervous anytime something went wrong with the car. She would call him, though he had told her many times it made more sense to call the AAA first. Bill liked her momentary helplessness. Anyway, they could afford to get a new car every two or three years, so car troubles were rare.

He waited for another hour. The phone was silent. Did Maud get no reception under some bridge or something? She could be stuck on a deserted street and afraid to leave the car. Maybe she asked someone to call the club for her, and now she might sit, shivering with fear with all the doors locked. Maud was a real chicken and didn't hide it. She could have asked them to call him, too. It had been over two hours now. She ought to have realized that he would worry. But then again, who knows, she may not have had a coin for another call....

Now he was worried. Could he be a victim of one of those stupid blows of fate you read about in the papers sometimes, or see on TV? Once someone at work had told him a story about some inexperienced thug who tried holding up a gas station. Something must have spooked him, and he fired at random. A stray bullet struck the father of a family, a recent immigrant from Mexico. It hit him on the day he had just gotten his first job in his new country. He had been on his way home, where his whole family was expecting him with dinner to celebrate the occasion.

Could it be that some criminal had noticed Maud waiting for the tow truck, and got into the car, kidnapping her at gunpoint? No. Things like that only happened in movies, or to somebody else, not him.

Bill had always considered himself lucky. Everything had always gone the way it ought to, the way he expected it to, the way he planned. He graduated from high school, then college. After sending out some resumes, he got the job he wanted. Maybe the work wasn't as fascinating as, say, working at Cape Canaveral in a space lab, but it was a decent job, with good prospects for growth. He had met Maud just when he was ready to settle down and have a family. They devoted the first three years of their marriage to travel to all the places they had dreamed of since childhood (Paris, Barcelona, the Caribbean Islands, Hawaii, and Acapulco). During these travels, Maud got interested in photography, took a few classes at the local school, and freelanced for travel magazines. Once she even got a call from *National Geographic*....

Maud conceived as soon as they decided to have a child. Their son was born healthy. For the first three months, Maud would not use the baby formula, but nursed the boy, though she complained she would pay for it one day when her breasts would lose their shape and firmness.

She had read that breastfed babies grew up healthier and were better adjusted. It must have been right. Patrick grew into a sound, strapping boy.

Another hour passed, and Bill called the police.

"How long's it been since you last saw her?" they asked.

"Three and a half hours."

"Do you have any reason to worry? Did you fight? Maybe she went to see a friend?"

"No, no, I'm telling you...."

Bill slammed the receiver down. What could he say to this moron of a cop? Maud didn't have any close friends, no one who she could just barge in on so late at night. The police were thinking Maud had some brief fling on the side. Ridiculous! Anything was possible. But with Maud? She wasn't the type. Sometimes Bill felt he hadn't met his wife in a college cafe, between computer science lectures, in a little courtyard squeezed between two campus buildings, but he had picked her out of a catalog. Maud fulfilled everything he had ever wanted in a woman. She just wasn't cut out for a cheap minor affair. And even if she were to—let's assume—sleep with someone else, would she do it like this? Would she just vanish off the face of the planet? That wouldn't be some insignificant romance; that would be something a lot more serious. No, no, this had nothing to do with love affairs.

The night was awful. It was stuffy. As if to spite him, the air conditioning broke down. He had to wait until morning to call a serviceman. Bill could not sleep. He drank weak tea, then strong coffee, hour after hour, flipping through the TV channels, watching parts of a western, then a 1930s musical, a show for intellectuals about the decline of trust in elected officials, a drama about the murder of a young actress who had some rather interesting relationships with the city bigwigs. Bill tensed, listening for the phone, sometimes reaching out to pick it up when a phone rang on the screen. Toward morning when they began to show young women stretching and exercising, exposing as much skin as seen on the Playboy channel, he took a shower, drank some Turkish coffee, and again called the police. They could find neither Maud nor her car on their list of traffic accidents for that night.

"Come down to the city morgue, if you're sure that your wife is a victim of a homicide," said the cop, "I'm telling you, though, that the computer doesn't show her either on the list of identified victims, or arrests."

Before leaving, Bill called his mother-in-law, Mrs. Root, at the "Quiet Sunset" retirement home. The old lady recognized his voice and asked what happened. Bill called Mrs. Root rarely, but Maud visited with her weekly, on Sundays, between lunch and dinner.

"Has Maud called you by any chance?"

"Why? Was she supposed to? What's the matter with her?"

Bill calmed her down as best he could and hung up the phone. He drove to the coroner's office, trying not to think about the corpses as people who, a short while ago, were living as if they had decades ahead of them. They had a woman who fit Maud's description. Horrified by the thought he might see his wife dead, Bill walked into the mortuary which reeked of formaldehyde. He recalled his grade-school biology lab where he had once dissected a frog. He loathed everything there—the fat biology teacher, Mr. Goursky, the frog with its eyes, which seemed to stare at him in disbelief at its sad fate, and that awful smell....

The woman was much shorter than Maud; he saw it right away, even before they exposed her face. The one under the linen was hardly over five-two. Didn't he tell that moron-on-duty that Maud was 5' 10", a tall woman by anyone's account? Why had he made him go through this ordeal? With a sigh of relief and hope that Maud was at least alive somewhere, he drove away.

A few more days passed in the quiet apartment; a chill would grip him every time the phone rang. It was clear. His wife had disappeared without a trace.

It was Saturday, the day Maud visited their son at boarding school. Lawrence Academy was a three-hour drive from the city. Bill drove there, even though he could not think of what he could tell Patrick about his mother. At the last minute, he decided he would stall for time and say to him she wasn't feeling well. He'd promise that Patrick would see her next time.

They opened the gate when he showed his parent's pass, which he used on those rare occasions when he wasn't on call, stayed in town in case of an emergency with his bank computer program, and could join Maud when visiting Patrick.

He did not drive up to the dorm but went to the main building. At this hour, they had extra classes on European history, and he remembered Maud mentioning that Patrick had signed up. The teacher—"the Old Ms. Higgins," as Patrick called her—greeted Bill when he peeked into the classroom. Bill apologized, closed the door, and waited for recess. Twenty minutes later, the kids poured out into the hall. He did not see Patrick among them. Ms. Higgins was the last out of the classroom.

"Excuse me," Bill said, "where's my Patrick?"

"Patrick?" the teacher smiled. "Which Patrick? We have two. Patrick Swanson and Patrick O'Brien. They're over there in the corner, shoving each other."

Bill looked at the far end of the hallway.

"Ms. Higgins, I don't visit here too often, my wife comes. My name is Masters. Patrick Masters is my son."

"Your face seems familiar, but there are no Patrick Masters in my class, and I'm afraid there never has been."

"Ms. Higgins," said Bill. "You say you remember me, but you don't know my boy, even though he's been at school here for a year."

"I assure you, sir, that you are mistaken. I am not a young woman, but I am not so old I wouldn't remember my students. Come, you can see for yourself."

She invited him into the classroom and led him to the podium, where there was a class attendance log. Bill checked it twice but did not find his son's name. For a moment, he thought he was dreaming. He was asleep, and in his dream, he visited Patrick, who turned out to be not listed among students at his boarding school. Maybe he had somehow ended up in the wrong place. But they had opened the gate for him, had recognized him! Maybe Maud had transferred Patrick to a different school and had not told him? But that was just impossible. Maud would never do such a thing without talking to him. But then, where was his son?

Feeling he was on the verge of insanity, Bill rushed to the headteacher's office, shoved the pass in his face, and demanded an explanation. The headteacher found his behavior to be distressing and ordered his assistant to straighten out the mess at once. The assistant went to search the school archives and returned with the lists of students for the last few years. It was true; there was no sign of Patrick. And the assistant promised to find out who allowed Bill on the premises when he had no right to be there.

On his way home, he could not get a hold of himself. Patrick, where is Patrick? He speeded through the streets, forcing himself to stop at red lights and thinking about what he would do first. School bills! There should be paid bills somewhere. He would pick them and come back to Lawrence and make them look harder. If they refused to cooperate, he would call the police. As he entered his apartment, without removing his coat, he rushed to his desk and searched the stacks of papers on a spiral stand where he kept his bills.

He combed them twice and didn't find a single one from the school. Checkbook! The last time he paid was about a month ago. Bill leafed through the carbon copies in his checkbook and found no trace of the check he was looking for. All copies seemed in order. There were no missing numbers....

This is ridiculous! He recalled he should have a copy of the school's open-house invitation last summer. He spent almost an hour going through every piece of paper on his and Maud's desks. And found nothing.

Now Bill was sure that something strange was happening. To lose a wife and a son within a matter of a few days! He didn't even know if he should grieve for them as if they were dead. After all the panic, the sleepless nights, the gulping of sedatives to get some rest and to get some work done, the coffee drunk to stay awake while he waited by the phone for the call from the police—after all that, he didn't believe in anything.

At one point, an incredible thought struck him that his wife and son had gone out of his life as if they had never existed. All that was left were some pictures on his desk of a tall, slim woman and a boy with a shock of hair that had that same tinge of red as his own.

Left alone, Bill tried long and hard to remember his family life. Even though it had been happy, he couldn't remember anything. His profession, civil engineering, had turned out to be well chosen: he'd made a good living. His family life had been just as smooth. On Fridays, with his wife's blessing, Bill would go with his colleagues to bowl and drink beer. His wife would invite her high-school friends to play a few hands of bridge and gossip. In the summer, once a month, they would picnic at Crooked Lake. In the winter, there were ski trips to Aspen with Maud. And then there were his mother-in-law's birthdays when the whole family would gather at the "Quiet Sunset," and take her out to a restaurant where a surprise birthday cake would be brought out by servers singing "Happy Birthday." He could remember nothing else, no matter how hard he tried.

And now it had all evaporated. He couldn't believe it, but days passed, and nothing changed. He would drive to work. There would be no talk with colleagues about what happened in his life since he couldn't explain it even to himself. To Maud's high-school friends, he said that Maud had gotten an assignment from *National Geographic* to travel to Kenya and then Zanzibar; she wouldn't be back soon and would call them as soon as she arrives. The only family whom they befriended and invited in turns to each other homes, the Mathewsons—Tom, Paula, and their son, Jerry—left for Texas after Tom, Bill's regular partner in the pool, got transferred to Austin with his firm.

In the evenings, Bill would warm up a frozen dinner and sit in front of the television with his phone next to him, channel hopping with his remote control. He always had the mute button under his thumb, so when the phone rang, he could turn off the sound and speak without taking his eyes away from the screen. The only calls he got were from his brother Gary in San Francisco, on the other side of the continent, wanting to know if there was any news of Maud and Patrick. Bill spoke to him, letting him know that there was no news, then pressed the mute button again and continued to flip through the channels until he felt himself falling asleep. The screen would flicker out, with a final noise as if it were spilling metal powder on the floor, and Bill would often fall asleep right there, in the chair, never making it to bed.

Two months passed. Then three more. Half a year had passed, during which nothing happened. Now, as the pain of the loss of wife and son subsided, to his embarrassment, Bill felt something he never expected to feel: a certain shy joy that his family no longer kept him in its tender, but firm embraces. He caught himself thinking that for the first time in his married life he could allow himself, on his way home from work, to stop his black BMW at the corner of 14th and Main, at the entrance to the city park, and for an hour stroll along its large pond. The pond with a bushy little island in the middle reminded him of the template he used for his designs at the firm.

He watched the alabaster white swans diving into the dark, cold fall water, their reddish web-footed pads up, and a small flock of drakes swam by him. As on cue, they turned their dark-green velvet heads, staring at him now with their left eyes, now with their right ones. The scene prompted him to recall his early childhood years spent at his grandfather's farm in Connecticut. This change in his daily routine wasn't some out-of-this-world manifestation of freedom: he often would come here with Patrick and Maud. Yet, now there was quite a difference.... Before, the very thought that he would do something just for himself was impossible for him.

Bill walked along the pond bewildered by the fact that time had collapsed, and not decades, but just a few weeks, separated him from those childhood days of bliss and wonder of the world. He felt himself not a grown man, a civil engineer, a project head of a reputable construction firm, but that five-year-old kid on his grandfather's farm. He would force himself to leave the park to break off this illusion....

Somehow, a date floated to the surface—June 13. Bill remembered it was the anniversary of his father's death, and on Saturday closest to that date, he drove to the cemetery. Bill recognized the wrought-iron Phoenix on the gates. The first time he had been there, his father was still alive. The old man was worried and wanted his son to make sure he would be buried in plot number 723, and not stuck into some other, cheaper one, with dried-out or damaged grass.

Bill hurried to the plot with his heart in his throat. He had loved his dad and had felt uncomfortable watching him survey his future place of burial in such a business-like manner. Bill had wanted to hug his father then, to hold him close, to say "Don't die, please, don't ever die, won't you do that for me?" His dad may have been old, but he was healthy. Why not just keep on living forever? Why should one expire just because it was time? He did not hug his father then. It felt awkward somehow. His father was a shy person and could not stand any sentimentality. But now Bill regretted his awkwardness and indecision.

He found his way over the familiar lawn, searching for his father's grave marker. Suddenly something went through him, like an electric shock, like the one he had felt at that moment when he realized Patrick had vanished forever. His dad's grave was not there. He remembered that, on his last visit, there had been a black marble marker with his father's name and the dates of his birth and death. No matter how intensely Bill peered at the grass, he could see no evidence it had ever been disturbed. This time, he did not rush to the cemetery office or try to find out what had happened. He knew it would do no good. They would not find his father's grave, just as they had not found Patrick, as they had not found Maud.

Bill left the cemetery and went to a bar where, for the first time since his misfortunes had begun, he got drunk, so drunk that the bartender offered to call him a taxi. Bill refused and got behind the wheel of his black BMW. Luckily for him, the traffic was heavy, despite the late hour, so no matter how much he wanted to step on the gas, to tear up the street, there was no room for speed. He was hardly moving. The alcohol was making him sick, and he was thinking of leaving the car and walking, but he got hold of himself and drove the rest of the way home. He barely made it to the bathroom before he threw up. Then he dragged himself to the bed, where he fell asleep, grateful that it was Saturday night and he would not have to get up for work the next morning.

Six months passed. Whenever loneliness got to him, Bill would go to Joe's Bar, close to home. There he could meet some people while sipping Jack Daniel's. Once he planned to go to a ball game with one regular, a middle-aged man with a beard touched with gray. They exchanged business cards. But when he dialed the number on the man's card, he was told there was no one by that name working there, and never had been. He made no more contacts.

About a year later, he was preparing to go overseas on business and needed a photograph for his visa. At lunchtime, he walked into the nearest photo studio and, after a brief wait, stepped up in front of the screen. A little old man with enormous glasses and a smile full of gleaming dentures clicked the camera and took the film into a curtained-off cubicle. Moments later, he came out bewildered and embarrassed.

"I'm sorry, sir, something must have gone wrong," he said. "Allow me to do it again."

He changed the film and took a few more shots. Apologizing for the delay, he once again disappeared into the lab. Soon he came out, shrugging:

"It looks like there's something wrong with my camera. I'm sorry, but I can't figure out what it is. Your face isn't there. Can you come back after work? I'll check everything, and we can do it then."

17

Who Are You?

Until now, all my archival discoveries confirm the ancient wisdom reflected in the Hebrew Bible: a person over the age of twenty, who was born and raised in captivity, carries the slave psychology throughout his entire life. This seems to be indisputable. The question, however, remains open: couldn't it be that living under the new circumstances of freedom helps such a person shake off at least some of the habits born of his or her slavish past?

One day, I ask myself a question: is there some sign that my work produced in America bears an imprint of the fact that it was produced by a person who not only crossed the borders of the country in which he was born and raised but also that he left behind at least some of his old self? That is, could the proverbial "country boy" get rid eventually of at least some of the "country" in which he grew up and spent his formative years?

After digging through my archive, I came across one manuscript that, in my view, proves this is possible. The evidence that such a thing could take place is in the very title of that Russian-language book-length manuscript, *Kto ty takoj: Odessa 1945–53* (Who You Are: Odessa 1945–53).

What's so remarkable about this quite unassuming title? An American reader could even be perplexed. Why, when choosing it, did the publisher violate the fundamental rule of making it catchy?

The gist of the matter is that this title, "unassuming" in American culture, violates the postulate of the Russian culture in which the author grew up. Since the book is a memoir, the "you" in its title refers to the author's "I."

While in English the pronoun "I" is always a capital letter, in Russian it always is rendered as a lowercase letter (unless it starts a sentence). The Russian everyday expressions referring to the speaker's feelings avoid the usage of the "I" in the nominative case. While in English we say, "I'm cold," "I'm bored," and "I'm shaking," in Russian, it

199

is always expressed through impersonal sentences: *mne kholodno, mne skuchno, menia triaset.* At every attempt to use the "I" when talking about things one takes credit for doing, he or she runs the danger of being interrupted with "Stop saying 'I, I, I' [*ia, ia, ia*]. Don't you forget the 'I' is the last letter of the alphabet!" (Compare it with an old American saying, "If you don't toot your own horn, there won't be any music.")

There are a lot of Russian proverbs and sayings meant to put people down, such as "What a one you are! You have a finger in every pie," "Don't you get in someone else's [belonging to a pro] sleigh," "Every cricket should know its hearth," and many others. A reference to a person's career, the very word (*карьера*) was used in a negative context only.

These proverbs and sayings exist not to just discourage bragging and promote modesty. If you want a certain sign of what distinguishes an expatriate from the Soviet Union from others in North America, it is how he or she uses the word "I." A Westerner emphasizes individualism, but a native of a communist state emphasizes collectivism. Even if his or her life-altering decision to emigrate is in itself a rejection of the way of life in his or her homeland.

There are deep sociological reasons for this suppression of the personal in Russian culture. One's lowliness bordering on self-abasement comes from the culture of the Russian peasant communes, in which all personal interests were subordinated to the interest of the commune, making the "we" always prevail over the "I." This collective mentality lingered in Russian culture for centuries and spilled over into Soviet time. As Konstantin V. Kustanovich points out, "the contemporary Russian population bears the collectivist and authoritarian spirit and values of the old Muscovites."[1]

In Russia, the degradation of human dignity has been an integral part of the centuries-old tradition. The belittling of a person in Russia has been an absolute necessity, given the fundamental principle of Russian civilization—the primacy of the state over the individual. According to the logic of this principle, an individual must be subordinated for the sake of strengthening the state.

It is characteristic that, in the first attempts of the Soviet regime to liberate the individual from his or her dependent position, the collective pronoun "we," not the individual one "I," was used. One of the most widely used slogans of the era when, in Soviet Russia, the eradication of illiteracy among adults was carried out en masse was "We aren't Slaves, and Slaves aren't Us" (*My ne raby; raby--ne my*). The pronoun "we," not "I," was used to emphasize the imperative of being part of the collective. The overwhelming cultural demand for the dominance of the collective's interests was thoroughly observed for the whole length of the Soviet time.

Here are the lines of popular songs played out over the Soviet radio *ad nauseam*:

> My address is not the house number or the street name.
> My address is the Soviet Union.
> [*Moi adres—ne dom i ne ulitsa,*
> *Moj adres—Sovetskij Soiuz!*][2]

and

> As long as my dear country is okay,
> I don't have anything else to worry about.
> [*Zhyla by strana rodnaia,*
> *I netu drugikh zabot'*][3]

The social rules to suppress individuality had to be observed unequivocally. Nevertheless, back in my Soviet days, that "I"-suppressing culture felt natural neither to me nor to other people I knew.

"What are you talking about!" one of my acquaintances, a well-known literary critic, said to me one day when I shared my feelings with him. "I keep my ready-to-go articles in my desk drawer waiting for the time to send them to a newspaper or a magazine.... Still, my coworkers keep whispering behind my back that I am *too visible* in the press."

I couldn't help myself but compose a piece poking fun at the shaming of any personal achievement as purportedly hostile to the interest of the collective. Needless to say, I didn't even think of showing it to any editor.

"How I Died of Modesty"

One day, one of my co-workers said to me:

"Arkady, don't you get tired of showing off?"

"What are you talking about?" I said. "Showing off?"

"You know perfectly well what I'm talking about. Why are you always rubbing your success into people's faces?"

"Rubbing it into people's faces?" I was flummoxed. "My! Where does that come from? Have I ever uttered a word about my work?"

"Worse than that," he said, "it's not your words that make people cringe, but your deeds, pal. Look how much work you have done in the last six months! Shame on you! Don't you realize you're antagonizing all the members of our collective? Don't you see that everybody else takes it easy...? People live and breathe in measured steps. And you? Whenever we see you, you're puff-puff-puffing away.... What is it with you? Are you better than everyone else? Step on the brakes, Arkady. I give you this advice out of the goodness of my heart. You should hear what they say about you after learning about one of your achievements! 'Like everyone else, he'll die eventually,' they say, 'but it won't be of modesty.'"

I felt ashamed, and, not to rouse anybody's censure, began to do as little as possible, working at half my ability, and then at a quarter of it. However, even that didn't help. The derisive expression didn't leave my co-worker's face, and now and then, as he walked past, he would whisper:

"...Of something, of something, but not of modesty...."

I felt sad. I always hoped, when my time comes, to die not of some tormenting disease, but of something not too painful. And so, trying to make my colleagues feel better about me, I decided on a drastic measure. I ordered myself to do nothing.

This turned out to be not that easy. The disgusting habit of working at full capacity didn't yield right away. I kept doing a lot of things out of inertia for a while.

However, in the end, I succeeded. I forced myself to lie down on the sofa and do nothing.

As I lay down, I listened to my body, trying to find the source of my antisocial instincts, apparently nestled somewhere deep inside of me....

I began with my head. My brain was still churning things around. This was a patent outrage, nothing but colossal insubordination. I ordered it to stop. It resisted for a while, but then it unwillingly submitted.

I noticed that my lungs were puffing up importantly from time to time.

"What is that!" I got enraged. I shushed them—and they wilted.

I lay there, breathless. Still, inside me, as before, something kept working, demonstrating its activity, calling unhealthy attention to itself....

This was my heart. I raised a ruckus, upbraiding it for the gross wish to show off at all costs. "Ugh, you little worker," I shouted. "What is it with you? Are you better than everyone else?"

My heart stumbled and began skipping every other beat. I threatened it with a citizen's lawsuit for treason against the collective interest, and my heart stopped.

There was a hellish silence. I was happy, like a baby. Well, now, nobody—just nobody will accuse me of immodesty.

And I died.

At the funeral, my co-worker whispered into the ear of a colleague:

"Of course, it's a sin to speak ill of the dead, but he died as he lived—not like other people."[4]

The writing of my book-length memoir titled *Kto ty takoj* (*Who Are You*) was the result of long internal processes, a gradual understanding of where I come from and traveling to my past.

The impetus that pushed that boat of memories into a long voyage was a colleague's remark. In 1989, that is, a decade and a half after fleeing the country where I was born and grew up, at lunch at a local restaurant following my lecture at the University of Albany, I got into conversation with the head of the Russian department, Professor Toby Clyman. Since my lecture was devoted to the sociological functions of Jewish humor in the Soviet Union, she, a long-time immigrant from Poland, began recalling related episodes of her childhood in her homeland. To keep the conversation going, I also began remembering my formative years spent in Odessa, Ukraine, a city considered the cradle of Russian Jewish culture.

At some point, my interlocutor said: "I noticed that, when pronouncing the word 'Jewish,' you lower your voice. Why? American Jews don't do it. They say it in a regular voice."

It was a startling discovery. Little by little, I recalled my reaction when encountering anything related to Judaism in America. Soon after I arrived in the country, on one of my first visits to an American supermarket, I winced in surprise. Seeing the marking "Hebrew National Wieners" on the packaging of hot dogs made me feel uncomfortable. I realized that the very sight of a Star of David produced an unsettling feeling in me. It brought back my childhood memories of cartoons in *Pravda* portraying Israel as a disgusting enemy. At that time, if the authorities found the Star of David in your belongings, you could be accused of "bourgeois nationalism."

Since that fateful lunch in Albany, I caught myself thinking hard, trying to remember when the whole thing had started. My memory gradually took me back to the time of my growing up in the above-the-board anti–Semitic, post–Holocaust Soviet Union when "Shush!" was the word I heard most frequently from my parents trying to protect me. "Shush!" they would whisper to me, "Don't use your Jewish name in public.... Shush! ... Don't speak a word of Yiddish.... Shush! ... Don't cry over your relatives murdered in the Holocaust."

It was the time of loud campaigns in the Soviet media against "Cosmopolitans," those Soviet cultural figures of Jewish origin who the powers that be accused of glorifying Western culture and downplaying Russian cultural achievements.

It was followed by "the night of murdered poets," the secret execution of a group of Jewish writers and poets, many of whom were members of the Anti-Fascist Committee raising money for the war effort. It all culminated in the notorious "Doctors' Plot," in which a group of mostly Jewish medical luminaries was accused of contemplating the murder of Soviet leaders.

In 1967, after Israel's victory in the Six-Day War, the Soviet Union again severed ties with Israel, and a new wave of the anti–Semitic campaign, thinly disguised as an "anti–Zionist campaign," was unleashed in the country.

Back in my Soviet life, all these developments created in me an unrealized habit, as much as possible, to hide my belonging to "persons of Jewish ethnicity," as it was customary to call Jews in the Soviet press.

Having started to publish my satirical pieces, on an editor's prompting, telling me that my real name was "not-for-newspapers," I hid my Jewish surname under a Russian-sounding pen name.

Recently, looking through my old scrapbook with my Soviet-time publications, I came across a clipping of my story titled "The Ticket." It was published in the Moscow regional newspaper *Lenin's Banner* (*Leninskoe Znamya*) back in 1968. Rereading it so many years later, I remembered what inspired me to write it. In the story, to save money on a ticket, the mother hides the boy's age, and he eventually revolts. He craves to be accepted for who he is, no matter the expense.

Although autobiographical, the story is fictional. I have never been of small stature for my age. What prompted me to write this story was a latent wish, at least metaphorically, to free myself from the feeling of being assumed inadequate, not being equal with everybody else, for just being different, in my case, Jewish. My human dignity suffered. I wanted to free myself from the feeling of being treated as an inferior human being, to overcome the fear of the power that dominated my life back then, in my Soviet past. In the story, it is rendered as the power of the boy's mother. Of course, under the circumstances of my Soviet life, I couldn't express all these feelings publicly without resorting to artistic license, to do it through an allegory.

"The Ticket"

Oh, how he wished that people would understand that he wasn't a baby anymore. But they didn't get it. His mother would take him to school on the bus and she always refused to buy a ticket for him from the conductor. If the conductor was very insistent, his mother would push Vova into the center of the aisle[5]:

"Well, see for yourselves!"

And, to Vova's grief and shame, usually, the conductors would agree. Some grumbled, of course, but all the same, they let it pass. He would stand in the aisle with his head hunched and his shoulders raised,—more like a bowling pin than a boy.

It was even worse for Vova when he had to sneak onto the bus unnoticed and hide behind someone's coat because his mother wouldn't give him any money.

"It's nothing! They won't get poor!" She would say about someone, he didn't know who, as she prepared Vova for school.

"What if they notice my satchel?"

"Tell them that you study in the music school. There they accept six-year-olds."

Fortunately, no one asked him to pay. The trips only took ten minutes, but for him, they were a year-long blizzard full of danger, wind, and cold.

One day, Vova couldn't stand it anymore. He set out from school on foot. The road went along a construction site and was mucky with puddles of melted ice. His new boots made a quick acquaintance with lime, clay, and red brick crumbs.... Vova washed them in a puddle. At first, they were okay, but when they dried, they cracked and turned gray. That day, he was mercilessly spanked. Sobbing quietly, he listened as his mother spoke to him in a strange, far-away, unmotherly voice:

"Don't you dare, don't you ever lie to me!!"

What could he do? How could he go on?

That night, he came to a decision. For a long time, Vova rocked on his bed from side to side in quiet joy, curled up with his knees under his chin.

It was hardly daybreak when he slipped out of bed, quietly got dressed, grabbed his satchel, and made his way to escape. A door locked with a metal hook blocked his path. The Iron Goose from a fairy tale stood guard at all entrances and exits. His heart was beating heavily in his chest like a lead ball in a wooden clapper.

Vova tried to push the hook out of the goose's beak with his finger. It didn't work.... He grasped the cold gooseneck and yanked it up. The goose honked but did not give in. Then Vova quickly squatted, raised his shoulders, leaned with his legs, and jerked his whole body upwards.

With an iron clang, the door slowly swung open and thudded against a drainpipe. Vova squinted his eyes shut and held his breath.

He had gotten past the wicket gate when he heard a bellow from the window:

"Where do you think you're going? Get back in the house! Eat your breakfast!"

The milk had a sour taste, the bread was musty, and his usual cup looked ugly. An hour later, when they were going towards the bus, Vova looked numbly down at the tips of his boots poking out from under his coat. Right, left, right, left....

They sat down on the bus. The mother paid with a five-kopeck coin. The elderly conductor examined the coin under his nose and said with a sniffle:

"Lady, isn't the little boy yours? What, is he by himself?"

His mother turned and said to no one in particular:

"Not supposed to pay. Doesn't go to school yet."

Her face got spiteful and haughty. Vova became hot-hot, his temples pounded, he clenched his teeth and tore himself from his mother's hands, and burst out sobbing:

"I already go to school! I am in third grade! I ... I am almost nine years old! It's just that I'm small!"

He reached the conductor in the aisle, jerked open his satchel, and, still crying, began to pull out his notebooks.

"Here ... here is one for Russian! There you see, it says third grade.... Here is one for arithmetic! Here ...!"

Leaves of blotting paper were fluttering out of his notebooks. Vova caught at them, wet from his tears, as they fell at the passengers' feet. He dropped to the floor to collect them, glancing fearfully at his mother from the corner of his eye.

A ruckus began above him. Vova could not make out what they were shouting about. He cried.

The next morning, his mother led the resistant Vova to the bus stop. At the last moment, he tried to break away from her, but she swiftly picked him up and pushed him onto the bus.

She extended a coin, hesitated, but said, as indifferently as possible:

"Two."

Upon hearing this, Vova straightened and grew quiet.[6]

Of course, the mere discovery of lowering my voice when pronouncing the word "Jewish" didn't cure me of this mental affliction at once. The colleague's remark just brought it to the forefront of my consciousness. It made me think back, trying to recall when and how such a contemptible habit had taken root in me. It took seven more years before I thought of making my memory public.

It happened as a result of my emotional response to a work that broached this issue related to another minority—the Irish. In 1996, reading Frank McCourt's wonderful memoir, *Angela's Ashes*, I was startled by one phrase on the opening page of the book: "People everywhere brag and whimper about the woes of their early years, but nothing can compare with the Irish version...." As soon as I read this line, I said to myself, *Oh yeah? Nothing? How about growing up a Jewish child under Stalin?*

Because so little about that time was known in America at the time, I felt compelled to tell the story of my formative years, no matter what.

It took another seven years when, in 2003, my memoir *Who Are You* appeared in Russian. It was followed by its expanded version in English titled *Shush! Growing Up Jewish Under Stalin: A Memoir* (University of California Press, 2008).

Afterword

It would be wrong to assume that the road to Americanization is straightforward and smooth. In the reality, it is far from it; it's full of unexpected twists and pitfalls. The longer I live in America, the more I discover both about the country and myself, about my hang-ups conditioned by my past life in the old country. The process of Americanization never ends for a newcomer from a different culture.

A recent event in my life proved this to be true beyond any doubt. I called my old friend, also a UCLA grad school alumnus, who lived at the other end of the American continent, in a small California town. He picked up the phone and said hello. However, his voice was weak, and I realized by the short beeps that something had happened to him. Alarmed, I contacted a mutual friend of ours and told her about my worry. Not an immigrant like myself, she, a red-blooded American, threw herself into action. She asked me to verify our friend's home address. I was puzzled. Why did she need it?! She replied that she was going to contact the local police precinct and ask them to check out what's happened to our friend.

I was flabbergasted. To call the police for help? I recalled how amazed I was on my first steps in America reading the lettering on the doors of American police cars, "To protect and serve." What?! Police— *to protect and serve*?! Over the nearly forty years of my Soviet life, police for me were there for one reason only—to arrest people for any wrongdoing (real and imagined wrongdoings). And it was up to them to decide which of my "doings" were wrong and warranted an arrest.

I was by far not alone in such a perception of what the Soviet police were for. We, immigrants from Soviet "civilization," brought that fear of the police along with us to America. A friend of mine, a well-known Soviet scientist in the past, confessed to me one day that, even here, in America, whenever he sees a uniformed police officer, to be on the safe side, he tries to keep as much distance from him as possible.

He was just part of that culture in which the government at any level was always right, and there was no point even arguing with it. This attitude toward the Soviet police by regular Soviet citizens finds its reflection in the classic Soviet film *Cranes Are Flying* (1957). As the film opens, German troops had already invaded Russia. The young heroine Veronica, holding her boyfriend in her arms, contemplating her wedding, says to him in a gesture of intimacy: "When I'm with you, I'm not afraid of anything. Not even the war. Though," she says after a giggle, "I'm afraid of the police."

Her humorous admission reveals the mindset of any Soviet person. The fear of the police was so ingrained in any Soviet citizen that even war seems to be less threatening.

(In time, I learned that the reaction to the police that I describe here is typical for Soviet immigrants and refugees and is also typical of Americans who happen to be Black. So, the instinct to trust police is not universal in America, rather it is universal or nearly universal in White America.)

Back to the story of my friend's sudden break from our telephone conversation: Our mutual American friend called the town's police precinct. They contacted the building manager, asked for the key, and entered the man's apartment. They found him lying on the floor having fainted. They called an ambulance and brought him to the ER of a nearby hospital.

They saved his life.

As far as self-discovery is concerned, looking back and recalling the circumstances that led to writing the first volume of my memoirs gave me hope. The overcoming of the cultural ban on the word "I," which occurred fifteen years after I set foot on the Promised Land, promised a gradual liberation from other shameful habits of slavery.

However, that transformation turned out to be just another step toward my inner freedom, a journey that may well turn out to last my whole life. The following occurrence could serve as an example of never-ending self-discovery, pointing out that cultural standards laid down in one's early years linger in one's mind much longer, often lasting a lifetime.

Before making official my desire to retire from my college, of reducing my pace of teaching from full-time to part-time, I stopped in to see the head of our department, Professor Tamara Green. Over our friendly talk, I shared with her the reasons for my decision to lower my teaching responsibilities at the college. After citing being very busy with my literary work at that time, I also mentioned the recent public disclosure that our college was experiencing financial hardship. I said that my retirement from the full-time position would help the college somewhat, to which Professor Green told me point-blank: "Emil, you should do what's best for you, not for the college."

I am sure this episode of my American life is not the last reminder of cultural baggage lodged deep in the consciousness of one brought up in a different culture. It sounds like the wisdom laid down in the Exodus story of the Old Testament, the story of the flight of slaves from ancient Egypt has proven to be worthy of recognition. *Exodus* tells us that those who got out of slavery as adults, as was my experience, are forever incapable of saying farewell to their upbringing in slavery. Steeped in the wisdom of many millennia that preceded it, the Exodus story seems to suggest that even if those who came to the border of the promised land as adults would enter it, they wouldn't be able to live their lives as free people in that land. They would inevitably bring along their slave mentality with them, and thus, ultimately, could never be truly free.

Chapter Notes

Foreword

1. *Russian and American Cultures: Two Worlds a World Apart* (New York: Lexington Books, 2018).
2. Emil Draitser, *Farewell, Mama Odessa: A Novel* (Evanston, IL: Northwestern University Press, 2020), see Chapters 7, 17, 19, 21, 29, and 31.

Preface

1. I dedicated my autobiographical novel, *Farewell, Mama Odessa,* to two Americans, Si Frumkin and Zev Yaroslavsky, who, among many others, were instrumental in pressuring the Soviet government to allow our emigration. For a detailed history of the involvement of American Jewry in the movement, see Gal Beckerman, *When They Come for Us, We'll Be Gone: The Epic Struggle to Save Soviet Jewry* (Boston: Houghton Mifflin Harcourt, 2010).
2. Alexander Pushkin, "195. P.A. Viazemskomu // Pis'ma" (*195. To P.A. Vyazemsky: Letters*). *Polnoe sobranie sochinenii v 10 tomakh* (*Complete Works in 10 Volumes*) (Moscow: Nauka, 1965), vol. 10, 208.
3. Leonard Feinberg, *The Satirist: His Temperament, Motivation, and Influence* (New York: Citadel, 1964), 90.
4. *Ibid.,* 92.
5. Mark Tolts, "A Half Century of Jewish Emigration from the Former Soviet Union: Demographic Aspects," accessed November 29, 2022, https://daviscenter. fas.harvard.edu/sites/default/files/ files/2021-04/Tolts%20M.%20A%20 Half%20Century%20of%20Jewish%20 Emigration%20from%20the%20Former %20Soviet%20Union%20-%20Harvard4 %20_0.pdf. Compare to the biblical numbers cited at https://www.jewishhistory. org/the-exodus/, accessed November 29, 2022.
6. Josef Brodsky, "Kolybel'naia" ("A Lullaby"), 1992, accessed November 3, 2022, http://www.world-art.ru/lyric/ lyric.php?id=7826.

Chapter 1

1. Vladimir Mayakovsky, "My Soviet Passport," *Sputnik* 12, 1982, translated by Herbert Marshall, https://www. marxists.org/subject/art/literature/ mayakovsky/1929/my-soviet-passport.htm.
2. Emil Draitser, "Temnyi ehkzempliar" ("A Dark Copy"), *Krokodil* [Crocodile] 27, September 10, 1973, 12.
3. Emil Draitser, "Kak doma" ("Like Home"), *Literaturnaia gazeta* (*Literary Gazette*) 24, October 7, 1970, 16.
4. "MIA: History: Soviet History: Sounds of the Soviet Union: Lyrics," https://www.marxists.org/history/ussr/ sounds/lyrics/moskva-majskaia.htm, accessed November 29, 2022.
5. Emil Draitser, "Futbol v polovine shestogo" ("Soccer at 5:30 pm"), *Novoe Russkoe Slovo* (*The New Russian Word*), New York, July 12, 1978, 3.
6. Emil Draitser, "Ostryj sluchaj" ("The Special Occasion"), *Chaian* (*Scorpio*, Kazan), September 1, 1973, 6–7.

Chapter 2

1. Emil Draitser, "Uroki Montrealia" ("The Lessons of Montreal"), *Novoe*

Russkoe Slovo (*The New Russian Word*), August 25, 1977, 2.

Chapter 3

1. Alexander Pushkin, *"K Chaadaevu"* ("To Chaadayev"), in *Russkie poety XIX veka: Antologiia dlia studentov (Nineteenth-Century Russian Poets: Anthology for Students)*, ed. Emil Draitser (Tenafly, NJ: Hermitage,1999), 31.
2. Emil Draitser, *"Pyl'"* ("Dust"), *Novoe Russkoe Slovo* (*The New Russian Word*), March 22, 1991, 17.

Chapter 4

1. *"Kto ect' kto"* [Who's Who], *Novoe Russkoe Slovo* [The New Russian Word], March 29, 1979, 3.
2. Mayakovsky, "My Soviet Passport," 34.
3. Emil Draitser, "Increditability," *Confrontation* 20 (Spring/Summer 1980), 185–88.

Chapter 5

1. Emil Draitser, "Would You Buy a Used Soul From This Man," *Los Angeles Herald Examiner*, April 10, 1983, A12.
2. For the description of the boarding house Bettina in Vienna, Austria, in October 1974, see my autobiographical novel, *Farewell, Mama Odessa* (Evanston, IL: Northwestern University Press, 2020), 96.
3. For other real-life stories about the ex–Soviet work ethics, see *Farewell, Mama Odessa*, 175–88. On the historical origins of the Russian work ethic, see Konstantin V. Kustanovich, *Russian and American Cultures: Two Worlds a World Apart* (New York: Lexington, 2018), 49–65.
4. Emil Draitser, *"Tiazhelyj sluchaj"* ("A Difficult Case"), *Novoe Russkoe Slovo* (*The New Russian Word*), August 13, 1991, 16.

Chapter 6

1. Emil Draitser, "He Won't Make It," *Studies in Contemporary Satire*, Summer 1987, 15–22.

2. Emil Draitser, "Gone into Literature," *Chicago Literati*, December 4, 2016, www.Chicagoliterati.tumblr.com, accessed October 30, 2022.

Chapter 7

1. Si Frumkin, "Understanding Russia Through Its Humor," *Los Angeles Times*, June 4, 1978, 15.
2. P.G. Wodehouse, "Quotes," *Goodreads*, https://www.goodreads.com/author/quotes/7963.P_G_Wodehouse, accessed November 29, 2022.
3. "Rosa Klebb," *Wikipedia*, https://en.wikipedia.org/wiki/Rosa_Klebb, accessed November 4, 2022.
4. Emil Draitser, *Forbidden Laughter: Soviet Underground Jokes* (Los Angeles: Almanac Press, 1980), 68.
5. Abraham Brumberg, "The Funny Side of Russia," *The New Leader*, July 31, 1978, 8–10.
6. Draitser, *Forbidden Laughter*, 9.
7. *Ibid.*, 29.
8. Mary Kerner, "Maybe Americans and Russians Have Something in Common After All," *Vision*, June 1980, 14–18.
9. Linda Black, "Acch, Comrade, Not Another Bolshoi joke," *Los Angeles Magazine*, May 1980, 12.
10. *Atlantic Monthly*, February 1980, 18.
11. *"Anekdot da i tol'ko"* ("Such a Joke"), *Krokodil* (*Crocodile*), May 1980, 13.
12. I address this issue in my book, *In the Jaws of the Crocodile: A Soviet Memoir* (Madison: University of Wisconsin Press, 2021), 190–91.
13. Quoted in Terrance McGarry, "The Moscow Yockline: Emil Draitser and the Ironic Curtain," *Washington Post*, April 1, 1980, B1 and B4.

Chapter 8

1. Dratiser, *Forbidden Laughter*, 71.
2. Sam Cooke, "Don't know Much about History Lyrics," *Songlyrics*, https://www.songlyrics.com/sam-cooke/don-t-know-much-about-history-lyrics/, accessed November 14, 2022.
3. *Ibid.*

4. *Ibid.*

5. Isaac Asimov, "The Cult of Ignorance," *Newsweek*, January 21, 1980, 19.

6. *Ibid.*

7. Alvin Parker, "Literacy Statistics in The U.S. For 2022 (Data & Facts)," https://www.prosperityforamerica.org/literacy-statistics/, accessed November 3, 2022.

8. Celia Fernandez, "These are the 10 best universities in the world, and 8 of them are in the U.S.," https://www.cnbc.com/2022/11/02/best-universities-in-the-world-us-news-ranking.html, accessed November 2, 2022.

9. Ilya Ilf and Evgeny Petrov, *Zolotoj telenok* ("The Golden Calf"), in *Collected Works in Five Volumes* (Moscow: State Publishing House of Artistic Literature, 1961), vol. 2, 76.

10. Emil Draitser, "Buglet," *Raconteur* 3, no. 7, February 1996, 44–45.

11. Emil Draitser, *"Rodnaia dusha"* ("A Close Soul"), *Novoe Russkoe Slovo* (*The New Russian Word*), November 23, 1990, 7; reprinted in *Literaturnaia gazeta* (*Literary Gazette*) 24, June 16, 1993, 16; *Kur'er* (*The Courier*), New York, June 24, 1993, 32; *Vesti 2* (*The News 2*), Tel-Aviv, March 11, 1994, 22; included in Emily Tall and Valentina Vlasikova, *Let's Talk About Life: An Integrated Approach to Russian Conversation* (New York: John Wiley & Sons, 1996), 229–30.

12. Lynn Visson, *Wedded Strangers: The Challenges of Russian-American Marriages* (New York: Hippocrene Books, 1998), 171.

13. Evgenii Evtushenko, *"Staryi drug: Stikh"* ("An Old Friend: A Poem"), https://rustih.ru/evgenij-evtushenko-staryj-drug/, accessed November 14, 2022.

14. Emil Draitser, *"Druzhbu nado tsenit'"* ("One Should Cherish Friendship"), *Novoe Russkoe Slovo* (*The New Russian Word*), November 13, 1987, 11; reprinted in *Vecherniaia Moskva* (*Evening Moscow*), March 22, 1993, 6.

Chapter 9

1. Emil Draitser, *"Podruga Dzherri"* ("Jerry's Girlfriend"), *Vestnik* (*Herald*) 12, no. 3, June 16, 1992, 49–50.

Chapter 10

1. For the historical roots of Russian legal nihilism, see Kustanovich, *Russian and American Cultures*, 97–98.

2. Emil Draitser, *"Babochka schast'ia"* ("Butterfly of Happiness"), in *Poterialsia mal'chik: Rasskazy sovsem ne detskie* (*The Lost Boy and Other Stories*) (Moscow: Moscow Worker, 1993, 71–81.

3. Emil Draitser, *"Sluchaj v banke, ili kak ia stal rasteniem"* ("An Incident in a Bank, or How I Became a Vegetable"), *Novoe Russkoe Slovo* (*The New Russian Word*), June 13, 1983, 12–13.

Chapter 11

1. Emil Draitser, "In a Baseball Cap and Sunglasses," *Studies in Contemporary Satire* XX (1996), 109–12; *"V bejsbol'noj kepke, v chernykh ochkakh"* ("In a Baseball Cap and Sunglasses"), *Novoe Russkoe Slovo* (*The New Russian Word*), September 8, 1977, 3; reprinted in *Russkii kur'er* (*The Russian Courier*, Moscow) 38, 1991, 32.

2. *Ibid.*

Chapter 12

1. Emil Draitser, "Blame It on Uncle Sam—It's the American Way," *Los Angeles Herald Examiner*, February 29, 1984, A12; *"Spasite Kisu!"* ("Save Kisa!", *Novyj amerikanets* (*The New American*] 110, March 23–29, 1982, 48–49; reprinted in *Ogonek* (*The Little Light*, Moscow) 36, September 1990, 33.

2. *Ibid.*

Chapter 13

1. Emil Draitser, *"Ushi vianut"* ("Ears Wither"), *Trud* (*Labour*), August 11, 1968, 2.

2. *Ibid.*

3. *Ibid.*

4. Fyodor Dostoevsky, *Dnevnik pisatelia 1873. Malen'kie kartiny* (*A Writer's Diary 1873: Little Pictures*) complete works in 30 volumes (Leningrad: Nauka, 1980), vol. 21, 108–09.

5. Emil Draitser, *"Volshebnye slova"* ("Magic Words"), *Chaian* (*Scorpio*, Kazan), September 20, 1970, 6.

6. Emil Draitser, *"Pochem diuzhina oskorblenii"* ("How Much for a Dozen of Insults?"), *Russkii kur'er* (*The Russian Courier*, Moscow) 23, August 1991, 11; reprinted in *Novoe Russkoe Slovo* (*The New Russian Word*), September 24, 1991, 4.

Chapter 14

1. See, for example, in Emil Draitser, *Making War, Not Love: Gender and Sexuality in Russian Humor.* (New York, NY: St. Martin's Press, 1999), 131.

2. Emil Draitser, *"Futmol"* ("Footmall"), In *Poterialsia mal'chik: Rasskazy sovsem nedetskie* (*The Lost Boy: Stories Not-for-Children at All*) (Moscow: Moscow Worker, 1993), 112–19.

Chapter 15

1. Emil Draitser, "Let's See … a Socko Ending to This Disease Might Be…," *Los Angeles Times,* December 12, 1980, Part II, 3; reprinted in *San Francisco Chronicle*, April 5, 1981, 11, under the title "Everybody's Got a Script."

Chapter 16

1. Emil Draitser, *"Icheznovenie"* ("Disappearance"), *Russkii kur'er* (*The Russian Courier*, Moscow) 38, no. 28, November 1991; included in *Poterialsia mal'chik*, 127–31.

2. Emil Draitser, *"Odin den'"* ("One Day"), in *Poterialsia mal'chik*, 160–66.

3. Lew Anninsky, *"Sud'ba soldata v Amerike"* ("The Fate of a Soldier in America"), in *Poterialsia mal'chik*, 4–12.

4. *Ibid.,* 11.

Chapter 17

1. Kustanovch, *Russian and American Cultures*, 64.

2. V. Kharitonov, *"Moi adres- Sovetskii Soiuz"* ("My Address Is the Soviet Union"), https://www.karaoke.ru/song/1064.htm, accessed November 29, 2022.

3. Lev Oshanin, *"Pesnia o trevozhnoi molodosti"* ("A Song about Our Troubled Youth"), https://www.youtube.com/watch?v=x3KVAByJids, accessed November 29, 2022.

4. Emil Draitser, *"Kak ia umiral ot skromnosti"* ("How I Died of Modesty"), *Vestnik* (*Herald*, Baltimore) 12, no. 3, June 16, 1992, 50–51.

5. In the USSR, children of preschool age were not required to buy a ticket to ride a bus or tram, but children seven years and older, who are of school age, had to pay the fare.

6. Emil Draitser, *"Bilet"* ("The Ticket"), *Leninskoe znamia* (*Lenin's Banner*), August 17, 1968, 2; reprinted in *Novoe Russkoe Slovo* (*The New Russian Word*), October 2, 1981, 4; included in Tall and Vlasikova, *Let's Talk About Life*, 22–24.

Bibliography

Asimov, Isaac. "The Cult of Ignorance." *Newsweek*, January 21, 1980, 19.

Beckerman, Gal. *When They Come for Us, We'll Be Gone: The Epic Struggle to Save Soviet Jewry*. Boston: Houghton Mifflin Harcourt, 2010.

Brumberg, Abraham. "The Funny Side of Russia." *The New Leader*, July 31, 1978, 8–10.

Draitser, Emil. *Farewell, Mama Odessa: A Novel*. Evanston, IL: Northwestern University Press, 2020.

_____. *Forbidden Laughter: Soviet Underground Jokes*. Los Angeles: Almanac Press, 1980.

_____. *In the Jaws of the Crocodile: A Soviet Memoir*. Madison: University of Wisconsin Press, 2021.

_____. *Kto ty takoj: Odessa 1945–53 g.g. Avtobiograficheskie zapsiki* (*Who Are You: Odessa 1945–53. Autobiographical Notes*). Baltimore: Seagull Press, 2003.

_____. *Poterialsia mal'chik: Rassakzy sovsem nedetskie* (*The Lost Boy and Other Stories*). Moscow: Moscow Worker, 1993.

_____, ed. *Russkie poety XIX veka: Antologiia dlia studentov* (*Nineteenth-Century Russian Poets: Anthology for Students*). Tenafly, NJ: Hermitage, 1999.

_____. *Shush! Growing Up Jewish Under Stalin: A Memoir*. Berkeley: University of California Press, 2008.

Feinberg, Leonard. *The Satirist: His Temperament, Motivation, and Influence*. New York: Citadel, 1964.

Frumkin, Si. "Understanding Russia through Its Humor." *Los Angeles Times*, June 4, 1978, 15.

Kustanovich, Konstantin V. *Russian and American Cultures: Two Worlds a World Apart*. New York: Lexington, 2018.

Mayakovsky, Vladimir. *Stikhotvoreniia-Poehmy* (*Verses and Narrative Poems*). Moscow: State Publishing House of Artistic Literature, 1963.

Visson, Lynn. *Wedded Strangers: The Challenges of Russian-American Marriages*. New York: Hippocrene Books, 1998.

Index

www.ingramcontent.com/pod-product-compliance
Ingram Content Group UK Ltd.
Pitfield, Milton Keynes, MK11 3LW, UK
UKHW040052060325
455897UK00006B/40